PELICAN BOOKS

1917
The Russian Revolutions and
the Origins of Present-day Communism

Leonard Schapiro was born in Glasgow in 1908, and educated at St Paul's School and University College, London. He was called to the Bar in 1932 and practised until 1955, with interruption for war service. In 1955 he joined the Department of Government at the London School of Economics, where from 1963 until his retirement in 1975 he was Professor of Political Science, with special reference to Russian Studies. Professor Schapiro was elected to Honorary Membership of the American Academy of Arts and Sciences in 1967 and to Fellowship of the British Academy in 1971. In 1980 he was made an Honorary Fellow of the London School of Economics and was appointed CBE in the same year. His many publications include, *The Origin of the Communist Autocracy* (1955), *The Communist Party of the Soviet Union* (1960; second edition, 1970), *The Government and Politics of Soviet Russia* (1965, sixth edition 1979), *Rationalism and Nationalism in Russian Nineteenth Century Political Thought* (1967), *Totalitarianism* (1972) and *Turgenev: His Life and Times* (1979). He also translated, with a critical essay, Turgenev's *Spring Torrents* for the Penguin Classics. Professor Schapiro died in November 1983. In its obituary *The Times* wrote: Professor Leonard Schapiro ... was widely regarded as Britain's most distinguished analyst of Soviet history and politics and he was one of the most influential scholars of his generation in Russian studies in the entire non-communist world.'

D1494018

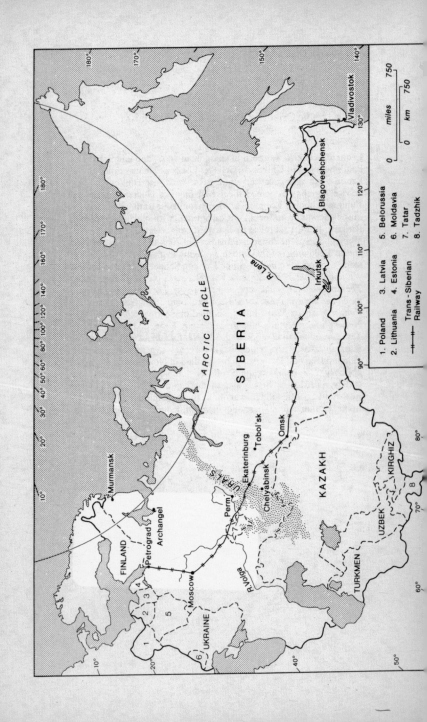

ARCTIC CIRCLE

SIBERIA

URALS

R. Lena

R. Volga

KAZAKH

FINLAND

UKRAINE

TURKMEN

UZBEK

KIRGHIZ

Murmansk

Archangel

Petrograd

Moscow

Perm'

Ekaterinburg

Tobol'sk

Chelyabinsk

Omsk

Irkutsk

Blagoveshchensk

Vladivostok

1. Poland
2. Lithuania
3. Latvia
4. Estonia
5. Belorussia
6. Moldavia
7. Tatar
8. Tadzhik

┼─┼ Trans-Siberian
     Railway

0   750
   miles
0   750
   km

Leonard Schapiro

1917

The
Russian Revolutions
and the
Origins of
Present-day Communism

PENGUIN BOOKS

Penguin Books Ltd, Harmondsworth, Middlesex, England
Viking Penguin Inc., 40 West 23rd Street, New York, New York 10010, U.S.A.
Penguin Books Australia Ltd, Ringwood, Victoria, Australia
Penguin Books Canada Ltd, 2801 John Street, Markham, Ontario, Canada L3R 1B4
Penguin Books (N.Z.) Ltd, 182-190 Wairau Road, Auckland 10, New Zealand

First published by Maurice Temple Smith Ltd 1984
Published in Pelican Books 1985

Copyright © Leonard Schapiro, 1984
All rights reserved

Made and printed in Great Britain by
Cox and Wyman Ltd, Reading
Typeset in Plantin

Except in the United States of America,
this book is sold subject to the condition
that it shall not, by way of trade or otherwise
be lent, re-sold, hired out, or otherwise circulated
without the publisher's prior consent in any form of
binding or cover other than that in which it is
published and without a similar condition
including this condition being imposed
on the subsequent purchaser

Contents

Dedication

*For Robert, James, Arabella and Jemima.
In the hope that their generation will
never be duped by promises of utopia.*

Preface

This book is primarily concerned with one aspect of the Russian revolutions of 1917 — the loss of control by the Provisional Government which succeeded the overthrown monarchy, and the capture of power by the Bolsheviks in the eighth month of the new liberal, and by then republican, government. However, since the story is so closely interwoven with the personality of Lenin, I thought it right to extend it to the end of his life in January 1924. This has enabled me to deal in greater detail with the consolidation of the Bolshevik hold over the country. It has also given me an opportunity to consider the, somewhat mysterious, last years and months of Lenin's life when severe illness and almost complete severance of contact with political affairs produced a period of reflection which was exceptional for the energetic revolutionary leader.

These matters have, of course, all been dealt with before in the vast literature which exists in several languages on Lenin and on the Russian revolutions, including some of my own books. What I have tried to do here may be summarized under two headings. First, to provide a concise narrative of the events in Russia of 1917 to 1924 which takes account of the labours of the many scholars who have devoted themselves to one or other aspect of the period, and in many cases produced works of great merit. (It is a curious fact that no comprehensive history of the Russian revolutions has appeared in English since 1935, when W.H. Chamberlin published his excellent two-volume history, which has never been superseded. The first three volumes of E.H. Carr's *The Bolshevik Revolution* do not, of course, deal with the fall of the monarchy and are, in any case, mainly confined to official policy, which is nowadays recognized as an inadequate guide by itself to the politics of communist régimes.) I have also tried to make full use of the many collections of documents which have appeared in the Soviet Union, though, with some notable exceptions, compilations produced after 1934 are of little scholarly value.

My second object has been to bring to the consideration of the

Russian revolutions the reflections produced over many years of study and teaching on the subject. Several questions seem to me to arise which perhaps have not yet received the full attention they deserve. One is the failure of the Provisional Government and of the leaders of the socialist parties, both inside and outside the government, to take effective steps to deal with the threat which, in retrospect though possibly not at the time, seems obvious: that of an impending Bolshevik seizure of power. I have tried to deal with this failure at different stages covered by the narrative. Another is the Bolshevik technique of victory. Any objective student of 1917 in Russia cannot fail to observe the fact that by September or October the majority of the articulate portions of the Russian population had rejected the leadership of the middle-class parties, and stood for a soviet government composed of a coalition of all the socialist parties represented in the soviets throughout the country. The Bolsheviks derived their support in the main from two sources: from the army and navy, which wished to see an end to the war and believed that the Bolsheviks were the most likely to achieve this; and from those, including many in the army and navy, who were persuaded that what the Bolsheviks intended to win was real power for multi-party soviets. The essential feature of Bolshevik technique was aimed at ensuring that a soviet victory in the end meant the emergence of the Bolshevik party with a monopoly of power. This device has been frequently repeated by fascist and communist parties since, but this was the first occasion of its use and for that reason seemed to me to be worth studying in some detail.

The reader will soon discover that this is a book mainly about power. He, or she, will not, I hope, reproach me for not dealing with such matters as economic problems or social questions, on which excellent studies exist.

Writing about Soviet Russia always poses the question of objectivity, and it is well to explain the criteria which I have always applied before, and which are used in this book. Objectivity in a subject of scholarship which arouses political passions means, so far as I am concerned, that scrupulous regard is paid to the accuracy of the facts set down, and to the presentation of opposing points of view. It does not mean for me suppression of unpalatable facts about left-wing or right-wing politicians, let alone their obfuscation by means of sociological jargon. I have tried my best to observe these principles this time, as I have done in the past.

I have been fortunate in the assistance provided by friends. Dr George Katkov and Dr Harold Shukman read and commented on the first two chapters. Professor John Keep generously gave me the benefit of his great learning by reading and criticizing the whole manuscript. I am immensely grateful to these three scholars, and have benefited much from their advice. But I am, of course, responsible for errors and omissions. I am indebted to Professor Donald J. Raleigh of the University of Hawaii for letting me read in manuscript a forthcoming work on the revolutions of 1917 in Samara, which is most illuminating on the little-studied question of the Bolshevik take-over in provincial Russia. I am glad to acknowledge a special debt to Mrs Ann Kennedy of the Government Department of the London School of Economics who, with great skill and patience, typed the first draft of my untidy manuscript; and to Mrs Pugh of the Geography Department who drew the excellent maps of Russia. I am particularly grateful to my old friend Maurice Temple Smith for his sensitive editing.

Above all, I wish to thank my wife Roma. Her editing of my manuscript in draft was of immense value. Any elegance it may be found to possess is due to her, not to me.

London School of Economics and Political Science
July 1983

Chapter One

The Seeds of Revolution

This is the story of the collapse of the Russian Empire, and of the revolution which caused it, though the origins of this momentous happening — sudden, violent and anarchical — must be sought in the problems of the generations that went before.

The new, free Russia came into being in March 1917 in the midst of a terrible war, on a tide of idealism and euphoria. Within eight months, the fate of the country was in the hands of a small band of more extremist revolutionaries. Riding to power on a wave of clamour from the soldiers for peace at any price, lavish in promises of that peace, as well as of bread for all and land for the peasants, they brought civil war and famine, and, so far as the countryside was concerned, little land but much strife and repression. How far this was their fault will be argued about for a long time: this book offers a contribution to the debate in two ways. It examines the rule of the Bolsheviks while Lenin was alive. It also looks at the controversial question of the extent, if any, to which Stalin's appalling tyranny was a consequence of the system which Lenin devised.

More than six decades span the distance in time from 1917. Yet many of the questions about the events which have affected the lives of all of us still remain the subject of heated controversy. Was the coming to power of the Bolsheviks a *coup d'état* or a popular revolution? Was this event in line with Russian tradition or was communism an alien system imported into Russia from outside? Was the nature of the Soviet régime directly derived from the theories on which it was founded, or was it the result of the hostility of the outside world, fearful of the infectious social appeal of bolshevism?

There are no such things as 'answers' in history, but the continuous attempt to find them is part of the duty of responsible citizens.

The clash between society and the monarchy, which in 1917 was eventually to lead to the downfall of Nicholas II, had its origins in Russia's Age of Reform.

Under Alexander II (1855 to 1881) a series of far-reaching reforms had begun the process of modernizing Russian society. The impetus for the changes came from the Emperor and from his more enlightened state servants, and the unlimited power which the Emperor enjoyed was the main factor which made it possible for the reforms to be put through. He was not inspired by the radical and liberal ideas which were then current in many parts of Europe: while resolute in overcoming the resistance of many of his subjects to the changes he strove to effect, he was at the same time fully determined to maintain intact the plenitude of royal power which he had inherited from his ancestors.

Of all Alexander's reforms, the most influential was the emancipation from serfdom of the peasants, who formed the overwhelming majority of the population. This transformation of Russian society, which occurred in 1861, had two very disparate consequences. First, the disappointments which the long-awaited liberation from bondage brought to the peasants stimulated a revolutionary movement. This would have been inconceivable in the rigid police state of Nicholas I, but the more relaxed conditions of the new reign now made it possible. Second, the stimulus which the abolition of serfdom gave to the economy led, by the time the First World War broke out in 1914, to a not inconsiderable industrial development.

There were around twenty-two million adult serfs in the possession of the landowners at the time of the accession of Alexander II, and a further nineteen million adult state-owned peasants. The landlords had considerable power over their serfs: they could require them to work for them, and maintained discipline by penalties such as birching (of both sexes and all ages), exile or forcible recruitment into the army. Of course, there were good landlords as well as bad. Not all were tyrants — but those who were seldom suffered the penalties nominally prescribed by the law.

Alexander II came to the throne determined to force through the emancipation of the serfs. His motives were economic and practical — the Crimean War at the end of his father's reign had demonstrated the inefficiency of the Russian state. In a speech to the nobility of Moscow on 30 March 1856, Alexander used words which became famous: 'It is better to abolish serfdom from above than to wait until the serfs begin to liberate themselves from below.' In fact, although peasant revolts were a fairly common feature of Russian life, there is no evidence to suggest that the kind of revolution the Emperor hinted at was imminent.

The emancipation, naturally enough, provoked strong opposition from the landlords, especially when it became apparent that the serfs were to receive some land as well as their freedom. As against this, the Emperor was supported by all enlightened opinion of the day, in his own family, among his officials, and also by a minority of landlords — both those whose sense of what was right outweighed their economic interests, and those who anticipated material advantage from the employment of free labour. The reform was put through by a Main Committee which based its recommendations on reports submitted by committees of landlords in the various provinces,* two members of each committee being elected and two appointed. An important precedent of consulting elected opinion was thus established; but when some of the committees attempted to broaden the scope of their brief, by making such additional proposals as extension of civil freedoms, the Emperor soon made it clear that this kind of advice would not be tolerated.

The Emancipation Act of 19 February 1861 was a compromise of conflicting interests which satisfied no one. As the poet Nekrasov wrote, 'The great chain broke — one end struck the landlords, the other the peasants.' The landlords faced loss of revenue. The peasants were given personal freedom, but remained in practice, as they saw it, as much enserfed as before; and, moreover, were endowed with (or rather promised) less land than they expected. The peasant received outright no more than his house and the plot of land surrounding it. Within two years a system was to be put into operation intended to confer on him the ownership of a quantity of land related to the land that he had tilled before emancipation; but the amount was to be settled by a complicated formula which the landlord could often manipulate in his own favour, and in many cases the peasant received less land than he had disposed of in the past. While the amount was being settled, he remained in a state of 'temporary obligation' which meant that he was obliged to render services to the landlord or work independently and make over a proportion of his earnings. During this period of 'temporary obligation' he was subject both to the local state authorities and to a new 'rural community'. In practice, the 'temporary' situation often dragged on for years. The landlord was anxious to retain his free labour, and the peasant usually believed that some new and better Emancipation Statute was in preparation. When the bargain was complete, the state paid a redemption price to the landlord and recovered it by instalments from the peasant, who was therefore forced to pay for what he regarded as his own property. Exact calculations are not possible; but the reduction of the peasant's allocation of land, while not universal, was certainly highest in the fertile 'black earth' zone, and it was not surprising that this area should have become the scene of the most frequent and violent peasant revolts.

*Russia was administratively divided into *gubernii*, or governments, and each *guberniia* was subdivided into *uezdy*, or provinces.

One of the worst features of the emancipation was the fact that it preserved intact the traditional peasant commune. This institution was much favoured by some romantic intellectuals who saw it as the embodiment of Russian virtues, and by the fiscal authorities who valued it as the best way of ensuring that the peasant paid his redemption dues; but it was a drag on economic development, since it perpetuated the most primitive methods of cultivation. In particular, it discouraged land improvement through the traditional practice of periodic redivision of allotments among families. It also had the effect of preserving the peasant in a state of *apartheid* within the community — largely subject to special laws and separate courts and to penalties (such as corporal punishment) from which others were exempt. The peasant was thus precluded from full participation in the new legal system, which was to be inaugurated in 1864 as one of Alexander II's most successful reforms. This state of affairs would not be put right until the following century: meanwhile the overwhelming majority of the country remained second-class citizens.

Revolutionary activity, hitherto almost unknown, emerged immediately after the emancipation. The first organization, named 'Land and Liberty', was set up in June 1861. (Its name was suggested by an article in *The Bell*, a revolutionary paper edited in London by Alexander Herzen.) There followed over the next few years a spate of revolutionary pamphlets and proclamations, couched in the most bloody terms. Revolutionary ardour, especially among students, was kindled by the covert support of the radical authors whose publications in Russia, in the conditions of relaxed censorship, stimulated uncompromising opposition to the government of the Tsar. Herzen, though not an unqualified advocate of revolution, helped to fuel the flames by criticism of abuses voiced in the pages of *The Bell*, which circulated freely, though clandestinely, inside Russia, at any rate until 1863. There were student disturbances and peasant revolts, to both of which the government responded with violent and extreme measures. In 1866 there was an attempt on the life of the Tsar. While the government could not be blamed for taking steps to preserve order, the severity of its methods, and its failure to enlist the support of enlightened society, left unhealed the deep breach which had opened up in the grim reign of Nicholas I. Even so staunch a supporter of moderate reform as the Chief Censor Nikitenko (whose diary is a good barometer of opinion) thought by 1867 that 'our most dangerous enemies' were neither the Poles (who had rebelled against Russian rule in 1863) nor the revolutionaries, but the lack of sincerity and good faith of the authorities. He was bitterly disillusioned and 'convinced that it was our fate to begin fine deeds, but not to carry them through to their conclusion'. A few years earlier he had recorded that 'the cream' of the 'thinking sector of society' was distressed and irritated by many measures which exposed the 'weakness or ineptitude' of the government.

As for those who saw the only solution in the violent overthrow of that government, to be followed by the rapid development of capitalism which would bring stability to the bourgeois state (as the statute of the revived 'Land and Liberty' expressed it in 1878) they had singularly little idea of how to achieve this. Their only success, if such it can be called, was the assassination of Alexander II on 1 March 1881.

One of the main reasons why the cream of the thinking sector of society was turning against the government was its failure to do what many hoped it would — crown the reforms of the sixties by some modification of the central imperial autocracy which would enable the moderate, liberal supporters of those reforms to participate in public life. Throughout the reign of Alexander II, proposals for the modification of central government were put forward by several enlightened leaders of opinion and state servants — including the Grand Duke Constantine, the Emperor's brother, who had played a leading part in putting through the emancipation, and the Minister of the Interior, P.A. Valuev. These schemes varied in detail but were all broadly similar. What they suggested was not a full constitutional monarchy, but the addition to the State Council,* which consisted of members nominated by the Emperor, of a number of elected representatives who would have an advisory voice in legislation. The proposals were all ignored or rejected by the Emperor, except for a plan advanced by Count M.T. Loris-Melikov (1825-1888), who had been appointed chairman of a Supreme Administration Commission to deal with the rising tide of revolutionary activity, which included assassinations of prominent people and repeated attempts on the life of the Emperor. Loris-Melikov was convinced that peace could not be restored to the country unless measures to maintain order were combined with concessions to the aspirations of enlightened elements in society, which would enlist their support. To this end he put forward to the Emperor in January 1881 a modest scheme for the participation in certain selected spheres of legislation of two pre-paratory commissions which would submit bills for examination in a general commission, for eventual forwarding to the State Council. Representatives of the elected local government institutions (*zemstva*)

---

*An advisory body which had important consultative functions in the process of legislation. It is not to be confused with the Council of Ministers, which was the name given to the body of ministers who headed the various departments of state and, under the Emperor, formed the government of the country.

were to participate in all instances. The scheme was approved by the Emperor shortly before his assassination, but in the reaction that followed under Alexander III the Loris-Melikov 'constitution' (as it was ineptly entitled both by Alexander III and later by Lenin) was abandoned.

The *zemstva* mentioned above were authorities of local goernment set up in 1864 in some of the 'governments' (*gubernii*) and 'provinces' (*uezdy*) and eventually extended to all European Russia. The members of the *zemstvo* for each province were chosen by three electoral colleges, one each for nobles, townsmen and peasants, the peasants' college being elected by 'elders' in the communes. The executive authority of the *zemstvo* was an elected board of three, whose chairman had to be confirmed by the central authorities through the governor of the province. These provincial *zemstva* in turn elected the *zemstvo* of the *guberniia*, the chairman of whose executive board had to be confirmed by the Minister of the Interior.

The subjects assigned to the jurisdiction of the *zemstva* were purely local — roads and buildings, famine relief, charitable institutions, health and education, and the like. Although they were empowered to levy a rate, the *zemstva* had to rely on the police for executive enforcement. A situation soon developed in which, in the words of an eminent constitutional lawyer, 'power without competence' remained in the hands of the central government and its officials, 'competence without power' in the hands of the *zemstva*. It is no exaggeration to say that the frustration which developed from this source of conflict was one of the causes of the fall of the monarchy.

In the opinion of the Minister of the Interior, who in 1863 prepared the law creating the *zemstva*, this concession to the landed nobility would take their minds off the political ambitions which they had been manifesting. Nothing could have proved further from the truth. The *zemstva* developed and grew in size and importance with astonishing rapidity. The lack of any kind of adequate central government provisions in such matters as famine relief, public health and primary education meant that the local authorities became increasingly indispensable — during the First World War, after 1914, the Union of *zemstva* became virtually an alternative government so far as supply and medical services at the front were concerned. Out of constant exasperation with the failures of the central government grew mounting pressure by these genuinely representative institutions to play an adequate part in running the country. It should have been evident to all (and was indeed to all, except the government) that these institutions were the natural cradle of a future parliament. According to a shrewd observer in the early 1870s, there was no trace of antagonism between the peasant representatives in the *zemstva*, who were in the majority, and the nobles — even if most of the discussion was carried on by the gentry.

The large numbers of officials whom the *zemstva* employed (the so-called 'third element', who numbered around seventy thousand by 1903) became increasingly critical of a government which they despised. While not usually politically active in the socialist or liberal parties, when these came into existence, they provided an important section of the educated opposition-minded public, and helped further to widen the gap between the government and society. The government in turn, pursuing its resolute policy of making no concessions which could conceivably bring Russia nearer to a constitution, obstructed the *zemstvo* and their representatives in every way it could: it often removed, or refused to confirm, chairmen who had become prominent in *zemstva* activity, and in particular resisted any attempt by *zemstvo* activists of different assemblies to meet in order to concert policy. Central administrative supervision, and therefore harassment, was further increased by a statute of 1890.

When Nicholas II succeeded his father Alexander III in 1894, the hopes of society were aroused that Russia could now look forward to a more liberal era. Accordingly, some dozen *zemstva* presented addresses to the new Emperor, couched in the most moderate and loyal terms, expressing the hope that their voice would be heard when it came to deciding the needs of the nation of which they represented a part. These addresses were received with marked disapproval by the Emperor. Before long he took the opportunity, at a reception of deputies from the nobility and the *zemstva*, to dismiss the hopes of the *zemstva* as 'senseless dreams', and to affirm his intention of maintaining autocracy as firmly as his late father. This speech did much to increase the gulf between society and the government which was to culminate in the revolution of 1905.

By the turn of the century, an opposition movement in favour of a full constitutional system for Russia was beginning to form both among the more active *zemstvo* delegates and among members of the liberal professions — mainly writers, professors and members of the bar. In 1902 there came into being, in Stuttgart, a paper entitled *Liberation* with no definite programme beyond the replacement of absolute monarchy by a more liberal régime. By 1904 the 'Union of Liberation' had been formed as a movement now explicitly dedicated to the 'establishment of a constitutional régime' in Russia. This shift to the left involved a parting of the ways with the more moderate minority of *zemstvo* activists, who believed that the proper way forward was to begin not with a constitution but (in a manner reminiscent of the projects for reform put forward in the nineteenth century) with a national body with advisory powers only, composed of elected representatives of the *zemstva*. But, as became evident at an unofficial but tolerated *zemstvo* congress in November 1904 (made possible because of the appointment of a Minister of the Interior, Prince P.D. Sviatopolk-Mirsky, who was more liberal than past ministers) even the majority which favoured a legislature with full powers was nevertheless willing to forgo its demand for a constitution to be adopted at a constituent assembly. There was still room for compromise between the Emperor and the *zemstva*.

Sviatopolk-Mirsky, probably under the influence of the resolutions of the *zemstvo* congress, put forward to the Emperor a programme of moderate reforms which included a clause allowing elected representatives of the *zemstva* to take a part in the discussion of legislative proposals in the State Council along with the nominated members. When the question was debated at a conference presided over by the Emperor, the overwhelming majority of the participants (all state servants) were in favour of the minister's scheme for *zemstvo* participation. The Emperor, however, was subsequently swayed by his finance minister, S.Y. Witte (1849-1915) who, for reasons which are not clear, chose to argue that this clause would inevitably lead to a constitutional régime, and frightened the Emperor off it. Within less than a year, this same Witte was to draw up the memorandum which persuaded the Emperor, at the climax of a revolution, to divest himself of his absolute powers. Witte would have served his country better if he had supported Sviatopolk-Mirsky in 1904.

Many causes contributed to Russia's first revolution in 1905. There were reasons for dissatisfaction in all classes. Educated society, of which the Union of Liberation was the extreme voice, had been repeatedly spurned by the Emperor. The growing workng class had to suffer a very low standard of living: laws governing their conditions of work were frequently flouted, and there were no unions to act on their behalf. The peasants were even worse off. Ravaged by famines (in 1891 and in 1901, for example), they were also burdened by redemption payments and, if they sought to increase their holdings by buying or leasing, impoverished by the rising price of land. Unorganized, spontaneous peasant disturbances were a normal feature of Russian life. Above all, the wasteful, inefficient and tyrannical commune system inhibited any real agricultural progress. There were some concessions — redemptive payments were eased in 1883 (only to be wiped out in the revolutionary turmoil in November 1905) and corporal punishment was abolished in 1904; but it was not until 1905 that Witte grasped the real problem by proposing the abolition of the commune, and this had to wait some years before it began to be implemented.

There were good grounds for discontent among the national minorities who suffered from severe discrimination — especially the Jews. And in January 1904 a war had broken out with Japan in which Russia was to suffer ignominious defeat the following year. Although the war led at first to an upsurge of patriotism in some quarters, it was not long before its effects on the national morale were felt, especially after the shattering defeat of the Russian navy in May 1905.

Late November and early December 1904 (the last weeks of the liberal régime of Sviatopolk-Mirsky) witnessed the most outspoken and widespread campaign of intellectual opposition to the government that Russia had ever known. At *zemstvo* meetings, at gatherings of the nobility, and especially at a series of political banquets organized by intellectuals and professional men from all over Russia, outspoken and impassioned speeches and resolutions called for civil freedoms and, in some cases, for a constituent assembly.

But the most dramatic event of the year occurred on 9 January 1905. On that day, a march of many thousands of Petersburg workers converged on the Tsar's Winter Palace in an attempt to present a petition, calling not only for improvements in factory conditions but for a wide range of civil and political rights. The march had been organized by Father Gapon, an agent of the police recruited to distract workers' energies from political demands by encouraging them to concentrate on economic grievances. Evidently Gapon's sympathies for the strikers (he was a peasant in origin) outweighed his rôle as a police agent.

The marchers were dispersed by rifle fire from troops assembled around the palace, killing ninety-six and wounding over three hundred, of whom thirty-four later died. (Unofficial figures of casualties ran into thousands.) The horror evoked by this massacre of an unarmed crowd (though it is possible that the authorities believed them to be armed) stuck in the minds of all sections of Russian society and would never be eradicated. Gapon, who did more than anyone else to shatter the power of the autocracy in 1905, was subsequently (with inept political ingratitude) murdered by some socialist revolutionaries.

Russia was in a turmoil of rebellion for the whole of 1905. Students, intellectuals and professional men of all kinds demonstrated, protested and put forward demands. Peasant revolts, which the newly founded Socialist Revolutionary Party* did much to encourage, were never far below the surface and erupted with mounting frequency. Official estimates of the damage from these disturbances amounted to twenty-nine million roubles (over a million and a quarter pounds sterling, or five million dollars at the values of the time). There were

*A note on the main political parties will be found at the end of the book.

also disorders in the areas where minority nationalities lived, and especially in Russian Poland.

An imperial *ukase* of 18 February reversed all previous policy by permitting the Tsar's subjects to send him proposals 'for improving the public well-being', while a rescript later the same day to the Minister of the Interior, Bulygin (who had succeeded the disillusioned Sviatopolk-Mirsky) proposed the summoning of an elected assembly, or Duma, with consultative powers. The *ukase* was naturally interpreted as a sign of weakness, and stimulated further revolt; while the rescript, made public in August, which might have forestalled revolution a year before, had come too late for anyone to pay much attention to it. For example, the Union of Liberation movement for the most part rejected the Tsar's concession.

An ever-increasing wave of strikes culminated in October in a general strike, which threatened to paralyse life in the capital and in many provincial cities. The government floundered, apparently powerless in the face of catastrophe.

But if the imperial government was at a loss and groping for a solution, it had one great advantage: in spite of several significant mutinies and extensive radical influence in many units, the army retained sufficient loyalty, or habit of obedience, to be an effective instrument for maintaining power in the last resort. Equally important for the survival of the régime in 1905 was the fact that the opposition, though universal, lacked any kind of leadership determined to make a bid to seize power.

The Union of Liberation, by far the most important element in stimulating the mass revolt, was a movement rather than a political party, and lacked the organization, and determination, to lead a revolution. The Social Democrats (split since 1903 into Bolsheviks and Mensheviks, as described in the next chapter) were quite incapable of exercising any effective leadership over the vast wave of strikes throughout the country — if one excepts the Jewish Social-Democratic *Bund*, which operated in the Jewish Pale of Settlement far away from the capital. However, even without socialist leadership, the strikers increasingly added demands for civil and political freedom, such as were resounding throughout the country, to their appeals for economic justice. The Petersburg Soviet,* for example, grew out of one of the strike committees that sprang up in many cities of Russia, and for a short time acted as a kind of substitute government in the midst of the chaos of the general strike, maintaining order, ensuring food distribution and the like. The soviets lasted long enough to create a revolutionary legend of worker democracy which would play an important rôle in 1917. For around a month the one in

*The word soviet simply means council.

Petersburg also provided a forum for Trotsky's verbal pyrotechnics, though the soviet itself was largely non-party.

Faced with what looked like the imminent disintegration of his régime, the Emperor's first reaction was to use force. He was only dissuaded when his experts assured him that the bloodshed would be enormous, and even so not necessarily successful in preventing a revolution. Accordingly, he reluctantly yielded to the entreaties of Witte and the Grand Duke Nicholas and signed the Manifesto of 17 October. This manifesto promised to create genuine civil freedom. In particular, it promised that no law should go into force without the consent of the State Duma which was to come into being and which was to be elected on a wider franchise than that proposed in the Emperor's February rescript to Bulygin. The Duma would also have the power of supervising the legality of actions by the Emperor's officials. It marked the end of absolute, unlimited monarchical power in Russia.

The momentous year ended with an insurrection in Moscow in December, organized by the revolutionary parties, which was easily suppressed by military force. The government also weathered a general strike called by the Petersburg Soviet, the members of which were arrested on 3 December and eventually brought to trial. There followed some two years during which sporadic terrorist acts were put down with considerable ruthlessness. The socialist parties did not yet present any threat to the survival of the régime.

As to the manifesto, it was dismissed by the socialists as a trick which in no way altered the situation. Lenin even went so far as to prevent his Bolshevik followers from participating in the 1906 elections to the First Duma — a mistake which he later acknowledged, since the Duma was subsequently to provide them with a welcome and virtually unrestricted platform for propaganda. At the other extreme, the right-wing groups rejected the notion that the Duma should be able in any way to restrict the Emperor's sovereign power, and tried to pretend that the manifesto had changed nothing. For them, the Duma would become little more than an opportunity for the display of political hooliganism.

The Emperor had conceded the limitation of his power in the manifesto with extreme reluctance. But the evidence of his correspondence and his demeanour at private conferences does not bear out the contention often advanced by his critics on the left, that he did his best to sabotage the new order to which the manifesto gave birth, though it was probably true that he strove to reduce to the minimum the effect of the concessions which he had made. In this he had the full support of the extreme nationalist right, such as the 'Union of the

Russian People' party, for which he felt considerable sympathy. But the fate of the new order depended on the relation which would develop between the Emperor and his advisers on the one hand, and on the other the two liberal parties which emerged in 1905 — the 'Constitutional Democrats', or 'Kadets', and the more conservative 'Union of October 17' (the 'Octobrists').*

The new political order was mainly embodied in the Fundamental State Laws, published on 23 April 1906. There was no question of any constituent assembly. These laws were the result of a free act by the Emperor (after consultation with his advisers) and the constitution which emerged clearly derived its legitimacy not from 'the people' assembled for the purpose of devising it, but from the auto-limitation accepted by the Emperor. But it was not a 'pseudo-constitution', as the great German sociologist Max Weber described it, probably under the influence of its Kadet Russian critics. It did not, indeed, provide for a government responsible to the Duma — this had not been promised in the manifesto — but it did enact that no law could pass without the assent of the Duma, the State Council and the Emperor. At least half of the members of the State Council were to be elected by such bodies as the nobility, the *zemstva*, the Academy and the Universities. Civil freedoms were guaranteed, though with the ominous proviso 'within the limits of the law', or some similar phrase. Members of the Duma were also given the right to 'interpellate', or question, ministers on their actions, but the Emperor's administrative (as distinct from his legislative) powers remained unimpaired by the Fundamental State Laws. This left a wide discretion for limiting the exercise of civil freedoms, both by arbitrary action and by the exercise of emergency powers, which could be abused.

Of the two liberal parties, the Union of October 17 expressly accepted the manifesto, and hence the Fundamental State Laws, as a basis for cooperation with the government — even if things did not quite work out like that in practice. The Kadets rejected both. They won a substantial majority in the elections to the First Duma, and immediately presented the government with demands which it could hardly have been expected to accept — the formation of a government responsible to the Duma, abolition of all emergency laws, endowment of the peasants with land drawn from state property as well as that confiscated from the landlords, and a full amnesty for all those convicted of political offences or peasant rioting. The inevitable clash

*The name Kadet, which has no connection with the English word cadet, was derived from the Russian initials of the party's name. The Union of October 17 was, of course, named after the date of the manifesto. It should be noted that the use of the word 'constitutional' at the time implied very radical ideas, just as the term 'social democrat' meant, in Russian conditions, a party committed to revolution.

resulted in the dissolution of the First Duma after two months' existence.

The Second Duma promised little more hope of cooperation with the government, especially after the breakdown of several attempts to form a ministry composed mainly of members of the liberal parties in the Duma. The Prime Minister, P.A. Stolypin (1862-911), decided on a bold, if quite unconstitutional, course. His policy, like that of Count Loris-Melikov in the last years of Alexander II, was to combine stern repression of revolutionary assaults on the government with a far-reaching programme of reforms. To this end, he dissolved the Second Duma, and introduced, in clear violation of the constitution, a new and restricted franchise. This, together with some government manipulation of the ballot boxes, produced a Duma in which the largest element became the Octobrists, with 120 seats. Whatever one's view of Stolypin's methods, he certainly transformed the Duma from a scene of head-on conflict into a body with some semblance of a working legislature.

Opinions differ as to the extent to which the Duma in fact developed real cooperation with the government as Stolypin had intended. Professor G. Hosking, who has devoted special study to the subject, contends that 'the suspicions dividing Russia's élites, not having been cured in peacetime, proved fatal and ultimately opened the way for revolution.' There is no doubt that there were serious clashes between the Duma and the government on several major issues, but the Third Duma did survive for its legal term, until 1912. And it was in the Third Duma that Stolypin achieved his greatest success — the passing into law of his momentous plan for agrarian reform. The Agrarian Commission of the Duma played an important, if critical, part during the three years that it took for the legislation to be completed.

In broad terms, Stolypin's aim was threefold. First, to complete what the Emancipation Act had left unfinished by removing those restrictions on the peasant which had prevented him from becoming a full citizen, equal with all others. Second, to encourage the peasant to free himself from the commune, and to help the more ambitious peasant to become, with state aid, the owner of an adequate land holding, thus forming a stable basis of support for the constitutional order set up in 1906. Third, to reduce peasant misery in European Russia (which was mainly the result of a rapid increase in rural population) by encouraging and subsidizing emigration to Siberia.

Stolypin said in 1910 that a long period of peace would transform Russia, but the war of 1914 interrupted the process. As it was, even in the short time available, considerable improvements took place in Russian agriculture, which the more impartial critics attribute to

Stolypin's reforms. Many scholars take the view that if the transformation of Russian society envisaged by Stolypin had run its full course, the revolution of 1917 would have been avoided. This question obviously cannot be resolved one way or the other, but it is of interest that Lenin at the time took a not dissimilar view of the stabilizing effects of the reforms. Stolypin was assassinated in 1911 by a Socialist Revolutionary who was also a police agent. The question whether the agent acted out of socialist fervour or at the behest of the police remains unsolved. Stolypin had become very unpopular with right-wing politicians and with the Emperor, who seems to have failed to understand that Stolypin was the one man who might have saved him from disaster.

One of the consequences of the reforms was to release a growing number of peasants to fill the ranks of industry, which was rapidly expanding. Another result was to help industry by providing a strong home market for goods. In general, allowing for price alterations, total production between 1900 and 1913 increased by 74.1 per cent, and per capita production by 46.2 per cent. In percentage of world production of the principal commodities like minerals, steel, pig iron or textiles, Russia in 1913 came fourth — higher still in oil production (and top in alcohol!). But while there was no doubt that on the eve of the war Russia was quite rapidly entering an era of prosperity, it was also true that she still required a fairly long period of peace to remove such obstacles to economic development as illiteracy, and to improve the housing conditions of the industrial proletariat. The workers were impoverished by the government's protectionist policy, designed to nurture home industry, and this made them highly receptive to revolutionary ideas. Indeed, poor housing and working conditions, as well as the virtual absence of the right to unite for their own protection, were probably more effective than propaganda by the socialist parties in alienating the Russian working class from society. Industrial unrest increased, and there was a mounting wave of strikes in the years which preceded the war. The government, while making some minor concessions, remained convinced that the grievances of the workers should be dealt with by police measures.

Russia's declaration of war on 19 July 1914 (old style)* resulted in an immediate upsurge of patriotism in the educated classes. The reaction of the peasant was less enthusiastic, an important factor in an army consisting largely of rural conscripts. The catastrophe at Tannenberg (so brilliantly portrayed by Solzhenitsyn in *August*

---

*Russian dates up to February 1918 were behind those of Western Europe — in the nineteenth century by twelve days and in the twentieth by thirteen. In future, old-style dates will be used until the narrative reaches February 1918.

1914) was an inauspicious opening to military operations, and further defeats followed in 1915. But the situation improved considerably in 1916, and, in spite of losses reckoned at over a million, an offensive under General Brusilov was regarded as a military success; it certainly made an important contribution to the allied cause. As Major-General Sir Alfred Knox, who was a close and shrewd British observer of the Russian army throughout the war, recorded early in 1917, 'On the eve of the Revolution the prospects for the 1917 campaign were brighter than they had been in March 1916. . . .' An important factor was the dramatic improvement during 1916 of supplies of ammunition and transport, which had earlier been sadly inadequate.

There had, however, been enormous losses. In all, by the end of 1916 the number of males put into uniform had reached 14,600,000, of whom 6,900,000 were in the field, and 2,000,000 in rear garrisons. Over 5½ million, therefore, were casualties: of these over 2 million were taken prisoner, leaving around 3½ million dead and wounded. Total loss of life has been reliably estimated at between 1,600,000 and 1,850,000.

In such circumstances, it is not surprising to find that there was a widespread desire for peace among the troops at the front. There were also universal complaints about the quality of food, and officers particularly were disturbed by the rapidly deteriorating conditions at home. Nevertheless the evidence shows that morale had not collapsed: in the main, the front line troops held fast and carried out their duty. Politicization did not come until 1917, after the fall of the monarchy, and the impetus for this came from the capital, Petrograd,* and from the garrison troops, whose morale was far lower. When it came, however, the seeds of revolt fell on ready soil. As a recent historian, M. Frenkin, concludes, by 1917 the army could not make the first move against the Tsar's régime, 'but it was undoubtedly prepared for supporting a revolution.'

The upsurge of patriotism at the outbreak of war did not last long — indeed, it was that very patriotism that fuelled discontent as it became increasingly apparent that the incompetent, discredited and unpopular government of the Emperor and his ministers was incapable of prosecuting a successful war. From 1915 onwards, the record of the last imperial government is one of decline; but the mounting criticism from all quarters stiffened the Emperor's determination to hold fast to the autocracy which was rapidly slipping from his grasp, and which he sincerely believed it was his duty to preserve intact as a sacred heritage. In this belief he was constantly encouraged by his wife, the Empress Alexandra.

*St Petersburg was renamed Petrograd in 1914.

The opposition of the Duma was before long united against the government as never before, and was supported by an important part of the membership of the State Council. On 25 August 1915 the centre parties in the Duma, the Octobrists and the Kadets, joined with academic and centre groups in the State Council to form the Progressive Bloc. (In the Duma the Bloc represented 300 out of 422 deputies.) This called for 'a decisive change' in methods of government, including strict legality and the removal of military authority over matters in which it had no concern. It also called for an amnesty for purely political prisoners, removal of limitations on the rights of Poles and Jews, restoration of trade union rights and a broad programme of legislation in the interests of peasants and local government authorities. Such a programme, the signatories claimed, could only be achieved by a government 'supported by the confidence of the public'.

The chances of such a comprehensive programme being carried out in wartime were, of course, slight. It is also, with the benefit of hindsight, open to doubt how far this constant immoderate propaganda by the liberals in the Duma did not in the end help the very triumph of extremism which they were anxious to prevent. On the other hand, the intransigence of the Emperor in the face of mounting demands for political reform of itself generated extremes of passion. When the British Ambassador, Sir George Buchanan, pointed out to the Emperor in October 1916 that the only salvation lay in his regaining the confidence of his people, the Emperor replied: 'Do you mean that I am to regain the confidence of my people, or that they are to regain *my* confidence?' The tragic history of the last three Emperors of Russia is mirrored in those words.

Another potent centre of opposition to the government was provided by the voluntary organizations. These fulfilled vital functions in the war which the government was incapable of performing adequately. In 1915 an All-Russian Union of *Zemstva* was formed for the relief of sick and wounded soldiers. Prince G.E. L'vov (later to be the Prime Minister of the first Provisional Government set up after the fall of the monarchy) became its chairman. By the end of 1916 nearly eight thousand *zemstvo* agencies of various types were in existence throughout the country, employing hundreds of thousands and with a budget of over a hundred and eight million roubles. In the rear, the medical relief work of the Union of *Zemstva* was supplied by the local *zemstvo* organs, united in 1917 into unions of *zemstva* and towns. In September 1915, a network of War Industry Committees had been set up throughout the country, under the general direction of a Central War Industry Committee, with the object of helping 'government organizations to supply the army and the navy with all necessary military and food supplies'. These committees, in which representatives of both workers and employers participated, had very considerable powers to take over property, to conclude contracts and, in cooperation with the authorities, to arrange the supply of military material ordered by the state. They apparently succeeded to some extent where the government had failed — as is suggested by the improvement in supplies to the front which took place in 1916. (The Chairman of the Central War Industry Committee was A.I. Guchkov, a leading Octobrist, who was to become Minister of War in the first Provisional Government.)

In the general opposition to the government the revolutionary parties played a limited rôle. The Socialist Revolutionaries took the view that their proper course was to bide their time and prepare for revolution when the war came to an end. The Social Democratic deputies in the Duma voted against war credits in 1914, but there was a group of Social Democrats who were prepared to form a workers' group in order to cooperate in the War Industry Committees, with the twin aims of using those institutions as a forum for propaganda and of promoting the interests of the workers. Anti-government propaganda, as voiced in the War Industry Committees, did in fact become increasingly strident. The police tolerated the activities of these Social Democrats (of which they were well informed through an agent planted in their midst) until 26 January 1917, when most of them were arrested.

The Progressive Bloc in the Duma was not opposed to the monarchy as such, nor were the Voluntary Organizations. Their opposition was directed mainly at the Emperor Nicholas II, and more especially at his wife. Various abortive plots were hatched in the course of the war to force Nicholas to abdicate in favour of his young son, under a regency of one of the Grand Dukes. (The most developed conspiracy was headed by Guchkov, who had long nurtured a hatred for Nicholas II.) But none of the plots got very far, mainly because of the reluctance of the army commanders to become involved. In view of the record of the Provisional Government which came into being in 1917, one may be forgiven for doubting whether a 'government of confidence' or 'a responsible government' composed of the leaders of the liberal parties would, in the event, have proved more efficient than that of the Emperor and his ministers.

Opposition to Nicholas and a movement towards compromise with the Progressive Bloc of the Duma extended even to members of the Council of Ministers, and an attempt to reach such a compromise was made in August 1915. It coincided with an effort to dissuade the Emperor from assuming supreme command in the field. Both attempts were defeated by his resolute refusal. There were those who later took the view that this was the last chance to save the monarchy.

One of the main reasons for the opposition to the Emperor was the growing influence of Rasputin. This unsavoury adventurer, whose scandalous way of life had been notorious for years, exerted a hold over the Empress by reason of his well-attested power (witnessed by medical men) to stem the flow of blood of her haemophiliac infant son. She, as well as the Emperor, was prone to religious mysticism, and an easy prey to a charlatan of Rasputin's skill. Through her he was able to influence the Emperor in the selection of ministers — though probably not nearly to the extent that popular imagination believed.

Rasputin's actions were principally aimed at securing the appointment of those who were friendly to him, and the removal of any minister who showed sufficient courage to try to neutralize his influence. But rumours, especially after 1916, ranged far and wide to the effect that he and the Empress headed a camarilla of German agents whose aim was to bring about a separate peace with Germany. In the case of the Empress the evidence is conclusive that the rumours were devoid of truth, while the rascals who thronged around Rasputin were more concerned with sordid financial intrigues than with espionage. But the charge was widely believed, did more than anything else to discredit the Imperial family, and hence played a vital part in the downfall of the monarchy.

Frequent changes of ministers, and the appointment of some notorious characters (such as that of the corrupt Protopopov as Minister of the Interior in September 1916) helped to fuel the rumours — and further to discredit the government and the Emperor. The Progressive Bloc had no wish to topple the monarchy while hostilities were in progress, whatever its political aims might be after the victorious conclusion of the war, but it played an influential part in swelling the rumours of treason in high places. The leader of the Bloc, P.N. Miliukov, in a speech in the Duma on 1 November 1916, openly accused the Prime Minister and the Empress of treason. He could adduce no evidence, but the repercussions can easily be imagined, both in the country at large and in the army, where the text was widely distributed. (Miliukov would become Minister of Foreign Affairs in the First Provisional Government.)

The assassination of Rasputin in December 1916 was motivated by the desire to save the monarchy from an evil influence. All that the murderers (Prince Yusupov, one of the Grand Dukes, and an extreme right-wing politician) achieved was to deepen the already wide chasm between society and the Emperor and Empress. The decline of public standards in Russia and the weakness of the tradition of law were evident in the fact that no proceedings were taken against the murderers, whose identity was widely known.

As the year 1917 began, there were gathering premonitions of impending catastrophe, though few realized how close it was. In his Swiss exile, Lenin, in a lecture, expressed the opinion that 'we older men' might not live to see the revolution in Russia. The Russian police were nearer the mark. In a report in October 1916 they pointed out that dissatisfaction caused by rising prices and food shortages was strong in Petrograd and in Moscow. Opposition both to the government and to the Emperor personally was mounting and exceeded that observed in 1905 and 1906. Disorders, the police believed, could break out at any time, and the garrison troops could not be relied on to suppress them.

Chapter Two

The Emergence of Bolshevism

Bolshevism, the revolutionary doctrine of the party which seized power on 24-25 October 1917, owed its existence to Vladimir Ilyich Ulianov, who adopted the surname Lenin. Whatever influences may have shaped his ideas* — and there were many — his single-minded dedication to revolution far exceeded that of his fellow-theorists of marxism, and this certainly coloured much of his intellectual development. Without him the course of the Russian revolution would have been very different.

The future Bolshevik leader was born on 10 April 1870 in Simbirsk on the Volga, now renamed Ulianovsk. His father, of fairly humble origins, had risen by his own efforts to become Director of Primary Schools for the province, and had acquired the rank of hereditary nobility by virtue of his service. He was liberal-minded and enlightened, but did not discuss political matters in the family. Vladimir's mother came from a well-to-do family of Germans long settled in Russia. Both parents were believers but not active church-goers, and did not enforce religion on their five children. Vladimir, the third son, was outstandingly brilliant at school, and showed no interest in political questions until the age of seventeen.

In May 1887 his elder brother, Alexander, was hanged for his part in an attempted assassination of the Emperor Alexander III. Alexander's involvement in the conspiracy came as a shock to the whole family, including his sister Anna, the only one who knew of his membership of a revolutionary circle. By that date The People's Will, the main terrorist organization which had existed in the previous reign, had long been broken up, following upon the assassination of Alexander II. Such revolutionary groups as existed were either of the so-called 'preparatory' populist trend, or marxist, and did not engage in violence. The highly secret terrorist group of five to which

---

*Much of Lenin's doctrine was moulded by the modifications to marxism which were effected by its early Russian exponents who, unlike, say, German marxists, were dealing with a country in which four fifths of the inhabitants were peasants, and which lacked a strong middle class. For a convincing exposition of this view see Neil Harding, *Lenin's Political Thought*.

Alexander Ulianov belonged was probably the only one in existence. Since Vladimir was to devote much study to this organization, it is necessary to look at its programme.

This described the members as 'socialists', who believed that socialism was the inevitable result of capitalism, 'when once a country has embarked on the road of a money economy'. Socialism could only come about with the 'increase in the strength and consciousness of the working class': the peasants could at most provide unconscious support to the workers through their general discontent. Disagreements with the Social Democrats were 'merely theoretical' and of little importance. Since educational activity was impossible in Russia at the time, the struggle had to be political, which meant terrorist acts. The aim of these acts of 'systematic terrorism', in which the flower of the younger generation were to sacrifice their lives, was to prove to the government that it could not ignore public opinion indefinitely, and to force it to concede freedom. It was in line with this heroic view of the duty of the revolutionary that Alexander refused to plead for clemency after his conviction.

Under the impact of his brother's execution, Vladimir embarked on an intense course of reading, devouring whatever he could lay his hands on in his maternal grandfather's country house where he spent the summer. This, his first encounter with the radical Russian writers of the nineteenth century, made a lasting impression on him, as his widow revealed in her memoirs.

A now more serious youth, convinced that he was destined for the life of a revolutionary, he entered the university of Kazan' in the autumn of 1887, and promptly joined a circle which followed the traditions of The People's Will and which had had links with Alexander's organization. At the end of the year this group mounted a rowdy demonstration which resulted in many arrests. Vladimir, although not a ringleader, was among those arrested — the police were not likely to take any chances with the brother of a convicted terrorist. He was expelled from the university and ordered to live under surveillance on his grandfather's estate, Kokushkino. The family stayed there for some nine months, and Vladimir resumed his studies of the radical writers.

We know that Chernyshevsky was one of his main objects of study. Chernyshevsky's political novel *What is to be Done?*, though without much literary merit, had been the inspiration of generations of Russian revolutionaries, including Alexander Ulianov, since its publication in 1863. It deals with the lives of 'the new men and women' — a euphemism for 'revolutionaries' made necessary by censorship — and its effect on Vladimir was electrifying. 'It is a work which charges one up for the rest of one's life,' he told a friend years later.

Chernyshevsky was a materialist and an uncompromising revolutionary, much admired by Marx. It was from him that Lenin learned that nothing could be achieved by reform, and that the liberals would always betray. We do not know whether he also read the works of P.N. Tkachev during this period of exile though it is quite possible that they were available among an uncle's collection of periodicals at Kokushkino. He certainly read him at some stage, because in 1902 or 1903 he was advising young revolutionaries to read Tkachev's 'profound and original' works, and described him as 'undoubtedly closer than any other to our point of view'. The reason for this high praise was presumably Tkachev's insistence that a revolution could only be successfully accomplished by a disciplined organization which would seize power in the name of 'the people' and then put through radical measures.

By the autumn of 1888, Vladimir was allowed to return to Kazan' (though not to the university). He was well grounded by that time both in the Russian literary radical tradition, and in the methods of The People's Will, of which his first revolutionary experience had taught him something. As yet, he knew of the works of Marx only at second-hand from the articles on him which appeared in the back numbers of the political periodicals which he found at Kokushkino. He now applied himself to the thought of Marx, reading the first volume of *Capital*. He also frequented at least two revolutionary circles, one of which was run by an old member of The People's Will, while the other was probably more marxist in orientation. In the spring of 1889 the Ulianov family moved to Samara, where the future Lenin embarked on the serious study of marxism. He brought to this certain qualities which distinguished him from other Russian disciples of Marx: a quite extraordinary dedication to revolution; the realization that the 'systematic terrorism' of his brother could achieve nothing in the Russian police state; and possibly already the belief that the secret of successful revolutionary activity lay in the organization of the party which engaged in it.

While in Samara he also studied as closely as he could the organization and practices of The People's Will, through long discussion with two of its former adherents who lived there. Although The People's Will had in the end achieved no more than the assassination of Alexander II, which inevitably resulted not in revolution but in reaction, its programme contained elements which the future Bolshevik leader may well have pondered. It emphasized the growing importance of the workers in the movement, and laid particular stress on the need to win over the army: 'One can say that, with the army behind one, one can overthrow a government even without the help of the people; while if the army is against one, nothing can be achieved even with the support of the people.' The organization of The People's Will consisted of a highly disciplined, conspiratorial 'centre', in complete authority over the local 'groups', and over their individual members. The term 'party' was used for what in practice was a fairly indefinite category of like-minded people. Even if its achievements were minimal, The People's Will did hand down a body of tradition of conspiracy and of revolutionary technique which repaid study.

The failure of the movement was one of the main stimuli for the foundation in 1883 in Geneva, by G.V. Plekhanov, of the first fully marxist organization — the Group for the Liberation of Labour. This was a purely theoretical body which in its publications attacked the intellectual foundations of the populists who urged the need for Russia to avoid the evils of Western capitalism and to build the future on the foundations of the peasant commune. Plekhanov argued that the commune was already disintegrating, that capitalism would inevitably develop in Russia, and that the main aim must be to found a workers' party which could eventually take over in the distant socialist revolution. This would succeed the middle-class revolution which was bound to come in the wake of capitalism.

By the time Vladimir reached Samara in 1889, Plekhanov's Geneva organization of marxists had lost touch with the groups of younger marxists which were beginning to spring up in Russia. These were developing very much on their own lines, thus laying the foundation for future clashes with the exiled theorists when the Geneva group tried to exercise authority over the Russian committees. But Vladimir was, as yet, unaware of this impending conflict. He was fast making himself master of the works of Marx. These, and the classics of Russian nineteenth-century radicalism, as well as the work of Plekhanov, were closely studied by the future Lenin and his circle of like-minded believers in marxism. He became the undoubted leader of the Samara marxists, and engaged in spirited debates with populist theorists. He also studied the peasants as closely as he could, and his first known published work (in 1893) was an analysis designed to show the extent to which economic differentiation was taking place in the villages. In the same year, in a series of letters which were only published many years later, he argued that capitalism already existed in the villages and that it was essentially the same as the industrial kind (Plekhanov had never gone further than the contention that capitalism was imminent in Russia, or that the first signs of it were appearing).

The importance of this view of Lenin's, though perhaps not apparent at the time, is in its relation to the two stages of revolution — the bourgeois and the socialist — in which Plekhanov and his supporters believed. There is some evidence that by 1894 Lenin thought that the bourgeois revolution, when it occurred in Russia, would herald the collapse not only of the autocracy but of the bourgeois capitalist order as well. But, this apart, if capitalism was already established, as he would maintain with particular vigour in discussions on the party programme in 1902, then the next phase introduced by revolution must be socialism. His outright rejection of collaboration with the liberals, on which he eventually clashed with Plekhanov, was in tune with this kind of thinking.

In September 1893 Vladimir moved to Petersburg. This brought him into contact with a group of experienced social democrats whose activity had been entirely among factory workers. This contact with practical social democratic work was probably new to him — it is not certain that he had had any experience in the factories in Samara. In 1895 he spent between May and September on an extensive tour abroad, visiting Switzerland, Berlin and Paris. He met Plekhanov and his colleagues, and leading West European social democrats. He had long discussions with Plekhanov and Aksel'rod, his close collaborator, both of whom lectured the young man on his intransigent attitude to the liberals. But the veterans were deeply impressed with this serious, modest and above all determined marxist who seemed quite ready to accept the preeminence of the Geneva prophets on questions of theory.

Soon after his return to Petersburg Vladimir was arrested and after a year spent in prison was sent into Siberian exile, where he spent three years in relative comfort, amply supplied with books by his devoted sister, Anna. It was a time of intense intellectual activity. His major work of the period, *The Development of Capitalism in Russia,* argued that only capitalist development and class structure were possible in Russia. In 1896 he produced the draft of a programme for a Social Democratic Party, which won the warm approval of Aksel'rod. So far no such party existed in Russia, 'social democracy' representing only a general movement — in Russian conditions, of course, a revolutionary one — centring round marxist ideas. (The first, foundation congress of the party took place in 1898.) Lenin's draft programme recited the evolution of the workers' struggle in Russia, and stated that the first task of the party must be that of helping the workers to attain their main aim — political freedom. The draft programme demanded the summoning of a National Assembly which would ensure the basic civil liberties. In order to achieve this demand, the party would support 'every movement within society directed against the unrestricted power of the autocratic government' and against the privileged class of the exploiters. The explanatory section added that the workers must remember that 'the propertied classes can only be their allies temporarily, that the interests of the workers and the capitalists are irreconcilable, and that the abolition of the autocracy is only needed by the workers in order to be able openly to conduct their fight against capitalism on a broad front.'

Here we have the 'classical' two-stage revolution: make the bourgeois revolution jointly with the liberals, then turn against the liberals and destroy capitalism in a socialist revolution. This section also contained an exposition of the relations between the party and the workers. The task of the party did not consist 'in thinking up out of our heads some modern methods,' but in helping the workers to develop their class consciousness and to conduct their struggle. The consciousness of the need to struggle for political power would grow up among the workers in the course of their battle for their daily needs against the factory owners. This struggle 'of its own accord and inevitably brings the workers up against questions of government and of politics,' and to the realization that economic and political demands are indissolubly linked. Three years later Lenin (as we may by then call him) would argue virtually the opposite. Why did he change his mind?

His relations with Aksel'rod remained warm and friendly during the early years of his exile, and there seemed to be an identity of views between them. Lenin had evidently taken note of Aksel'rod's fears that the old People's Will tradition of conspiracy and *coup d'état* (against which Plekhanov had directed his most violent polemics) might manifest itself in the young Russian social democratic movement. A pamphlet written by Lenin at the end of 1897 was published in the following year with a preface by Aksel'rod, which included the following sentence: 'And let no simple-minded reader have any fear that he [i.e. the author] is proposing to summon the workers to the barricades, or to engage in conspiracies.' A year later, in a letter, Lenin expressed agreement with the view that the two main dangers facing the Russian movement were that it would either fail to develop beyond the stage of isolated conflicts in the factories, or dissipate itself in conspiracies and pointless violence.

The change in Lenin's outlook was apparently brought about by Eduard Bernstein's famous pamphlet *Evolutionary Socialism* which, published in March 1899, became the bible of 'revisionist' marxism. It argued that evolution was more effective in achieving socialism than revolution, and that much of Marx's analysis had been proved wrong. The work did not reach Lenin until 1 September, but some weeks before then his sister Anna forwarded a document to him, to which she added the heading 'Credo'. This looked like the programme of a new group, but was in fact a statement by two or three moderate marxists to the effect that in Russian conditions political action should be left to the liberals, while the workers should concentrate on economic demands. The effect upon Lenin of the two documents was electrifying, driving him into determined opposition to what he regarded as revisionism in the Russian social democratic movement, and by the end of the year he had evolved a plan of action which laid the foundation for Bolshevism. The first signs of it appeared in an article ('Our Immediate Tasks') which foreshadowed some of the arguments embodied in 1902 in the textbook of Bolshevism, Lenin's *What is to be Done?*.

Although the article remained unpublished, Lenin, after his exile came to an end at the beginning of 1900, set about putting into effect its main idea — to create a central party newspaper which would 'bring into the spontaneous worker movement certain specific socialist ideals'. After lengthy discussions with Plekhanov and his colleagues agreement was eventually reached. The paper was to be called *Iskra* (The Spark), and its editorial board was to consist of Plekhanov (with two votes) and his colleagues Aksel'rod, Vera Zasulich and Potresov, as well as Lenin and the future Menshevik leader Martov. The first issue appeared in Munich on 24 (old style 11) December 1900.

It was clear from the start that the main purpose of *Iskra* was to conduct an all-out battle against the marxists inside Russia who refused to accept directives from the Geneva prophets, and who were accused, without any real justification, of being 'economists', or followers of the 'Credo' line. One such group of Social Democrats was organized around another paper, *Rabochee delo*, and on Lenin's insistence a breach with them took place in October 1901.

Meanwhile, in the course of 1901 and 1902, work was going on in preparation for the Second Congress of the Social Democratic Party. (The First Congress of 1898 had achieved nothing, its nine members having been arrested immediately after it.) It was intended that the Second Congress should be solidly *Iskra*-orientated, and Lenin and his fellow editor Martov worked to that end, with the aid of Lenin's wife, Krupskaia. They were assisted in their task by twelve agents, paid out of party funds, whom they had recruited in Russia before leaving for Switzerland after their exile, and whose work was helped by the mounting industrial unrest (the annual number of workers on strike at least doubled between 1900 and 1903). The object of the agents was to win over to *Iskra* the Social Democratic committees inside Russia, and they were not over-scrupulous in their methods. Usually victory was achieved by splitting a committee into an *Iskra* group and an opposing group. In due course the opposing committee died a natural death, unable to compete either with the greater financial resources of *Iskra* or with the greater emotional appeal that *Iskra*'s message held for young revolutionaries.

An important part of *Iskra*'s campaign was Lenin's pamphlet *What is to be Done?*, published in March 1902. (The title, of course, was an echo of Chernyshevsky's novel.) Its main argument stressed the need for a centralized, disciplined party which would lead the workers' movement and not follow in its wake. At the head of this movement Lenin envisaged a network of professional revolutionaries, united in doctrine and devoting themselves full-time to the task. This, argued Lenin, was necessary because 'political class consciousness can only be brought to the worker *from the outside* [Lenin's emphasis] that is to say from outside the economic struggle. . . .' The accusation made by opponents of *Iskra* that it did not attach sufficient importance to the 'spontaneous' nature of the workers' movement was misconceived: workers had no social-democratic consciousness. 'The history of all countries bears witness that the working class by virtue of its own powers alone is only capable of developing a trade union consciousness, i.e. the conviction of the necessity of uniting in trade unions, of urging struggle against their employers, bringing pressure on the government to pass this or that law which is necessary for the workers, and so forth.' The vanguard of professional revolutionaries should not confine its activities to the workers: it should work among all sections of the population. It would necessarily take a long time before the proletariat could become the overwhelming majority in Russia, as Marx had envisaged they must be before they could take power in the capitalist systems of Western Europe. Lenin frankly offered a short cut: 'give us an organization of revolutionaries — and we will overturn the whole of Russia.' The argument of those who stressed the need for democracy in the party was dismissed: in conditions of underground secrecy such democracy was inconceivable. The whole conception of 'freedom of criticism' was false: 'People who were really convinced of the fact that they had advanced knowledge would be demanding not freedom for the new views alongside the old views, but the replacement of the latter by the former.'

It is perhaps possible to find some support for these views in the writings of Marx if one looks hard enough. The notion that social democratic consciousness has to be brought to the workers from the outside is certainly to be found in several of the works of the German socialist Kautsky. But the overall trend of Marx's views cannot be reconciled with *What is to be Done?*, though it is true that Marx was mainly writing about workers operating in conditions of liberal democracy and not in a police state. The views of Plekhanov and Aksel'rod certainly seem at variance with Lenin's. On the other hand, neither of them offered any serious criticism of the pamphlet when it first appeared. The explanation is presumably to be sought in the fact that they were strongly committed to the struggle of *Iskra* against the Russian committees who refused to follow it, and anxious to secure an *Iskra* majority for the forthcoming congress. To this end *What is to be Done?* was a valuable contribution: for one thing, it offered the prospect of a revolution much sooner than the somewhat leisurely 'classical' two-stage version promised by Plekhánov. 'Party democracy', 'spontaneity', 'freedom of discussion' were all slogans much used by the rival Social Democratic paper *Rabochee delo*, and a vigorous answer to them was much to be welcomed.

When the Second Congress met in Brussels on 30 (old style 17) July 1903 it looked as if the *Iskra* group could be sure of a substantial majority. There were 57 delegates, but only 43 of them had a vote and 8 of these delegates had two votes each. (This situation was due to the complicated basis of representation laid down by the Organizing Committee.) Of the total of 51 votes, 5 went to the Jewish *Bund*, whose demands for autonomy were certain to lead to its ultimate exclusion; 2 votes represented *Rabochee delo*, and 3 went to other opponents of *Iskra*. This left what looked like a comfortable majority of 41 to 10 — but things did not work out as expected.

No divisions appeared during the debates on the party's programme, which occupied the early meetings of the congress. The programme was passed unanimously — though one delegate took the opportunity of pointing out in the course of the discussion that the basic doctrine of *What is to be Done?* was inconsistent with the views of Marx. But by the time of the sixteenth and seventeenth meetings it became apparent that a number of *Iskrites* were voting against Lenin along with the *Bund* and the other dissenting delegates. These divisions were not in any way related to questions of theory or principle. They were in all probability to be explained by the fact that in a series of private meetings of the *Iskra* group organized by Lenin (there were five such in all) the future Bolshevik leader had antagonized many of the members by his intransigent demands for the exclusion from the congress of a marxist scholar with whom he had clashed in the past.

Among Lenin's opponents (the 'softs', as he called them) were Martov, Aksel'rod and Vera Zasulich. It was Martov who, at the twenty-second session of the congress, led the opposition to Lenin, with the result that Lenin was outvoted by 28 votes to 23. The disagreement was over the wording of the first paragraph of the Party Rules, in which membership of the party was defined. Lenin's wording suggested stricter party discipline than Martov's version, and the division on this issue at the congress has frequently since been cited as the main cause for the split in the party. In fact, in 1903 in

Russian conditions, the question was largely academic, and the reason for the split must be sought in the growing antagonism between the two kinds of social democracy — the tougher 'Leninist', and the milder, more traditional, sort.

Martov's majority included the five *Bund* votes and two 'economist' votes. A few sessions later the *Bund* delegates, followed by the two 'economists', left the congress after it had voted to deny the *Bund* the autonomy it sought to achieve. This now left Lenin and his supporters in a majority. Lenin was quick to exploit this advantage in order to secure control by his faction over the party organs. He could be sure, with his majority, of the three Central Committee members, who would operate inside Russia. But the supreme organ, the Party Council, consisted of five members — two appointed by the Central Committee, one by the congress (who was certain to be Plekhanov, who still supported Lenin) and two by the editorial board of *Iskra*, on which the 'softs' predominated. Lenin now proposed that the editorial board should be reduced to three — Plekhanov, Martov and himself — and caused an uproar, with accusations against him of bad faith. But his proposal was carried against the abstentions of his twenty opponents.

The split in the party, into what soon became known as 'Bolsheviks' ('majoritarians') and 'Mensheviks' ('minoritarians') was to prove permanent. The division was much less one of principle than of temperament. Neither faction had any real intention of permitting democracy in the party; and if once the principle was accepted that a (nominally) marxist revolution, was to be carried out in a peasant country by a strictly disciplined, conspiratorial party — and all *Iskrites* had accepted this — the emergence of Lenin as the dictator was logical enough. Who else was it to be, Lenin asked a confidant a few months later. Plekhanov — who, for all his erudition, was incapable of organizing anything? Martov — an excellent journalist, but an 'hysterical intellectual, who needs watching all the time'? Aksel'rod? Zasulich? Potresov? Trotsky? The very idea was enough 'to make a chicken laugh'. The future would show that Lenin's assessment of the practical abilities of most of his colleagues was not far off the mark.

The coming year was to prove turbulent for a party which, though nominally still a single one, was in fact under Lenin's influence moving towards a division into two.* Lenin was determined to keep the 'Martovites', as he called those who opposed his tactics, out of party life, though they were in fact in the majority. After some abortive attempts at compromise, Plekhanov changed sides and

*It was not until 1918 that the Bolsheviks formally ceased to call themselves Social Democrats, although after 1903 they began to maintain a separate organization.

coopted the old *Iskra* board, who now poured recriminations on Lenin's tactical theories. *Iskra* argued that the proper course for the infant Social Democratic party was to encourage the workers in every way to develop political consciousness in the course of the struggle for their rights. In the face of the threat from a stronger, richer and more popular organization, Lenin strove to build his own machine of loyal followers. The revolution of 1905 produced a strong demand among workers for unity in the party which claimed to speak for them, and for some years to come there were to be repeated attempts at genuine unity. The Menshevik leaders believed in this because marxism, as they saw it, had no room for more than one party of the proletariat. The evidence suggests that the Bolsheviks, or those who loyally supported Lenin, had no intention of allowing this unity to become a reality — and the view that their desire for it was never genuine is borne out by the fact that at all periods the Bolsheviks maintained their own separate organization. As time went on it became increasingly clear that the real division between the two factions was tactical rather than theoretical. While the Bolsheviks accused their opponents of being 'liquidators' — in other words of wishing to do away with the underground party — it would seem that in the overwhelming majority of cases the real cause of division was refusal to serve in a party directed by Lenin. This was due to resentment of his tactical methods in winning support for party committees, and above all to a number of scandalous incidents connected with the raising of funds.

The Mensheviks were fast assuming the rôle which they would play to the very last — that of willing the ends, but not being prepared to endorse the necessary means. There remained, however, the theoretical difference between the factions on the two phases of the revolution. Lenin appeared to be accepting the 'classical' view of the two-stage road to socialism when he wrote after the 1905 revolution that it was 'inept' and 'semi-anarchist' to believe that the maximum socialist programmes could be attempted immediately after the democratic revolution had succeeded. The workers had to acquire class-consciousness in the course of their struggle against the bourgeoise. This was a statement of the orthodox and Menshevik interpretation of Marx. What followed was less so. The democratic revolution must be succeeded, he argued, by a 'revolutionary democratic dictatorship of the proletariat and peasants'. This dictatorship would radically alter land tenure in the peasants' favour, introduce complete 'democratization', improve the conditions of the workers and 'last but not least' carry the flame of revolution across to the rest of Europe. There was no room in this programme for the kind of collaboration with the bourgeoisie envisaged by orthodox marxists

— as became clear in 1917 when Lenin's plan was in effect implemented by the Bolsheviks. That Lenin was already, in 1905, thinking in terms of an immediate socialist revolution became evident when, at the party congress the following year, he advocated nationalization of all land. As Plekhanov pointed out this could only strengthen the government, and therefore Lenin must be contemplating a socialist and not a hostile government emerging as the result of the democratic revolution. The Mensheviks at this congress advocated 'municipalization'.

In 1912 Lenin's assault on the Mensheviks became more determined. There was no longer any pretence of preserving a united party. At a conference in Prague the 'liquidators' were expelled from the party, and an all-Bolshevik Central Committee was set up. The Mensheviks continued to advocate unity, believing that no theoretical differences of importance divided the party, and that Bolshevik tactics were the 'growing pains' of a young movement. The rank and file of the party were also strongly in favour of unity, and the thirteen Social Democrats elected to serve in the Fourth Duma were returned upon their express promise that they would endeavour to preserve a single 'fraction'. For a time a kind of harmony prevailed, but in 1913 Lenin succeeded in organizing a split in the 'fraction'. The Mensheviks turned for help to the Socialist International, which offered its services as mediator. In the enquiries which the International conducted, and in the unification conference which met in July 1914, Bolshevik intransigence antagonized international socialists and found little support inside Russia. By the eve of the First World War, Lenin and his supporters were isolated and faced expulsion from the ranks of socialism when the Executive Committee of the International Socialist Bureau reported to the forthcoming International Socialist Congress. But the war came, and the congress never met.

Except for a short period in 1905/1906 Lenin lived abroad from 1900 until his return to Russia on 3 April 1917. The outbreak of war found him in Austria. After a spell of arrest, he moved to Switzerland, where he remained. He staked all his hopes for revolution on the war, and envisaged that the proletariat which first achieved victory would arouse the working classes of other capitalist countries to insurrection. He did not, however, believe that these upheavals were imminent, nor did he specifically expect a revolution in Russia. When the Russian revolution did come, he believed, it would be the completion by the proletariat, in alliance with the peasants, of the bourgeois revolution.

He repeatedly made it plain that in the emergent 'revolutionary democratic dictatorship' there would be no sharing of power with

Mensheviks. His pattern of action, as it was in fact to develop in 1917, was sketched by him in October 1915. It would not be enough merely to demand the summoning of a Constituent Assembly; the important question would be who was in power when the elections to it took place. Should soviets arise, as they had in 1905, they should be treated as organs of insurrection against the bourgeoisie. On no account must Social Democrats (i.e. Bolsheviks, in Lenin's terminology) participate in a provisional government side by side with 'social chauvinists' — meaning Mensheviks and Socialist Revolutionaries. If the 'social chauvinists' should be victorious in Russia, 'we should be against the defence of *their* fatherland in the present war.' The Bolsheviks would be against the 'chauvinists' even if they were revolutionaries and republicans, and stood 'for the union of the international proletariat for the socialist revolution'.

In the international sphere Lenin advocated a final break with the Second Socialist International, and the need to create a third, truly marxist, international, cleansed of 'opportunism' and 'chauvinism'. This decision, though fully consistent with his policy towards all socialists who did not accept his own leadership, was no doubt reinforced by the fact that the great majority of European socialists (the Russians and Serbians had been conspicuous exceptions) had voted in support of war credits, in spite of solemn pledges made in peace-time not to do so. However, the vote in the Duma notwithstanding, Russian socialists were divided on the question of the war. There were some who argued that it must be pursued to victory. Others, including Martov and Aksel'rod, repudiated it as an imperialist war of plunder and, like Lenin, saw the only solution in revolution. But, unlike Lenin, they believed that the one hope lay in restoring the shattered unity of international socialism. Nor were they prepared, as he was, to advocate the defeat of Russia as the 'lesser evil', regarding the victory of any imperialist belligerent as a disaster. As a first step they believed it necessary to mobilize the proletariat of all the belligerents, so that they would put pressure on their governments to conclude a speedy and just peace without annexation of territory or payment of indemnity. They saw the only prospect of lasting peace in the universal victory of socialism.

In the hope of implementing his policy, Lenin was active in 1915 and 1916 in international conferences of dissident socialists who opposed the war, organizing a left group which first demanded civil war as the only means of ending hostilities, and later called on the proletariat to 'lay down your weapons. You should turn them only against the common foe — the capitalists.' These activities brought severe reprisals on the Bolshevik underground in Russia, where its committees, both in Petrograd and in the provinces, had been heavily penetrated by police agents. They also helped to deepen the rift between the Bolsheviks and the Mensheviks. Neither did they escape the notice of the Germans, who attempted to enter into an agreement with Lenin. In this they were unsuccessful, but when the revolution had broken out Lenin did not hesitate to arrange with the Germans, through the agency of a Swiss socialist, for the famous 'sealed train' which they provided to enable him to travel to Russia through Germany. He arrived in Petrograd a month after the fall of the monarchy.

Chapter Three

The End of the Monarchy

In the early months of 1917 food was short in Petrograd, and there were widespread fears of still worse hunger to come. Official figures support the view that reserves of flour were indeed low after the middle of February, though probably little lower than they had been on occasions in the past. This shortfall was in part due to the serious decline in agricultural output — the production of cereals, for example, fell over twenty per cent in 1916-1917 compared with the pre-war level — but it was also due to administrative muddle and incompetence. The strident criticism of the government voiced by the Progressive Bloc and the voluntary organizations, combined with the failure of the authorities to publish adequate information, inevitably meant that in the public mind the blame fell entirely on the ministers and the bureaucracy. As always, rumours were rife.

A police report on the eve of the revolution predicted a hunger riot. This would, in their opinion, be sparked off not only by the steep rises in food prices between December 1916 and February 1917 (potatoes 25 per cent, bread 15 per cent, sausage 50 per cent, milk 40 per cent) but also by the widespread conviction that food was being made available to the rich and privileged while the poor starved. From other reports it is evident that, while the exact relation between rises in prices and increased wages is difficult to determine, the workers were convinced that the mounting cost of living far outstripped any improvement in their earnings.

Although there was plenty of explosive material spread throughout the country, in factories, among the peasants and in the largely peasant army at the front, there is no doubt that the impetus for the revolution came from the proletariat and military garrison of Petrograd. The capital city produced nearly a quarter of the total industrial output. The number of workers there increased from 242,600 in 1914 to 391,800 in 1917, or to over 400,000 (11.9 per cent of the entire industrial work force) if the regions adjoining the capital are included. The overwhelming majority of these workers were engaged in military production and were, in practice, exempt from conscription. They were highly literate, probably to the extent of nearly 90 per cent of men, and 65 per cent of women. The influx to the ranks of industry during the war was provided mainly by peasants, women and children, and while students of the Petrograd work-force are not agreed on the extent of the peasants' influence on industrial unrest, the impact of women in the bread riots of February 1917 was certainly strong. But all who have examined the question agree that the main impetus to the strike movement was provided by urban-born, better-paid, young skilled workers, who were relatively well educated and had a strong class consciousness. Patriotic fervour and fear of conscription kept strikes in Petrograd down to a low level up till the summer of 1915 — there were only 147 stoppages before July. Thereafter, up to 22 February 1917, there were as many as 1,163 strikes, involving more than a million people. Over half of these actions were politically, rather than economically, motivated.

Strikes, then, became a familiar feature of life in Petrograd. To keep them under control, the government relied on its police force, and if need be on the large garrison stationed in and near Petrograd. One cannot describe those responsible for the security of the capital in 1917 as impressive personalities. The Minister of the Interior, A.D. Protopopov, was, to the public, a symbol of the corruption and incompetence of the régime and a known protégé of Rasputin. The Minister of War, General M.A. Beliaev, and the general in command of troops in Petrograd, S.S. Khabalov, were military bureaucrats of mediocre talent who had seen no military service. Like Protopopov, both men were reputedly appointed through intrigues by Rasputin. Making use of a conflict between these two men on the one hand and the Commander of the Northern Front, General Ruzskii, on the other, Protopopov had succeeded in getting the Petrograd Military District detached from the Northern Front. If, as was widely believed (though there is no evidence to support the legend), Protopopov and Rasputin were German agents, they could hardly have served their masters better than by promoting these arrangements in the Petrograd Military District.

Under the contingency plans for the defence of Petrograd against revolution, order would first be maintained by the 3,500 (highly unpopular) police, with the help of 3,200 mounted Cossacks experienced in controlling crowds with whips. Only in the last resort would soldiers open fire. Exact figures on the strength of the Petrograd garrison are not available, but the total number of all troops in the city and in its immediate vicinity was between 322,000 and 466,800. The most important element was believed to be the fourteen guards battalions, numbering 99,000 men, which were to take over in each of the sixteen police districts.

There was no provision at any stage for seeking the support of troops from the Northern Front. The military authorities, Khabalov in particular, refused to contemplate the possibility that the loyalty of the garrison might be in doubt, or that some of them might be replaced with men from the front, whose morale was notably higher. Yet, in fact, the reliability of both soldiers and officers of the garrison troops was very dubious. Heavy casualties among officers at the front, followed by recruitment on a large scale, had meant that fewer than ten per cent of all officers were regulars, who could be trusted to impose ruthless discipline. The ranks were embittered by petty tyranny in the barracks, and demoralized by the monotony of life. Their numbers had been replenished by elements which undermined morale — soldiers in their forties who had replaced younger men sent to the front, evacuees from the front recuperating from wounds or illness, and strikers mobilized as a punishment. For the overwhelming majority of peasant soldiers, most officers appeared merely as landlords in uniform.

The year 1917 in Petrograd opened with a pattern of strikes that was by now familiar. The traditional one on 9 January, commemorating the 'Bloody Sunday' of 1905, was particularly successful: 300,000 were reported to have come out, and there were large stoppages in Moscow and elsewhere. Meanwhile, on 6 January, the reconvening of the Duma, which had been prorogued some time before, was postponed until 14 February. Calls were now issued by various worker organizations for a mass demonstration to be held on that day to demand a responsible government. But the most dramatic of the appeals came from the Menshevik-dominated Workers' Group of the Central War Industry Committee on 24 January. This condemned the autocratic system as incapable of conducting the war successfully, and moreover foretold disaster for the workers if victory were achieved while the present régime was still in power. The group therefore called for a mass demonstration on 14 February to demand the formation of a Provisional Government based on democratic principles.

The authorities, on Protopopov's initiative, made this appeal the excuse for arresting all but three of the Workers' Group, one of whom was a police spy. This move (made with the Emperor's approval) eliminated by far the most moderate element among the socialists, and destroyed any possibility of an alliance between the left wing of the Duma opposition and the working class, on which successful continuation of the war depended. The real reason for the arrests (if it was anything more than stupidity) was the influence which the Workers' Group was winning among the working class throughout the country. Its elimination played into the hands of the more extreme socialists. In the end, only some tens of thousands went on strike on 14 February and there were some student demonstrations. There was no mass demand for a democratic Provisional Government.

In the Duma, however, the Progressive Bloc did call for the formation of a government of national confidence, although such a request by the President of the Duma, M.V. Rodzianko, had been rejected by the Emperor a few days before; and in the State Council the supporters of the Progressive Bloc walked out of the chamber when a debate on the issue of a government of national confidence was refused by its President.

As the Petrograd workers moved towards their fatal confrontation with the government, the evidence does not suggest that the socialist parties were able to exercise anything like a controlling influence over them. In particular, the Bolsheviks, whom Soviet historians generally credit with virtually leading the revolution in February, were very far from exercising this rôle. On 10 February, for example, when they called for a general strike to commemorate the anniversary of the trial of members of the Petersburg Soviet of 1905, they virtually failed to evoke a response. Though there were said to be some three thousand Bolsheviks active in Petrograd their organization had been much disrupted by the arrests and exiles which followed on the determined stand against the war which Lenin had initiated from Switzerland. In October 1916 A.G. Shliapnikov (an honest, not very dynamic revolutionary whose memoirs form one of our most important sources on the events of 1917) returned from abroad and, together with the young V.M. Molotov and P.A. Zalutskii, revived the Russian Bureau of the Central Committee as an underground organization. The Bureau represented inside Russia the Central Committee, which functioned in exile, but it never succeeded in achieving leadership over the workers' movement and was even incapable of asserting authority over the Petersburg Committee,* which in turn was much harassed by police repressions and incapable of exercising leadership. The most effective Bolshevik influence over strike activity came from local committees, especially the one situated in the industrial suburb of the Vyborg District.

The Mensheviks were even less effective than the Bolsheviks, split by the war into several groups, including 'defencists', who believed in fighting the war to a successful conclusion, and 'internationalists' who believed that the war should be brought to an end on just terms. The only Menshevik body to make any mark was the Workers' Group of the Central War Industries Committee, and most of its members,

---

*This committee never adopted the new name Petrograd in its title.

as we saw, were arrested in January 1917. It was typical of the bitterness that existed between rival revolutionary groups that one of the main activities of the Bolsheviks during the war consisted of attacks on this group. There was also an extreme Social Democrat faction, the 'Interdistrict Group', not affiliated to either the Bolsheviks or Mensheviks, which became Trotsky's centre of operation until he joined the Bolsheviks, and which was active in anti-war propaganda.

The Socialist Revolutionaries were also split on the issue of the war. The spokesman for the defencist wing was A.F. Kerensky, the leading figure in the Duma opposition, a fiery orator who did much by his speeches to influence public opinion. He had not joined the Progressive Bloc and was a republican by conviction. All these parties and groups criticized the government by whatever means were available to them and, with the exception of the Workers' Group of the Central War Industries Committee, did what they could to encourage strikes — in so far as the Petrograd workers needed encouragement. But the evidence is clear that no socialist group saw the collapse of the monarchy as imminent in February 1917, and that all were equally taken by surprise by the rapidity with which the familiar pattern of strikes turned into a revolution.

With the benefit of hindsight, it is possible to discern that 23 February, traditionally International Women's Day, marked the beginning of the revolution. The strike that day was started in the textile factories in the Vyborg District by women who marched out into the street with cries of 'Bread!', calling on workers in other factories to join them. They were eventually joined by fifty thousand more, though not all took part in the demonstration. What distinguished this strike from others was not its size: it embraced at most twenty to thirty per cent of the Petrograd work force, and was, moreover, confined to two districts. There is no doubt that the police were fully able to control and disperse the demonstrators. Their reports of the day also suggest that the slogans exhibited or shouted were predominantly demands for bread. There had been food riots only a few days earlier, on 19 and 21 February, but the events of 23 February were notable for their militancy — in many cases those who initiated the stoppage forced the others to abandon work. Another new feature was the strikers' determination to stage demonstrations. There was also a good deal of looting, and it was evident that a number of ordinary criminals were taking advantage of the disorder. Above all, there were instances on that day in which the Cossacks were reluctant to charge the crowd.

The strike movement gathered momentum the following day, 24

February, when the largest number of workers came out since the war started — between 158,000 and 197,000, according to police records. On this occasion, all districts of the city were involved. Although the Bolsheviks had taken little part in the previous day's events, the local Bolsheviks, especially those in the Vyborg District, were now particularly active in urging militancy, but there were many more leaders involved, unconnected with any political party. The possibility cannot be excluded that some of them were paid German agents (as was widely believed at the time) but no conclusive evidence has come to light in support of this supposition. The other radical parties, notably the 'Interdistrict Group' were also active. On this occasion, in addition to demands for bread, political slogans against the war and the autocracy were noted by the police. The striking workers succeeded in penetrating, reportedly in as many as thirteen columns, to the centre of the city to hold demonstrations. Although the police and cavalry managed to disperse the demonstrators, the reluctance of the Cossacks was even more marked than it had been on the day before.

According to Shliapnikov it was on this day that the Russian Bureau of the Bolshevik Central Committee took the decision to try to involve the soldiers of the garrison in support of the workers' movement, though what effect this had on ultimate events is difficult to determine. Such evidence as there is suggests that the garrison revolt started in those units which had been least exposed to revolutionary propaganda. Propaganda was mostly directed at the men whose barracks were north of the River Neva in the Vyborg District, whereas the rebellion of the soldiers started in the guards regiments stationed in the centre of the town, south of the river. General Khabalov (in command of the troops in Petrograd) interpreted the unrest in the capital solely in terms of dissatisfaction over food shortages, and even issued a reassuring (and untrue) statement on the bread supplies. Although aware that the Cossacks could not be relied on to stem disorder, the general staff of the city's defence force decided against such measures as the arrest of revolutionaries or bringing in more reliable Cossack troops from areas near to the capital.

On the following day, 25 February, more than 200,000 joined in what amounted to a general strike, which virtually paralysed the city. There were mass marches and demonstrations in many districts, and the police both inflicted casualties with their bullets and suffered them at the hands of the infuriated crowds. The commander of a mounted police detachment was killed in circumstances which suggest that he may have met his death at the hands of a Cossack. Certainly the evidence shows that both Cossacks and other troops were reluctant to act against the crowds.

The Petersburg Bolshevik Committee, as usual more militant than the Russian Bureau of the Central Committee, unsuccessfully demanded arms from the latter in order to turn the strike into an insurrection, and Shliapnikov, as leader of the Russian Bureau, has been blamed by Soviet historians for his alleged lack of courage. But there seems to have been force in his argument that the correct tactics were to win over the troops, and that if the workers fired at them this could only destroy their sympathy for the crowds.

Police reports for the day took on a more alarming character. The Emperor at his Headquarters in Mogilev first heard that the disturbances were serious from his wife and from the palace commandant at Tsarskoe Selo, where the Empress and her family were resident. (Khabalov and the Minister of War, Beliaev, had sent the General Staff misleading reports that everything was under control.) In the evening, Khabalov received from the Emperor a telegram which was to have momentous effects. It ordered him to 'put an end, as from tomorrow, to all disturbances in the streets of the capital which are insupportable at this difficult time when we are at war with Germany and Austria.' Khabalov issued proclamations prohibiting street gatherings, warning that the troops would fire on demonstrators, and that those who continued on strike would be mobilized for service at the front.

Next day, 26 February, was a Sunday. The city was reported to resemble an armed camp, with police patrolling the street and stationed at all strategic points. The Red Cross had set up a headquarters post. Shliapnikov discovered that nearly all the members of the Petersburg Committee had been arrested early that morning. The functions of the Committee had to be taken over by the militant Vyborg District Committee, but Shliapnikov still firmly resisted the demands of its members for arms to be issued to the workers. According to the police reports, up to a hundred revolutionaries were arrested that Sunday, including five members of the Petersburg Committee and the two members of the Workers' Group of the Central War Industry Committee who had escaped capture on 26 January.

In the course of the morning, there were four major incidents in the centre of the town when troops of the guards regiments fired on marching demonstrators, inflicting quite heavy casualties. The units concerned were those in which selected soldiers were being trained for promotion as non-commissioned officers. The remaining guards were confined to barracks, and every attempt was made to isolate them from the demonstrating crowds. The success of the troops in dispersing the marchers seems to have had the twofold effect of raising the mood of the crowds to a state of fury but at the same time convincing all but the most militant revolutionaries that an incipient revolution had suffered defeat. As Shliapnikov had rightly predicted, the key to failure or success lay with the soldiers, and the omens were not very promising for the revolutionaries. News that demonstrators had been killed by the training unit did, however, reach the barracks of the Pavlovsky Guards Regiment, and caused a short-lived mutiny: a company of guards under the command of a non-commissioned officer went into the streets with the intention of attacking the men of the training unit responsible for the killings. The insurgents were promptly disarmed, and their ringleaders arrested and imprisoned; nevertheless, twenty-one soldiers were found to be missing, and had, it would seem, escaped from barracks, with their weapons. Also, the commander of the Pavlovsky Regiment had been killed in the street after he had left the barracks in the belief that the mutiny had been quelled. General Khabalov's optimistic report to Field Headquarters did not even mention the incident of the Pavlovsky Guards Regiment.

It was only on the following day, Monday 27 February, that the full impact on the garrison troops of the order to shoot at the crowds became apparent. For days before they had been mingling with the crowds in an atmosphere of friendship, and no doubt a good deal of sympathy: now they were told to shoot to kill. The rebellion of the troops started in the training unit of one of the guards regiments, the Volynskii, which had been involved in the shooting. Under the leadership of two non-commissioned officers, the soldiers worked out a carefully planned conspiracy and hoodwinked their commanding officer into leaving the barracks; he was shot dead from a window as he left. They then ran into the street and into the many barracks which, as it happened, were close to their own, in an endeavour to persuade other troops to join in the revolt. They met at first with refusal, even occasional resistance. But the rebellion gathered force. Some officers were shot when they tried to restore discipline; others abandoned the attempt and escaped.

The next few days can only be described as an orgy of anarchy. The ever-increasing number of soldiers who took the side of the rebellion joined with the crowds of demonstrators and supported them with arms. So far as the workers were concerned, there was no thought of going to the factories. There was widespread looting and lynching of policemen. The capture of the arsenal in the afternoon ensured a plentiful supply of weapons, while the storming of the city prisons not only liberated political prisoners but also released a large number of criminals into the streets, where they took part in the looting and raping. Whatever the revolutionary impulses that swayed this crowd on 27 and 28 February, there was much of the traditional Russian form of rebellion in the events of those days in Petrograd — 'senseless and pitiless', as Pushkin called it. One isolated instance of resistance by the Bicycle Battalion under the command of its colonel, of which the defeat by much larger and well-armed numbers of soldiers was inevitable, nevertheless proved that a disciplined military unit, if capably led, could effectively resist large numbers of rebels for a long time. The battalion's resistance ended on 28 February with the surrender of the troops and the murder of many of their officers.

It became obvious, as 27 February wore on, that the forces of revolt were degenerating into an anarchical mob, with no leaders, no plan, and above all no discipline, driven by pent-up resentment, with no thought but destruction. 'One disciplined division from the front would have been enough to quell the uprising,' commented one of the Duma leaders. But the momentum with which the soldiers' revolt gathered force took the command of the city by surprise: they were frightened, bewildered and unprepared. According to the estimate of Soviet historians 10,200 soldiers rebelled in the morning of 27 February, and by the evening the number had grown to 66,700. By the end of the following day the total had risen to 127,000 and by 1 March almost the entire garrison, 170,000 out of 180,200 in the city, had joined the insurrection.

The final defence of the old régime by the few thousand troops who still remained loyal was disorganized, incompetent and beset with mishaps. The commander of the city troops was absent, apparently on account of illness, and an inexperienced officer was appointed in his place by General Khabalov, whom several witnesses report as being in a state of panic. The military operations of the last hours of the old régime have been closely studied by Soviet historians. While the police force had to a large extent disintegrated by the early afternoon, there were still loyal forces left which, with better communication and leadership, could have been mobilized against the insurrection. In the end, the loyal troops in the city who, however reluctantly, had retained some degree of discipline, melted away to mingle with the crowds when all further resistance had become hopeless.

It was a symptom of the confusion reigning at Khabalov's headquarters that when, at long last, he requested reinforcements from the front in a telegram dispatched to field staff HQ at 12.10 p.m. on 27 February, this was followed an hour later by a telegram from the Minister of War, General Beliaev, to the Chief of Staff stating that all was well and that he was confident that order would be restored. Beliaev seems, by all accounts, to have lost his self-control to an even greater extent than General Khabalov — both were, after all, virtually civilians in uniform with no experience of warfare. In the

small hours of 28 February, a telegram reached General Staff HQ
from Khabalov to the effect that he had failed to fulfil the Emperor's
command to restore order in the capital. Khabalov was dismissed,
and General N.I. Ivanov appointed military dictator of Petrograd.
(Ivanov was at the time in the personal entourage of the Emperor.)

The government, in the shape of the Council of Ministers under its
last chairman, Prince Golitsyn, did not meet after the disturbances
on the 23rd until midnight on 25 February. By a majority, the
ministers decided to seek a political solution by negotiation with the
Duma, and delegates were selected to initiate the discussion. But on
the following day the short-lived optimism to which the apparent
success in repressing insurgency had given rise emboldened the
government to prorogue the Duma (which was regarded by all except
the most enlightened ministers as responsible for provoking the
disorders). The Chairman of the Council of Ministers followed the
accepted practice of effecting this by means of a decree which had
been signed by the Emperor for use at his discretion, with the date left
blank.

On the evening of 27 February the Council of Ministers was faced
with the imminent prospect of mob violence. A few hours before,
Prince Golitsyn had announced the resignation of his cabinet in a
telegram to the Emperor, and requested the formation of a temporary
dictatorship under the regency (in the Emperor's absence) of his
brother the Grand Duke Michael. The solution was quickly rejected
by the Emperor. By the following day, control over events — or such
control as there was — was assumed by two new bodies which had
come into existence on 27 February: The Committee of the Duma
and the Petrograd Soviet.

The leaders of the Progressive Bloc in the Duma viewed the events of
27 February with dismay. In spite of the fact that they had done all
they could to discredit the régime, they had not intended its
collapse — indeed, it had probably not occurred to them that the
Russian régime could even be shaken by verbal assault, however
extreme. Its downfall now seemed to threaten what they most
ardently desired — the successful prosecution to victory of the war.
The President of the Duma, M.V. Rodzianko, had, in telegrams to the
Emperor, pleaded for a 'government of confidence' to be appointed,
but had been ignored as a panic-monger. He sent the last such
telegram on 27 February, warning the Emperor that the fate of the
dynasty as well as that of the war was at stake, and urging him to
reconvene the Duma. There was, indeed, a strong demand from some
of the deputies after the Duma had been prorogued that it should
ignore the decree of prorogation, and assume power, as the only

institution now left with any legitimate authority. This Rodzianko, as well as many Kadet deputies, was unwilling to do.

The President also refused to allow the Duma to continue to meet in defiance of the decree, because he feared this could be interpreted as a revolutionary act. However, reluctantly and under pressure, he agreed to hold an *unofficial* meeting. This meeting, which was boycotted by the right-wing Duma members, showed little enthusiasm for any courageous or demonstrative act, but it did agree, at 3.30 p.m. on 27 February, to elect a Committee, headed (after hesitation, lest his acceptance be construed as rebellion) by Rodzianko, and consisting, in effect, of the leaders of the parties composing the Progressive Bloc. This Provisional Committee of the Duma (as it called itself) lacked authority because it stemmed only from an unofficial meeting, and not from the Duma as a whole. The Duma itself, by its pusillanimous and indecisive lack of action, lost the opportunity, which would never recur, of taking over power with a semblance of legitimacy.

As time went on, and the reality of the insurrection became even more evident, the Provisional Committee of the Duma issued two proclamations at 2 a.m. on 28 February, one appealing for order, the other explaining that the Provisional Committee 'has found itself compelled to take the responsibility for restoring national and public order'. As 28 February progressed, the victory of the insurgents became ever clearer. The last loyal troops, embattled in the Admiralty building, were evacuated by order of the Navy Minister so that the building should be spared destruction. The remaining military units in Petrograd, in its outskirts, and elsewhere in important centres like Kronstadt, Oranienbaum and Helsingfors, joined the insurgents, after a large number of officers (certainly no fewer than a hundred, including the Admiral of the Baltic Fleet, Nepenin) had been murdered in particularly brutal circumstances. Even the troops in the Tsar's residence, Tsarskoe Selo, joined the revolutionary forces. There were numerous arrests of former ministers and other prominent figures of the old régime, sanctioned by Kerensky in the name of 'revolutionary justice'. The memoirs of the time abound with accounts (probably largely apocryphal) of Kerensky's theatrical exhibitions in saving ministers and others from lynching. Those detained were kept in custody in a pavilion which formed part of the Duma building, the Tauride Palace, built by the Empress Catherine for her favourite lover, Prince Potemkin. The fever of arrests was to rage for some days.

The Provincial Committee, somewhat reluctantly, took further steps on 28 February. It appointed a number of commissioners who were despatched to the main ministries to take over the conduct of affairs. A.A. Bublikov, who had earlier in the day succeeded in persuading Rodzianko to let him take over the Ministry of Transport, immediately sent out a telegram to all railway stations in the name of Rodzianko, saying that the old régime had fallen and that 'the State Duma' had formed a new government — which was, of course, very far from the truth. This message spread the news of the revolution far and wide throughout the country. Rodzianko followed with a more cautious telegram to the commanders of all fronts.

The main obstacle to the restoration of order was the mass of insurgent troops who roamed the city and besieged the Tauride Palace, where, in a separate wing from that occupied by the Provincial Committee of the Duma, another body had come into being — the Petrograd Soviet and its Provisional Executive Committee.

The revolution of 1905 had left a tradition of the Petersburg Soviet which, as mentioned in Chapter 1, spontaneously developed from a workers' strike committee and acted for a short time as the only organ capable of maintaining essential order. When the strikes began on 23 February, some calls for the election of a soviet were heard, and the idea was mooted at the gatherings of socialist intellectuals which took place daily during the turbulent last days of February. For the Mensheviks, a soviet represented a means of worker self-government but was in no manner regarded as an organ of future state power. For Lenin, who treated it with contempt in 1905, it became, in his subsequent writing, an organ of insurrection, and 'the embryo of a provisional revolutionary government'. Among the other Bolsheviks, Shliapnikov did not support the idea, while the Petersburg Committee only envisaged a soviet as eventually emerging from the factory committees which they urged should be immediately set up.

The main impetus to create the Petrograd Soviet undoubtedly came from the defencist Menshevik members of the Workers Group of the Central War Industries Committee who, along with other socialists, had been liberated when the troops stormed the prison at noon on 27 February. By 2 p.m. on that day a group of predominantly Menshevik socialists had already formed a Provisional Executive Committee of the Petrograd Soviet, and had issued an appeal to soldiers and factory workers to elect deputies — one for every thousand workers and one from every company. The Bolsheviks, somewhat belatedly, now also called for elections to a soviet 'which will create a Provisional Revolutionary Government'. There was little support for the view that the soviet should become a government, and the Bolsheviks did not press this demand. The overwhelming conviction of socialists was that the business of ruling was for the bourgeois parties of the Duma, and that the functions of the soviet were worker self-government and the maintenance of order.

By 9 p.m. the first session of the rough and ready assembly that called itself the Petrograd Soviet of Worker Deputies opened in a wing of the Tauride Palace at the opposite end from where the Duma Committee met. Between forty and fifty delegates had arrived. Three socialist deputies from the Duma, N.S. Chkheidze, A.F. Kerensky and M.I. Skobelev were elected respectively its Chairman and two Vice-Chairmen. It soon became evident that Kerensky, a master of theatrical demagogy, was the leading figure of the revolutionaries, so far as the crowds were concerned. The session elected a predominantly Menshevik Executive Committee (the right-wing socialist preponderance on the Executive Committee was still further increased the following day) but a group of Bolshevik intellectuals was, for the time being, entrusted with the publication of the soviet newspaper, *Izvestiia* ('News'), of which the first issue appeared next day. The Soviet also took some measures relating to the restoration of public order, which was its urgent concern: it approved the Military Commission, which had been set up by the Provisional Executive Committee for control over the troops of the garrison, and took steps to ensure supplies of food. Immediately after the first session of the Soviet, the Executive Committee began the creation of a militia. It also elected Chkheidze and Kerensky from among the members of the Provisional Committee of the Duma to act as Soviet representatives on it — with the task of ensuring that it did not attempt to 'do a deal with the remnants of tsarism', in Shliapnikov's words.

The next two days were to show that the men who were going to dominate the revolution were the insurgent troops. This was not surprising. They, and not the workers, were the plain victors in the revolt which had taken place. They had suffered by far the heaviest casualties — according to figures of street fighting casualties published by the Bolsheviks, the soldiers lost 869, as against 237 workers and 276 students and others. (According to another Soviet calculation, of nearly two thousand killed and wounded 48 per cent were soldiers as against 30 per cent workers). They were full of pent-up resentment at the degrading and harsh treatment to which they had been subjected for years. They were demoralized by long months of idleness. The many peasant soldiers were driven on by the traditional hope that there would be landlords' land for the taking. Their sympathy lay with the strikers and demonstrators and not with the government and police, and they were repelled by the order to shoot at the crowds. And at length, having committed themselves to mutiny and having murdered their officers in many cases, they had the strongest interest of all in making sure that the revolution survived any attempts to defeat it — by bringing up disciplined troops from the front, for example. The Duma, as the only elected body, was the first point to which the insurgent troops rallied in thousands. But a Duma committee of liberal gentry, known for their support of the war, could scarcely hope to compete with the attraction of heady, revolutionary excitement furnished by the new Petrograd Soviet.

In the small hours of 28 February, the Military Commission which had been set up by the Soviet was taken over by the Provisional Committee of the Duma. There was surprisingly little resistance from the Soviet — its leaders were, after all, seriously alarmed by the military anarchy which prevailed in the city and believed the Duma members to be more capable of restoring order. At that stage they probably regarded them as more able to exercise authority.

The Military Commission worked hard in the next few days. It attempted to calm the anarchy and, to allay the suspicions of the garrison troops, arrested officers suspected of sympathy with the old régime. The two objectives — imposing discipline and safeguarding the revolution — were difficult to reconcile and the Duma Committee added to the growing suspicions of the troops when, in an endeavour both to restore discipline and to maintain the fighting capacity of the army, it issued proclamations calling on soldiers to return to barracks and to obey their officers. Rodzianko's order on these lines of 28 February provoked a storm of protest from many of the troops — it was much embellished by rumour that soldiers were to be disarmed, and that this was already taking place.

From the early hours of 1 March excited crowds of soldiers thronged the Tauride Palace, where the Soviet was due to meet at noon. When the session opened, somewhat later, it was attended by numerous delegates elected by the soldiers. (At this session the name of the Soviet was expanded to 'The Petrograd Soviet of Worker *and Soldier* Deputies'.) There was heated debate on the subject of relations with officers, disarming of troops, and the competence of the Military Commission. The general decisions reached in debate were handed on to the Executive Committee to formulate exactly in cooperation with ten soldier delegates elected to the Executive Committee. In fact, no socialist members of the Executive Committee participated in the drafting of the document which was given the title of 'Order No. 1' (by *Izvestiia* when it was published, with some distortion of the text, on 2 March. It was also printed in large numbers in the form of a leaflet.)

Several socialist members of the Executive Committee later maintained that Order No. 1 was issued without its approval, and there seems little doubt that the main motive force behind the document was that of the Bolshevik N.D. Sokolov and of delegates from the military units. Nevertheless, there is evidence to support the suspicion that some extreme left-wing members of the Soviet welcomed the destruction of the army as a disciplined force, believing that this would be the safest way to remove the threat of a counter-revolutionary coup.

It was N.D. Sokolov who, surrounded by a group of soldiers, produced a hurried draft of the document, which he then read out to the rapturous approval of the troops who thronged the chamber where the Soviet met. Order No. 1 consisted of eight points issued in the name of the Petrograd Soviet and limited in its application to the Petrograd Garrison: 1 Committees to be elected immediately from the ranks of all military and naval units; 2 One delegate from each company to be elected to the Petrograd Soviet; 3 The armed forces are subordinate to the Petrograd Soviet in all their political actions; 4 The orders of the Military Commission of the Duma to be carried out in so far as they do not conflict with the orders of the Petrograd Soviet; 5 All weapons to remain under the control of company and battalion committees, and in no circumstances to be handed over to officers; 6 While on duty soldiers must observe strict military discipline, but off-duty soldiers enjoy the same rights as other citizens; saluting off duty is abolished; 7 Honorific titles of officers ('your excellency' etc.) are abolished; 8 All coarse conduct by officers towards soldiers (in particular the usage of 'thou') is abolished, and cases of it must be reported to the committees.

The immediate effect of this order was to establish the Soviet as the body to which the allegiance of the troops was primarily due. The longer-term effect was to destroy discipline in the armed forces. Though it may not yet have been apparent, the fate of the Duma Committee, and of the Provisional Government which would come into existence on 2 March, was already sealed.

By 1 March there were signs that the insurgents were taking the first steps towards self-government — Order No. 1 and the new committees which it set up in military units could be expected to deepen this process. An inflammatory proclamation to the soldiers, calculated to increase anarchy, had been issued by the hot-heads of the Interdistrict Committee, but was suppressed by the Executive Committee of the Soviet. The Executive Committee also faced imminent demands from the insurgents that the Petrograd Soviet should seize power as a revolutionary government in opposition to the Duma. For the great majority of the Executive Committee this was a very unwelcome prospect, though it had some half-hearted support from the left wing. The majority had both doctrinal and practical reasons for the view that ruling should be the responsibility of the bourgeoisie. Doctrinally, the formation of a government by the liberal parties corresponded to the socialist belief that a bourgeois revolution had to precede the socialist revolution, and that socialists should not participate in the governing body that emerged. The Executive Committee, in fact, voted by 13 to 8 against the inclusion of socialists in the government. In practical terms, the possibility that the revolution would be put down by the arrival of troops from the front could not be excluded. The assumption of power by revolutionaries could be expected to lead to civil war, but a Duma government might prevent it. Also, the main socialist leaders were still abroad, and the Executive Committee may well have had little confidence in its own ability to deal with internal anarchy. Besides, so far as the general administration of the country was concerned, such vital services as railways, banks, telephones and telegraphs and power stations were under the control of the Provisional Duma Committee. It was therefore understandable that the Executive Committee of the Soviet should have seen as its function the duty of, at best, ensuring that the Duma Committee should put into practice a democratic policy. After much discussion, the main points of what this policy should be were agreed: complete amnesty for political prisoners; freedom of speech, publication and strike; a democratic republic; immediate convocation of a constituent assembly; a people's militia; democratic local administration; abolition of class, national and religious discrimination; election of army officers; and no disarming or withdrawal from Petrograd of the units of the garrison.

When joint discussions with members of the Duma Committee took place at midnight (most probably on the initiative of the Soviet Executive Committee) only two points proved contentious. Miliukov, on behalf of the Duma Committee, insisted that the monarchy must be preserved in the form of a regency by the Grand Duke Michael during the infancy of the heir, and refused to agree to election of officers. In the end, the Executive Committee delegates abandoned both these points. Even so, the agreement concluded by the Duma Committee made the ultimate collapse of any Duma Government almost certain, if only because it contained no mention of the explosive issue of the war. The Duma Committee did not yet appreciate that the acceptance of Order No. 1 had ranged the Petrograd Soviet on the side of the insurgent troops and against the Duma. It could therefore hope that the Soviet would act as a restraining influence and would help the Duma Committee to keep the support of the garrison.

Hindsight must not be allowed to obscure the fact that the genuine, almost universal, euphoria evoked by the revolution made such an agreement seem reasonable and desirable. Nevertheless, the seeds of destruction of the régime which emerged in the early days of March 1917 were already inherent in the fact that two irreconcilable policies were being pursued by the socialists of the Petrograd Soviet: concession to the demands of the garrison troops in the interests of what they believed was 'preservation of the revolution', on the one hand; and continued prosecution of the war and support of the Provisional Government, however half-hearted, on the other.

The events which led to the abdication of Nicholas II and which filled the four days from 27 February to 2 March are difficult to disentangle with any certainty: accounts of them by participants are numerous, but incomplete and contradictory, and coloured by motives of self-justification. Rodzianko's appeals to the Tsar on 26 and 27 February for the appointment of a ministry that would command public confidence were ignored, as well as similar appeals from the elected members of the State Council and from the Emperor's brother, the Grand Duke Michael. Advice from the Commander of the Northern Front, General Ruzskii, that the Emperor should adopt politically conciliatory, rather than repressive, measures, also fell on deaf ears — the Tsar did not get on with Ruzskii and in any case was not fully aware of the seriousness of the situation in Petrograd. He believed that the problem could be solved by the despatch of reliable troops from the front, and a force under the command of General Ivanov had already been despatched. In the early hours of 28 February, the Tsar left General Staff HQ at Mogilev in order to travel by royal train to Tsarskoe Selo to join his wife and children, who were ill and worried. It proved to be a long and eventful journey, and there is some ground for suspicion that the royal train may have been deliberately impeded by the railway authorities (who were under the control of the Duma Committee) for fear that reunion with his wife would strengthen Nicholas's resolve not to make political concessions.

By 1 March, the Duma Committee (now under the leadership of Miliukov, whose standing had rapidly risen against that of Rodzianko) had decided that the Emperor must be persuaded or forced to abdicate in favour of his infant son, with the Grand Duke Michael as Regent. Rodzianko, whose ambitions to head the future government clashed with those of Miliukov, was opposed to this solution — whether from ambition, or loyalty, or both can only be surmised. His plans to save the throne for Nicholas involved a further attempt, with the aid of the Emperor's uncle, to create a responsible government with himself as head of it, and it was presumably with this plan in mind that he proposed to visit the Emperor at one of the points on his complicated train journey. The visit was opposed both by the Soviet Executive Committee and by the Duma Committee who, not unnaturally, suspected an intrigue by Rodzianko.

Meanwhile, General Ruzskii and General Alekseev, the Chief of the General Staff, were active in trying to find a solution that would enable the Duma Committee to gain effective political control. They were better informed than the travelling Emperor on conditions in Petrograd and, moreover, the news they received from the Duma Committee was coloured in order to gain the support of the army in the field. General Ruzskii met the Tsar at Pskov in the evening of 1 March. With considerable difficulty, and with the aid of a telegram from Alekseev, he persuaded him that the situation could not be solved by military measures, and that the only solution was to set up a responsible ministry headed by the Chairman of the State Duma. A manifesto to this effect, prepared at Staff GHQ, was signed by the Emperor, and Ruzskii sent a telegram halting all operations to General Ivanov, who, with his troops, had by now reached Tsarskoe Selo (which is very close to Petrograd).

At 3.30 in the morning of 2 March, Ruzskii was awakened and informed that Rodzianko wished to 'speak' to him on the Hughes apparatus — a kind of primitive teleprinter. The record of this conversation, which lasted four hours, shows Rodzianko confused, contradictory and undecided. He had failed to keep his appointment with the Emperor, and gave two explanations for this, both of which were untrue — that the troops sent by Ruzskii to form part of General Ivanov's punitive force had rebelled at Luga, which is on the line between Pskov and Petrograd, and were making his journey to Pskov impossible; and that his own presence was essential in Petrograd because the 'raging popular passions' could only be appeased by his orders.

In reply to Ruzskii's news of the manifesto setting up a responsible ministry, which had been agreed to by the Emperor, Rodzianko said that it had come too late, and that there was now a demand by the troops and by the people for the abdication of the Tsar in favour of his son, under the regency of the Grand Duke Michael. He could offer no advice on whether the manifesto should be published. The confused picture which Rodzianko presented — of troops everywhere joining the Duma, yet of anarchy prevailing in the capital — may have been due to simple panic; or again, bearing in mind his prevarication, to a desire to preserve his position both with the army leaders and with the Duma Committee by playing for time. It would seem that this conversation persuaded Ruzskii that abdication was the only solution. By ten a.m. on 2 March the Chief of Staff General Alekseev was also of this opinion. Alekseev now despatched a circular telegram to the commanders of all the five fronts and of the navy explaining the situation: all replied endorsing abdication. General Ruzskii, accompanied by several other generals in the Emperor's entourage, put the telegrams of reply before Nicholas. After Nicholas had read the telegrams, Ruzskii asked him to hear what the generals of his entourage had to say. They supported the view that abdication was now inevitable. The Emperor then crossed himself, and announced his intention to abdicate in favour of his son. He embraced Ruzskii and thanked him for his past services. It was an emotional scene, but all were struck by the calmness which Nicholas preserved. He was religious, with inclinations to mysticism, and accepted his fate with submission and dignity. It may also have been easier for him to abdicate than to agree to the constitutional solution which he had been persuaded to accept the day before and which contradicted all his convictions about the nature of absolute monarchy. But in the entry for the day in his diary some rare signs of emotion appeared: 'All around me — treason and cowardice and deceit.'

The speed with which the front commanders were prepared to break their oath of allegiance would indeed be surprising were it not for the fact that their primary concern was the patriotic one of preserving morale in the army, and this had been undermined by the scandalous rumours of the 'Rasputin era', both the true and the false, involving the imperial family. When the delegates of the Duma, Guchkov and V.V. Shul'gin, arrived in Pskov some hours later with the mission of persuading the Tsar to abdicate, they learned from him that the decision to do so had already been taken. But when, in the course of discussion, Nicholas realized that the proposed regency would in all probability involve separation from his son, he decided to abdicate for his son as well, and in favour of his brother Michael — a procedure of doubtful constitutional validity. The manifesto of abdication, prepared at GHQ, was signed by the last Emperor of Russia and handed to the Duma delegates at 11.40 p.m.

Chapter Four

The Provisional Government

On 2 March a Provisional Government came into being. It emerged from the agreement reached between the Executive Committee of the Petrograd Soviet and the Provisional Committee of the Duma at the midnight meeting mentioned in the last chapter, and the rapidity with which it was formed seemed to indicate that its composition had been agreed some time before. Although the leader of the Kadet party, P. Miliukov, became Foreign Minister, the Prime Minister, Prince G.E. L'vov, was not associated with the Kadet party, but had been prominent in the *zemstvo* movement. The Octobrist A.I. Guchkov became Minister of War. The remainder comprised several Kadets, a further Octobrist, a few who were members of no party, and the solitary socialist, Kerensky. The inclusion of Kerensky, who was also a member of the Executive Committee of the Soviet, ran counter to the policy of that committee of not joining a bourgeois government (Chkheidze, the Social Democrat chairman of the Soviet had declined the offer of a seat). But Kerensky's appointment as Minister of Justice, though made without the prior approval of the Soviet, was ratified by it with storms of applause after he had made a speech charged with virtually hysterical emotion. A statement issued on 3 March by the Provisional Committee of the Duma listed the ministers which it had 'appointed', as well as eight principles by which it would be 'guided'. These were in effect identical with the points agreed on by the committees of the Duma and the Soviet the day before the government was formed.

Many years later, in a letter written in 1955 but only published in 1962, E.D. Kuskova, a moderate Social Democrat, disclosed that the main influence on the formation of the Provisional Government had been a peculiar Russian masonic organization, formed in 1906 or 1907. This was an underground movement, based on the principles of 'Liberation' and pledged to work for the overthrow of the autocracy. It was therefore considerably to the left of the Kadet party, let alone the Octobrists. Kuskova's evidence is reinforced by the fact that most of the prominent members of the Provisional Government, including

Kerensky, were masons; that Miliukov, who was in a minority of one in the Government and was soon forced out, was not; and that the other discordant element in the Cabinet of the First Provisional Government, Guchkov, although a mason, was the object of much criticism and hostility in the lodge.

Too much sensational importance should not be attached to this issue of masonry — indeed Kuskova did not suggest that the influence of the lodge extended beyond the formation of the government — but it was a factor in bringing into being a government considerably to the left of the Kadets, and of the Progressive Bloc of the Duma generally. This fact is relevant to the notion much canvassed at the time — that a state of 'dyarchy' subsisted between the Provisional Government and the Soviet. The term was invented by Guchkov, who indeed eventually resigned on the ostensible grounds that the Provisional Government had no real power in face of Soviet obstruction. 'Dyarchy' was enthusiastically adopted by Lenin, after his arrival in Petrograd on 3 April, since it was part of his policy to polarize the Soviet and the government as much as possible. Certainly, as will be noted, there was considerable difference between the government and the Soviet on the issue of the war. But so far as domestic policy was concerned the divergences should not be exaggerated. The members of the Provisional Government — if one excludes Miliukov — were radical revolutionaries and republicans at heart, and there is no evidence to support the view that the great majority of extensive reform measures which they adopted in refashioning the country to conform to the prevalent mood of revolutionary euphoria were forced on them by the Soviet.

The new government was 'provisional' in the sense that the future government of the country was to be decided by a Constituent Assembly, the election of which in due course had always been the ultimate aim of the revolution. Meanwhile, a question that was to bedevil the Provisional Government was that of its legitimacy. Miliukov was very anxious that the continuity of legitimacy and of power should be preserved in the person of the Grand Duke Michael in whose favour Nicholas had abdicated. When on 2 March Miliukov addressed an excited crowd in the Tauride Palace to announce the formation of the new government, a voice from the crowd cried 'Who elected you?' It was a pertinent question, to which Miliukov replied, with more rhetoric than sense, 'We were elected by the Russian Revolution.' But the real question was not resolved: from whom or from what did the new government derive its authority? It had certainly not emerged from any election; and its links with the Duma, through the self-appointed Provisional Committee, were slender. On the same occasion Miliukov referred to a proposed regency by the

Grand Duke Michael, during the infancy of Aleksei (in whose favour at that time Nicholas was still expected to abdicate). This remark was ill-received not only by the crowd but by Miliukov's fellow ministers, and later that day, in the face of angry protests mainly from a group of officers, he was forced to explain that he had merely expressed his personal opinion.

Popular feeling against the imperial family certainly ran high, and found a sympathetic response among the overwhelming majority of the Provisional Government. This was, presumably, the explanation why the last official act of Nicholas II, an appeal to the army to defend Russia and to obey the Provisional Government, was forbidden by order of the Minister of War from being distributed beyond the staff HQs of armies in the field. On 5 March the Soviet protested against the appointments of Prince L'vov as Prime Minister and of the Grand Duke Nicholas as Commander in Chief on the grounds that these emanated from the former Emperor. In a speech in Moscow on 7 March, Kerensky promised the removal of the Grand Duke, and he was in fact replaced on 11 March by his Chief of Staff, General Alekseev.

On 3 March the President of the Duma, Rodzianko, and members of the Provisional Government called on the Grand Duke Michael. With the exception of Miliukov and Guchkov, all were fiercely determined that he should reject accession. It was a fairly heated meeting, and in the end the Grand Duke refused the throne until such time as the Constituent Assembly had expressed 'the will of the people' on the question of monarchy. It may, indeed, be doubted if he had any power of retaining the accession in view of the temper of the Petrograd crowds — or for that matter, if he had the mettle for the job. His manifesto of refusal was carefully drafted by a leading constitutional lawyer with a view to conferring legitimacy on the Provisional Government. This, according to the terms of this document, had 'come into being at the invitation of the State Duma and . . . is endowed with full power until such time as the Constituent Assembly, to be convened in as short a period as possible. . . expresses the will of the people.'

The ex-Tsar and the members of his family were meanwhile being held as virtual prisoners at Tsarskoe Selo. Their arrest was ordered by the Provisional Government — the evidence is confusing, but for some ministers, at any rate, the motive may have been a desire to protect them from the crowds. This is borne out by the fact that on 8 March Miliukov asked the British Ambassador to request asylum in England for Nicholas and his family. The Imperial War Cabinet had in fact decided to offer them refuge even before it received Sir George Buchanan's cable informing it of Miliukov's request, and the invitation was conveyed to Miliukov by the Ambassador on 15 March. Before Miliukov's request, on 7 March, Kerensky had dramatically assured the Moscow Soviet that he would personally escort Nicholas to the ship which would take him to England. However, two days later, according to Chkheidze, the Provisional Government and Kerensky 'guaranteed' that Nicholas would not be allowed to leave Tsarskoe Selo without the consent of the Executive Committee of the Soviet.

What is certain is that the Provisional Government did not immediately take advantage of the British offer. The real reasons for this are not clear. The reluctance of the ex-Tsar to leave Russia; the vigorous opposition of the Soviet which was prepared to mobilize the railwaymen and the soldiers to prevent the ex-imperial family from travelling to Murmansk, the port of embarkation for England; and the desire of the Provisional Government to wait for the result of the Extraordinary Commission of Enquiry which they had set up on 4 March to examine former members of the government in order to see whether it would produce evidence of the Tsar's or Tsaritsa's treason; all have been advanced in memoirs as reasons for the delay. (Not a jot of evidence of treason against the Tsar or his wife was in the end produced by the commission, as was stated both by Kerensky and by the chairman of the commission, Muraviev.)

A change of mind by the British Government has also frequently been alleged as the reason for the failure to rescue the Tsar. The minutes of the British War Cabinet do indeed show that on 31 March (13 April) it was considered that, subject to the advice of the Ambassador, the offer of asylum should be withdrawn. The reasons given were 'strong feelings hostile to the Czar in certain working class circles', and the risk that if differences of opinion between the British and Russian governments should arise, this would be attributed to Nicholas's presence in England. Certainly, King George V was opposed to English asylum for his Russian kinsfolk. However, Sir George Buchanan maintains in his memoirs that the offer was never withdrawn, and the subject does not appear to have been discussed by the British Cabinet after 31 March (13 April). In July 1917 the members of the ex-imperial family were moved to Tobol'sk, in Siberia, apparently for fear by the Provisional Government that they might become the centre of a counter-revolutionary plot. It was the first stage on the road to massacre by the Bolsheviks a year later.

The life of the Provisional Government was to prove very harassed, shaken by four major crises, in April, June, July and August, which will be related in the next chapter. The Bolsheviks played an important part in these dramatic events.

Lenin's attitude in March 1917, when a bourgeois democratic revolution was supposed to have occurred, is only consistent with the view that the revolution which had just taken place must immediately be transformed into one in which power was (theoretically) vested in the people. His first reaction to the news of the revolution was a telegram to a close supporter in Petrograd: 'Our tactics: absolute mistrust, no support of new government. Kerensky particularly suspect: to arm proletariat only guarantee; . . . *no rapprochement with other parties*'. (Lenin's emphasis.) Victory must be won by his own party: all others who called themselves socialists were in his view compromisers, and therefore traitors to the workers. His intentions in Russia appear even more clearly from a letter which he wrote on 3 (16) March 1917 to a confidant and admirer: 'After a week of bloody battles by the workers and Miliukov and Guchkov and Kerensky are in power!! The "old" European pattern . . . Well, what of it? This "first stage" of the first revolutions (engendered by the war) will not be either the last, or only Russian. Of course we shall remain opposed to the defence of the fatherland, opposed to the imperialist slaughter directed by Shingarev [a Kadet minister] and Kerensky and Co. . . . The main things now are the press, and the organization of the workers into a *revolutionary* SD party. . . . The greatest misfortune now would be if the Kadets now promised a legal workers' party, and if our people went for "unity" with Chkheidze and Co!!'

Meanwhile, in Lenin's absence, under the leadership of Stalin and Kamenev, returned from exile, the Bolsheviks in Petrograd were doing exactly what Lenin said they should not do. The slogan 'down with the war' was useless, Stalin wrote in *Pravda* on 16 March. The proper course was 'pressure on the Provisional Government' to induce it to open peace negotiations. At an All-Russian Party Conference, which was still in progress when Lenin arrived on 3 April, agreement was reached to embark on exploratory discussions on unification with the Mensheviks. There was, however, also a more radical group headed by Shliapnikov and Molotov. In his 'Theses', published in *Pravda* shortly after his arrival, Lenin urged that there should be no support, even qualified, for the Provisional Government, and that the party should work for a 'republic of soviets of workers', soldiers' and peasants' deputies . . . confiscation of all landlords' estates . . . nationalization of all land . . . a single national bank . . . elimination of the army and police'. As for the war, Lenin urged the widest propaganda in the army of the view that there could be no genuine peace without the overthrow of capitalism, and advocated 'fratern-ization'. The Petrograd Bolsheviks thought that he had taken leave of his senses — but not for long. Shliapnikov, who was knocked out of action by a tramcar, returned a few weeks later to discover that his party was now solidly behind Lenin. By the end of the month of April the All-Russian Bolshevik Conference had adopted unanimously a resolution embodying Lenin's Theses, which henceforth became the Bolshevik programme.

Already, by March 1917, the possibility of real cooperation between the Bolsheviks and the two main socialist parties was negligible. The socialists, in the main, were prepared to cooperate with the middle-class Provisional Government, and indeed before long some of their number would enter it: the Bolsheviks believed that it should be destroyed. But there were elements within both socialist parties who stood much closer to the Bolsheviks. Among the Socialist Revolutionaries there soon began to form a left wing, which would eventually break off to become the Left Socialist Revolutionaries (LSR). Within the Menshevik ranks, there was a quite separate group known as the Internationalists, led by Martov, who were opposed to the war and whose general position was so close to that of the Bolsheviks that they were often nicknamed the 'semi-Bolsheviks'. On the other hand, there were also men like Kamenev among Bolshevik leaders whose opposition on the issue of the war or cooperation with the Provisional Government was at times closer to that of the Mensheviks than to the attitude of Lenin.

The Provisional Government was thus faced with a determined bid for power by Lenin and the Bolsheviks, as well as other problems virtually beyond its control. In the course of its attempts to wrestle with these problems the government underwent substantial changes. The April crisis led in May to the First Coalition, in which a number of socialists in addition to Kerensky now joined the cabinet — making five socialists out of fifteen, including the Ministers of Agriculture, Food and the Interior. A further reorganization of the cabinet took place in July. Prince L'vov resigned as Prime Minister and Kerensky took his place. The cabinet once again included socialist members, such as the Socialist Revolutionary leader V.M. Chernov, who was appointed Minister of Agriculture. The last coalition was formed at a time when the Provisional Government, after the disaster of the events associated with General Kornilov, was already in its death throes (see Chapter 7). It included seven socialist members out of a total of seventeen — five of whom were not members of any party. Throughout these tribulations the Provisional Government struggled to launch a legislative programme which might well have defeated even a stable government operating in normal conditions.

The government was pledged, both by its agreement with the Soviet and by its own declaration of principles, to dismantle the oppressive features of the old régime. No less than the Soviet, it was carried away by the general euphoria which characterized the days and weeks that followed the collapse of the Tsar's rule; and, above all, it was convinced that the natural instincts of the Russian people would lead it towards sobriety, discipline and voluntary restraint when once the shackles of the old tyranny had been cast off. None of its members seems to have considered the possibility that to remove at a stroke all constraints from a people accustomed for centuries to strict rule and a minimum of freedom might be a certain recipe for anarchy. One of the first acts of the new government, for example, was to oust from office the governors and vice-governors of the provinces, and to replace them by the chairmen of the local *zemstvo* councils (now to be known as 'Guberniia Commissars of the Provisional Government'). These men lacked authority and experience of administration, and in many cases proved unpopular as well as ineffective.

On his visit to Moscow on 7 March, Kerensky announced that he would sign a decree abolishing the death penalty on the following day. It was not in fact signed until 12 March and there was some criticism of the delay, which was apparently due to the desire in some quarters to retain the death penalty for use against former ministers and members of the imperial family. The decree applied to both civil and military offences. Six days before, a comprehensive amnesty was enacted for all those convicted of offences of a political nature. On 17 March brutal practices, such as flogging in prisons, were abolished, and on 26 April deportation to Siberia. On 17 April another promise of the new government was fulfilled when a law was passed establishing the militia, which had replaced the hated police almost at the very outset of the revolution, on a permanent basis: militiamen were placed under the overall control of the Minister of the Interior, their powers were very strictly limited, and they were made legally answerable for their actions. All limitations of rights based on religion or nationality were swept away on 20 March — a provision of particular interest to the Jews who had been severely restricted under the old régime — and full and unlimited freedom of press and public meetings was enacted soon afterwards. The Bolsheviks would, before long, take advantage of the latter enactment. Indeed, Lenin himself acknowledged on one occasion that revolutionary Russia had become the freest country in the world.

Whatever the wisdom of the Provisional Government in ushering in this era of freedom at high speed, there can be no doubt of the integrity of its intentions. Its policy in setting up, almost immediately after assuming power, an extraordinary commission of enquiry 'for the investigation of malfeasance in office of former ministers, chief administrators and other persons in high office' is, however, more open to criticism. The avowed object of establishing this commission was to ascertain whether there was evidence on which to base prosecutions. The spectacle of the victors in a revolution sitting in judgment on the government which it has overthrown is never an edifying one, and the commission was no more successful than other similar bodies in deciding where a judicial enquiry ended and revenge on the servants of a hated régime began. The question of prosecutions never arose (if exception is made for Sukhomlinov, a former Minister of War, who was sentenced to 'indefinite' penal servitude on 12 September) since the Provisional Government was overthrown before the work of the Commission was completed, and many of those detained for questioning were shot by the Bolsheviks without any semblance of trial. But men and women, often old and infirm, against whom no charge was ever brought, were kept imprisoned by the commission, often in conditions of greatest hardship, and subjected to insult and even brutality. There was, of course, the possibility that in some cases the acts of an individual state employee could amount to crime against the law in force at the time — treason, for example, or embezzlement of public funds; but in the majority of cases investigated — those of state servants carrying out the orders of an arbitrary government — one may doubt if it was possible, with any semblance of legality, to prosecute them, with perhaps the exception of cases where those orders were flagrant violations of elementary standards of humanity. The one thing that can be said is that, as a record for the historian, the proceedings of the commission, published by the Bolsheviks, are of great value.

One of the most ambitious, and least successful, endeavours of the Provisional Government was the complete overhaul of local administration. This was embarked on at the outset, although accompanied by frequent official assertions that the measures were only provisional, and subject to the ultimate decision of the Constituent Assembly. One of the main purposes of the new legislation was to broaden the base of representation in force in the existing *zemstva* and to extend the *zemstvo* system to lower administrative levels where it did not exist before. This expansion of the franchise and the bringing into participation in local administration of hitherto disenfranchised groups was regarded by the government as an essential preparation for elections to the Constituent Assembly. On 21 May two long statutes were enacted. One extended the *zemstvo* system to the rural areas, the *volost'*, which formed the lowest tier in the local government structure; the other introduced universal, in place of a restricted, franchise in elections to the *zemstvo* institutions which already existed at the two higher administrative levels — the provinces and the *gubernii*.

As in so many of its legislative changes, the government was putting its faith in the response it confidently expected from the liberated people to the new freedom they had now been granted. The results were very far from what was anticipated. A report prepared under the auspices of the Temporary Committee of the Duma (which still survived as a separate body even after the Provisional Government had emerged) painted a depressing picture of the first three months' functioning of the new and reorganized local authorities. The town authorities suffered from the apathy and indifference of the electorate. In the *volost'* 'complete disorganization and lack of system' prevailed. The work of these bodies was hampered by 'the enormous number of orators' who invaded the villages — presumably the hordes of soldiers and political agitators who constantly roamed the country. The *volost' zemstva*, when they eventually came into being, were not a success. Although they were set up on 21 May, legislation for the conduct of elections to them only followed on 13 June and 26 July. By the time elections were held, in August, the peasants, now completely disenchanted with the government, scarcely bothered to vote. The higher levels of local government were little more successful. In a sad speech in August, at a conference of *guberniia* commissars (emissaries appointed by the central government to administer the new system of committees), Kerensky regretted that 'there turned out to be too much ignorance and too little experience among the free people' for the reform of local government to work. A press editorial on the conference spoke of 'complete anarchy' in the authorities set up under the new legislation.

As the months wore on, it became increasingly apparent that the two gravest problems facing the Provisional Government were the question of land, which was the dominant topic in the minds of the millions of peasants both in the armed forces and in the villages, and, closely related to it, that of food supplies, at home and for the front. The fall of the Tsar was received very calmly by the peasants. Its immediate effect was to raise high their expectation that the long-awaited redistribution of all land would now take place which would put an end to the peasants' lack of adequate holdings, and stop what they regarded as the monstrous injustice of having to pay rent for land which they considered to be their own. For a short time they waited hopefully for the new government to act. Their first disappointment, which soon led to outbreaks of violence, was with the system of local administration, which seemed to them scarcely different from the old. The appointed commissars and the committees above the village level appeared to them to represent the rule of landlords, townsmen and intellectuals with little change. There were violent attacks on the 'land captains' — officials appointed in 1889 to maintain discipline on the land — and their office was suspended by the Provisional Government on 20 March, and later abolished, their judicial functions being transferred to the justices of the peace.

The peasants proceeded to establish their own village committees for the purpose of running their affairs, based on their traditional communal organs. These committees, which took on a great variety of forms, frustrated the government's efforts to create a system of local administration at village level. The informal *volost'* committees (which grew up before the abortive elections to the *volost' zemstva*) had become completely dominated by peasant aspirations: intended to be real organs of administration under government control, in effect they escaped all central direction until the very end. The chaos in the villages was naturally aggravated by the illiteracy of the peasants and by their total lack of political experience or understanding of what was happening. Their desire for self-government far exceeded their capacity for it. They therefore became an easy prey to the agitators, both indigenous and extraneous, such as deserters from the army, who swarmed into the villages and usually advocated violence.

The *volost'* committees in fact became the mainsprings of the rural disturbances which were to characterize life in Russia from April onwards during the survival of the Provisional Government. As Graeme Gill (a recent student of the peasant question in 1917) concludes, 'most committees established at the village and *volost'* levels as a result of government legislation were swallowed up by the peasant organizational structure arising out of the villages, thereby becoming instruments of peasant unrest rather than government authority.'

Statistics on peasant disorders, although very freely available, are contradictory, incomplete, and often quite misleading. Conclusions based on them are necessarily of dubious validity. In particular, attempts by different interpreters to draw political deductions from the rise and fall of violence in different months between April and October 1917 remain unconvincing. The most likely explanation for these variations is provided by the seasonal preoccupations of peasants — there is less time for riotous action when the sowing or the harvesting has to be done.

Violence took many forms: personal attacks, mainly on landlords, involving many deaths; disruption of the working of estates; seizure of land and timber; and forcible resistance to grain collection. Destruction of estates was at its height in September and October. Thereafter, seizure of land became more prevalent, reaching its peak in the late autumn and winter. Those who had responded to the attempt by Stolypin after 1906 to dismantle the commune, and had established private holdings outside it, became a particular object of peasant violence. The effects of the policy of 1906-1910 were largely undone during these turbulent months, and there was a resurgence of the peasant commune, which was to survive until Stalin's enforced collectivization. There were many factors which stimulated unrest in the villages, such as food shortages or proximity to the front, but it seems evident that there was least violence in districts where the peasants owned most land, and most disorder in the black earth area where communal holding was strongest.

The government was taken by surprise when peasant disturbances began to mount and completely lacked any policy for dealing with them. In line with the populist idealism which motivated many of its members, it was at first convinced that persuasion would be enough to ensure that the peasants would wait for the Constituent Assembly to bring them their long expected just dues. The prospect of using military force to deal with peasant violence appalled them. Their indecision, combined with their lack of real authority over the network of administrative organs, resulted in most cases in their policy being reduced to a string of pious exhortations, and half-hearted attempts to stem rural anarchy with a militia which lacked effective means, and with conciliation bodies totally devoid of power. The government did, on 8 April, authorize provincial commissars to call for military help in putting down disorders, and the soldiers were sometimes brought into action: they were used on 39 occasions during July and August (the Ministry of Interior reported over 1800 violent incidents for the same period) and 105 times in September. However, the government always had to reckon with the fact that a peasant army is scarcely a suitable instrument for suppressing rural violence.

Ensuring the supply of food both to the front and to the rear was a constant preoccupation of the government. In spite of the severe drain of man-power from the villages, the quantity of grain harvested did not fall too far short of the pre-war figure — perhaps by 23.5 per cent in 1916-17. The problem was to get it to its destination. Quite apart from the considerable breakdown in transport in 1917, the government was faced with determined refusal by the peasants to part with their produce. On 9 March the government set up a State Food Committee, and on 25 March attempted to tackle the problem of food supplies by decreeing a state monopoly of grain, a system of fixed prices and a network of local food committees. The system proved a failure for a number of reasons. The food committees were too large and unwieldy, and had little contact with the peasants. At the provincial and *guberniia* levels they tended to be urban in orientation, while the *volost'* committees, on whom grain collection ultimately depended, were dominated by the familiar peasant impulses: hatred of landlords and hostility to representatives of the *zemstva*.

Above all, the government at the centre suffered from severe handicaps. It lacked control over the subordinate agencies — and therefore had no effective means of coercion and had to rely on its favourite method, persuasion. But it was not easy to induce peasants to part with their grain without at the same time offering them the kind of necessities they lacked, rather than rapidly depreciating paper money; and one of the most serious failures of the Provisional Government was its inability to organize the production and distribution of the goods which the peasants wanted, at reasonable prices. That the inadequate supply of food was in part the result of incompetent administration is also suggested by the government's handling of rationing. This was introduced on 29 April, but it was only on 6 June that the methods to be adopted were prescribed, and it was not until the end of June that instructions were issued to the food committees to conduct a comprehensive survey of needs and resources within their areas.

By the time the Provisional Government was nearing its end, the supply of food was in a critical state. On 27 August the government, in desperation, doubled the price of grain, in spite of a solemn statement on 4 August that it would 'under no circumstances' do so. The measure did lead to a slight improvement in grain procurement, though at the cost of further loss of credibility by the ministers. By October the supply situation at the front was disastrous. On 16 October the Social Democratic Minister of Food made a statement which, while it described the situation as satisfactory, revealed that one front commander considered the food supply to be 'catastrophic', while the minister's own figure showed that procurement only reached around half the amount required to feed the soldiers and the civilians. One result of the breakdown of transport in 1917 was to make shortages in Petrograd particularly acute, providing fertile ground for agitators attacking the government.

So far as the land was concerned, the Provisional Government throughout its existence remained firmly committed to the view that any policy concerning the system of ownership which was to prevail in free Russia must be determined by the Constituent Assembly. This position was supported by the majority of the socialists. The failure of the Provisional Government to satisfy immediately the peasants' burning aspiration for land, which undoubtedly was one of the causes of Bolshevik victory, is sometimes ascribed to the fact that a government of landowners would be anxious to safeguard its own interests. This was the invariable theme of propaganda in which the government was attacked, and it was true that the Kadets' policy was that the landlords should only be expropriated to a limited extent and that compensation should be paid to them. However, the principal Kadet leaders were not great landlords, but professional men; nor did the Kadets dominate the government even at the outset, let alone in the three coalitions which came into existence between May and September. The socialist ministers in these governments were fully in accord with the Kadet view that all final decisions on future agrarian policy must await the Constituent Assembly. It was also true that immediate expropriation of the landlords' estates would have had serious effects on the country's food production, even though by this means, and in spite of the resulting chaos, the Provisional Government might conceivably have saved itself from defeat by the Bolsheviks.

The Provisional Government's first proclamation on assuming office, published on 6 March, was full of promises of liberty, which the Constituent Assembly would guarantee. On the question of the land, which interested the peasants much more, it was silent. The first reference to land was made on 19 March in a statement that deplored arbitrary action by the peasants, stated that an agrarian law could not be passed by the Constituent Assembly 'without serious preparatory work' and collation of materials, and promised to set up machinery towards that end. On 21 April a network of Land Committees was established, headed by the Central Land Committee. From the point of view of the peasants these organs appeared worthless, since they had no power to endow them with land. The local committees were, however, given the right to dispossess an individual landlowner who was said to be acting in a way that caused depreciation of his property. In practice these local committees often became a screen for peasants expropriating their landlords' property under cover of legality, and it was not until 7 September that any provision was made for challenging a committee's decision in the courts.

At the height of the peasant disturbances, in the summer of 1917, the task of the cabinet was made even more difficult by a serious clash of opinion on land policy between the Socialist Revolutionary, Chernov, who was Minister of Agriculture between 18 May and the end of August, and his colleagues. Chernov did not question the view that the final decision on agrarian policy must await the coming of the Constituent Assembly; nor was it true, as was sometimes alleged by his enemies, that he supported anarchic self-help by the peasants. But he believed that it was necessary to pacify the peasants by some assurance that they would eventually get the coveted land. He urged that the first step should be taken towards this end, even before the

Constituent Assembly met, by transferring the land to the control of the Land Committees. This was the policy which was agreed upon by the Socialist Revolutionaries at their Third Congress in May.

Since Chernov could not persuade his colleagues to adopt this course, he tried to achieve it by indirect means. For example, a circular to the Land Committees, issued by him on 17 July, included the directive that they 'must go quite far in satisfying the just demands of the toiling peasantry, but under the absolute condition that this does not lead to the disintegration of the national economy . . . to the lowering and loss of the crops so needed by Russia.' This advice was in direct conflict with a fiery circular issued on the same date by the Menshevik Minister of the Interior, Tsereteli, deploring self-help by the peasant and calling on the local commissars to take strict measures to repress such anarchy — though it is in truth difficult to see what they could do within the restricted powers granted to them. Chernov's period of office as Minister of Agriculture was a constant source of conflict with his colleagues, not only the Kadets but the socialist Ministers of Food and the Interior as well, whose responsibilities often overlapped those of the Minister of Agriculture. He did not make the last cabinet's task any easier by engaging in open polemics with his former fellow ministers after he had left the government.

Apart from participating in the various administrative committees — and in effect running them at the lower levels — the peasants also followed the fashionable trend of the day by forming soviets. These were dominated by Socialist Revolutionaries, whose advocacy of immediate division of all cultivable land for the benefit of those who tilled it was enormously popular in the villages. Until the Bolsheviks took power, the great majority of these soviets succeeded in retaining their independence from the parallel Soviets of Workers and Soldiers, in spite of Bolshevik efforts to bring about the amalgamation of the two in their effort to assert proletarian leadership over rural life. The absolute predominance of Socialist Revolutionary influence among the peasants (which was to be particularly evident in the elections to the Constituent Assembly in November 1917) did not in any sense signify political awareness, let alone aspirations, among them. They voted regularly for the Socialist Revolutionary activists because they knew them and because they promised them the land — the activity of the Socialist Revolutionaries in the government in the remote capital they neither knew about nor understood. There certainly were no political motives behind the great upsurge of the peasants in 1917, as Soviet historians often claim there were; but by increasing chaos in the country, they did help to bring the Bolsheviks to power.

No issue could have been more important to the new government than the summoning of the Constituent Assembly. This aim was a fundamental part of the programmes of all the parties involved. The failure in 1905 to base the new order on the will of the governed, with the emergence instead of a constitution founded on voluntary self-limitation by the Emperor, had been one of the factors which had helped to bring about the failure of cooperation between the liberal parties and the monarchy. Now, in 1917, the new government, which called itself 'Provisional', had urgent need of an authoritative, above all recognizably authoritative, body which could confer on it the legitimacy it so palpably lacked. It was characteristic of the weakness of the Provisional Government's position that before long popular imagination tended to regard it as the executive of the Petrograd Soviet, which was seen as the real legislature.

Election, if genuine, is a powerful symbol of legitimacy, and legitimacy in a polity is not just a matter of a legal formula. It is the sign of acceptance of a government, even an unpopular one. Without it a government is reduced to ruling by force alone — or floundering in chaos. The delay of eight months in summoning the Constituent Assembly also meant that issues which could not be postponed were being solved in disregard of it, so that summoning it became progressively less important. The survival of the monarchy (which, it will be recalled, the Grand Duke Michael's abdication had left undecided) was rejected in favour of a republic by a proclamation of the Provisional Government on 1 September. The question of the land was in practice being solved by peasant self-help. The problems of the non-Russian nationalities also would not wait for government action, and the attempt by the Provisional Government to postpone all decisions on the demands for autonomy with which it was immediately beset, was doomed to failure.

There was no lack of promises in the early days of the government that the Constituent Assembly would be convened without delay. The agreement to do so formed part of the pact between the Soviet and the Duma Committee on which the Provisional Government was founded, and the first statement issued by the government promised 'immediate preparation for the convocation of the Constituent Assembly on the basis of universal, equal, direct suffrage and secret ballot'. The oath of allegiance sworn by members of the cabinet included the obligation 'to take all the necessary measures to convene the Constituent Assembly at the earliest possible date'. However, at a press conference on 7 March, Prince L'vov, the Prime Minister, pointed out that 'owing to current events, a period of three to six months will be required for the preparation for the Constituent Assembly.' When, on 13 March, delegates from the

Executive Committee of the Petrograd Soviet stressed the urgency of the need to convoke the Assembly, they remained unsatisfied by the government's assurance that it would meet not later than mid-summer.

The government now set out on the long path which was eventually to lead to the much-awaited balloting. A special council was set up on 25 March to draft the statute on elections to the Assembly, but for one reason and another its first meeting was held only on 25 May. The further long delay which then ensued before the Electoral Statute was completed can be explained, at all events so far as some of those responsible were concerned, by a desire for perfection. This appeared from the speech of its (Kadet) chairman at the opening session. The quickest way to proceed, he explained, would be to create a small commission of specialists to work out the voting law. This course was rejected because 'the important thing is that the law conforms to the wishes and interests of various parts of Russia which may not be exactly known to the specialists.' This was essential, for an election which would be 'a unique historical fact in the history of Russia'. The first date set for elections, 17 September, proved impossible to meet. The usual administrative incompetence (which left-wing critics, probably unjustly, imputed to the government's lack of enthusiasm for the Assembly) explained the delay: the *volost' zemstva*, which were to be responsible for the compilation of registers, had not been elected in time, ballot papers had not been distributed, and the like. At the same time, it was probably true that for some members of the cabinet the delay was not unwelcome: if conditions in the country were to improve, the chances of greater success for the moderate parties could be expected to increase. The election was eventually held on 12 November, after the fall of the Provisional Government. The results of the voting and the fate of the Assembly belong to a later part of this story.

The revolution unleashed the national aspirations of the component elements of the former Russian Empire. The future pattern of relations between the Russians and the various non-Russian nationals was a subject on which the political parties were in sharp disagreement. The Kadets accepted national autonomy for certain groups, but totally rejected any solution which could threaten the unity of the Russian state. The socialists, at the First All-Russian Congress of Soviets in June 1917, favoured local autonomy, especially in such matters as the right to the use of language, and also accepted 'the right of self-determination of all peoples, including separatism'. The Bolsheviks, whose primary aim in 1917 was to hasten the disintegration of the empire, advocated the right of all nationalities to claim complete independence. In the end, the policies pursued by the Provisional Government, which led to bitter dissensions, remained incomplete when the government fell, and were overtaken by events after the Bolsheviks had assumed power. To some extent, painful decisions could be postponed by constant reiteration of the plea that policy on national questions could only be decided by the Constituent Assembly, but as the convocation of this body receded into the ever-distant future, its ultimate jurisdiction had increasingly to yield to the impatience of some of the component parts of the empire.

In the case of Russian Poland, which was under German occupation, the Provisional Government immediately issued a proclamation promising an independent Polish state, merely paying lip-service to the Constituent Assembly which 'will give its consent'. The avowed object was to encourage the Poles to resist Germany and to strengthen the morale of Polish units which had been formed within the Russian army. But a long period of Polish hostility to Russian rule had left its mark, and the Poles were not unanimous in their determination to throw their weight behind the remote prospect of a Russian victory over Germany and her allies.

The government was even less successful in its dealings with Finland, which had always enjoyed a privileged status in the empire. Finland now asserted its right to complete independence. The government took refuge in the contention that only the Constituent Assembly could decide the question — in spite of the fact that it had quite easily got round this difficulty over Russian Poland. The conflict with Finland led to a bitter clash between the Provisional Government and the Finnish parliament (the *Sejm*) which had not been resolved by the time the government came to an end.

Demands for various degrees of autonomy or independence were made by the territories which were eventually to become Latvia, Estonia and Lithuania, by Belorussia and by the peoples of the Caucasus. The Muslim peoples of the empire, in a conference held in Petrograd on March 15-17, called an all-Muslim congress. This congress met in May, and a second one was held in July. The main demand put forward by these congresses was for the widest possible cultural and national autonomy within a democratic Russian republic. The second congress also called for the implementation of this autonomy before the meeting of the Constituent Assembly.

The bitterest conflict arose over the Ukraine. Passions ran high on both sides: on the one there were long-standing aspirations for independence, on the other the determination that this important territory should remain a part of future Russia. Almost immediate pleas for the concession of autonomy for the Ukraine were curtly received both by the Soviet and by the Provisional Government. The matter was further complicated by the fact that non-Ukrainian parties within the area opposed the demand for autonomy, and that the Ukrainians resisted some of the Polish territorial aspirations. As time went on, the Ukrainian Central Rada (Ukrainian for soviet) which had come into being on 4 March on mainly socialist initiative, progressively extended its influence in the Ukraine, and in June set up a General Secretariat which assumed some of the functions of an executive organ. Although the Ukrainians continued to pay lip service to retaining a form of union with Russia, there was intense suspicion on the Russian side that their demands were merely a step to complete independence. An attempt early in July by the Provisional Government to reach a compromise agreement with the Rada outraged the Kadet members of the government and precipitated a crisis within it, but did not succeed in producing peace on the issue of autonomy. By the end of September, the Ukrainian Secretariat was calling for the convocation of a separate Ukrainian Constituent Assembly: by mid-October the relations of the Secretariat with the Cabinet in Petrograd were near to breaking point. But by that time the end of the Provisional Government was in sight.

Chapter Five

The First Bolshevik Onslaught

Although Lenin's ultimate objective — the overthrow of the Provisional Government — was not in doubt, he never allowed revolutionary enthusiasm to outrun prudence and he was well aware of the need to pick the moment for assault when victory seemed best assured. After initial hesitation, the Central Committee* of the Bolshevik Party accepted Lenin's leadership, but it remained in marked contrast to the reorganized Petersburg Committee, which, with the arrival of many Bolsheviks from exile, tended to become more radical than the Central Committee. This was equally true of the Central Committee's own Military Organization, dealing with all military questions, and headed by N.I. Podvoisky (who was to play a prominent part in the seizure of power in October).

Lenin's policy, at any rate at the outset, was to support the soviets against the Provisional Government (particularly its 'bourgeois' elements). At the same time he strove to win sufficient Bolshevik influence in the soviets, both in the capital and in the provinces, to make it possible for the Bolsheviks to squeeze out the socialists when once the soviets had taken power. The more radical Bolsheviks often wanted to chance their arm by force, while lacking a very clear idea of how to achieve this success, let alone the penetrating assessment of the balance of forces which usually characterized Lenin.

As suggested earlier, the great majority of the members of the First Provisional Government were above all anxious to maintain harmonious relations with the socialists who dominated the Petrograd Soviet. Indeed, they shared many of their ideals. One of them, however, the Foreign Minister, Miliukov, held views on the issue of the war that were far apart from the position of the Executive

*After the fall of the monarchy, when the Bolshevik Party could function legally inside Russia, it was organized hierarchically, with local committees which were in theory subordinated to the Central Committee in Petrograd. By the time of the Sixth Party Congress in August 1917 the total membership numbered 240,000, and 162 local committees and other party organizations were represented. The Central Committee elected by the congress is believed to have comprised 21 members and 10 candidates, but its full composition was never published.

Committee of the Soviet, and, as events were to show, from the policy accepted by his colleagues. This became clear during the first crisis into which the government was plunged.

The Allied Governments, headed by the British Ambassador, recognized the Provisional Government on 4 March on the basis of assurances that it accepted the obligations undertaken by its predecessor. These included the territorial war settlement which the Allied Powers had agreed among themselves as the rightful fruits of victory over Germany and her partners. But all talk of aims of conquest was anathema to the Soviet socialists. On 14 March, the Soviet published a manifesto to 'the peoples of the world', declaring its hopes for a peace settlement based neither on annexation of territory nor on indemnities. At the same time the document asserted the intention of the Russian people to fight in defence of its hard-won liberty.

This position, which was arguably very damaging to the morale of a war-weary peasant army, was totally unacceptable to Miliukov. His statement to the press on 23 March that Russia was fighting in order to unite the Ukrainian parts of Austria with Russia and to conquer Constantinople and the Straits raised a storm of soviet and popular protest, which led to lengthy negotiation between the Soviet Executive Committee and the government. The latter, with the sole exception of Miliukov, eventually accepted the Soviet position, and on 27 March the Prime Minister issued a declaration that Russia had no aims of conquest or domination but desired to establish at the conclusion of the war a stable peace on the basis of self-determination. On 18 April the declaration was transmitted to the Allied Powers, but accompanied by a note from Miliukov which contained the phrase 'decisive victory' and stressed that the government 'will fully observe the obligations taken with respect to our Allies'. This note found its way into the press, and for two days, 20 and 21 April, Petrograd was in a state of turmoil. Soldiers and workers, incensed by wild rumours that the Provisional Government was defying the Soviet, paraded with such banners as 'Down with Miliukov' or 'Down with the Provisional Government'. (There were also counter-demonstrations in support of Miliukov, and some banners bore the legend 'Down with Lenin'.) The soldiers and the worker militiamen were armed; there were also weapons at the disposal of those who demonstrated in support of the government. Shots were fired, and there were some casualties.

The hero of these 'April Days' was, beyond any doubt, the Soviet. On 20 April its Executive Committee persuaded the government to issue what, in effect, amounted to a retraction of Miliukov's note of 18 April, in terms approved by the Soviet, and moreover passed a resolution asserting more stringent control in the future over the government's political acts. Emissaries of the Executive Committee successfully persuaded the demonstrating crowds, who were mostly convinced that they had the authority of the Soviet to come out into the streets, to return to their barracks or factories. When General Kornilov, the Military Commander of Petrograd, attempted to station some of his troops around the Mariinsky Palace, which was occupied by the government, his orders were countermanded by the Executive Committee. Immediately after, this the committee issued a proclamation to the garrison stating that it alone had the right to call the troops out. Kornilov resigned soon after and took up a command at the front.

Bolshevik propaganda against the government obviously played its part in influencing the soldiers and workers. But if, as the examining magistrate on the disturbances reported, the factory workers, who were armed, had 'undoubtedly' been organized in advance, this must have been the work of the Petersburg Committee and the Military Organization. The Central Committee, headed by Lenin, was more cautious. As Lenin put it a few days later to a party conference, 'We wanted only a peaceful reconnaissance of our enemy's forces, and not to give battle. But the Petersburg Committee took a position "a wee bit to the left".' And indeed, in April 1917, for the Bolsheviks to have attempted to defy the Soviet and to seize power in its name, as some of the more radical Bolsheviks wanted, would have been to invite disaster. The great majority of the Petrograd garrison unswervingly supported the Soviet, and many of them were suspicious of the Bolsheviks. Lenin drew the correct inference that the motive force behind the demonstrations of 20 and 21 April had been the desire for peace, and not scholastic interpretations of Miliukov's note, and that propaganda for an end to the war was his strongest card.

The enhanced prestige of the Soviet Executive Committee and the obvious impotence of the Provisional Government during the April crisis, led to the government's decision to broaden its ranks by the inclusion of socialist ministers. Prolonged negotiations were necessary in order to overcome hesitations on both sides: the ministers, especially the Kadets, were doubtful about the possibility of such collaboration, while the socialists had to bury their doctrinal opposition to cooperation with the 'bourgeoisie'. The factor which probably helped the socialists to agree to a coalition was the unexpected resignation at the end of April of the Minister of War, Guchkov, on the grounds that the government enjoyed no real authority and was the slave of the Soviet — which was not entirely untrue.

On May 5 a government came into being, under Prince L'vov as Prime Minister. It included five non-socialists, without party allegiance; five Kadets; and six socialists. Kerensky was the new Minister of War, and the Socialist-Revolutionary leader, V.M. Chernov, a very controversial figure because of his internationalist activities before 1917, became Minister of Agriculture. Miliukov was, in effect, forced to resign, and his place as Minister of Foreign Affairs was taken by M.I. Tereshchenko, one of the non-socialists.

These negotiations took place against a background of mounting anarchy in the country. The 'semi-Bolshevik' chronicler of the revolution, N. Sukhanov, complained of the delight, as he saw it, with which the bourgeois press high-lighted stories of disorder. But his own account of the state of affairs at the end of May is horrifying enough: 'Lynchings, destruction of houses and shops, violence . . . against officers, provincial officials and private persons, unauthorized arrests . . . by individuals were recorded daily by the dozen or by the hundred. In the villages, setting fire to estates and their demolition had become frequent . . . . There were not a few excesses to be observed among workers too — against factory administrators and owners, against fireman . . . . But, of course, the free-roaming soldiers were the most responsible [for disorder].'

The industrial anarchy was in large measure encouraged by the Bolsheviks. They helped to organize a network of factory committees, designed to replace the more moderate trade unions, and by the end of May they had secured a majority in these committees in the capital. These factory committees were also used to reorganize the workers' militia into the Red Guard, which was to prove an important military force for the Bolsheviks in October. The Bolsheviks advocated workers' control of factories and agitated for higher wages, fomenting strikes which disorganized war industry and generally crippled the economy. Their arguments that exorbitant capitalist profits were the entire cause of the workers' low standard of living fell on ready ears. The fact that socialists now sat in the cabinet as delegates of the Soviet enabled Lenin to contend endlessly that the socialists had sold out to the capitalists and must share blame with the bourgeoisie for the catastrophic state of the economy. He argued that the Soviet should break with the middle-class ministers and their lacqueys, the compromised socialists, and assume full power.

That Lenin envisaged Soviet power mainly as the prelude to a Bolshevik take-over became evident in the course of June. Events were then dominated by the impending military offensive, which began on the 18th. From Lenin's point of view, a military success could mean a serious set-back for the Bolshevik policy of disorganizing the army at the front, while, in the capital, increased military activity raised the fears of the garrison troops that they might be sent forward into action. The First All-Russian Congress of Soviets met during the first three weeks of June. It was a predominantly socialist body, and fully supported the coalition which had been formed the month before. The Bolshevik delegation was small, but nevertheless had the satisfaction of knowing that at the end of May there had been a majority in the Workers' Section of the Petrograd Soviet for a Bolshevik resolution in favour of 'All Power to the Soviets'. On 4 June Lenin caused more amusement than alarm when he announced that the Bolsheviks were prepared to take power. He argued that a Soviet power which broke with the Provisional Government, and arrested the capitalists who were promoting the war in their own interests, could stop the war and restore prosperity to Russia. Clearly such a policy could not be put into effect by a government composed of relatively moderate socialists: what Lenin envisaged was the kind of all-Bolshevik government that would emerge in October, and not one based on the existing majority in the Petrograd Soviet.

Bolshevik activity was not confined to speeches. On 10 June an abortive armed demonstration took place. Around the middle of May, when preparations were afoot for the offensive at the front, the Bolshevik Military Organization had urged the Central Committee, without success, to organize a mass demonstration. In the following weeks, no doubt with encouragement from members of the Military Organization, a number of regiments of the garrison (60,000 troops in all, according to one estimate) pressed for such a demonstration, and the question was brought up again in the Central Committee. In the heated discussions two equally determined factions emerged, in favour and against the proposal. Lenin enthusiastically supported the move which, he claimed, corresponded to the will of the masses. Those who opposed the demonstration argued — with justice, as events were to show — that to be effective it had to have worker support, and that this would be harder to obtain than that of the garrison, which was directly affected by the proposed offensive. In view of the division of opinion, it was decided to postpone the final decision until a meeting to be held on the eve of the date proposed for the demonstration — 10 June. It was assumed throughout that those parading would be armed.

A relevant factor in the ultimate Bolshevik decision was an incident provoked on 5 June by the Petrograd Anarchist-Communists, when they seized the printing press and premises of a newspaper which was less than enthusiastic in its revolutionary fervour. The anarchist political programme was simple — the immediate elimination of all governments, whether autocratic or parliamentary, of the capitalist system, the war, the army, the police and of all state boundaries. The importance of these eccentrics, from the Bolshevik point of view, was that their extreme propaganda presented formidable competition for the allegiance of the more ignorant among the population which was the vital Bolshevik constituency. An attempt by the Minister of Justice to evict the Anarchists from their headquarters (after liberating the newspaper office) led to an appeal by them to factory workers to support them. This was followed by a mass strike in the factories. The Soviet succeeded in persuading the workers to return to work, but only at the price of postponing the eviction of the Anarchists. This incident not only increased the tension in the capital: it demonstrated to the Bolsheviks the weakness of the Soviet and the government.

Thus emboldened, the Central Committee, late on 8 June, decided to organize a mass worker and soldier demonstration for the afternoon of 10 June. The eve of the march, 9 June, was spent in feverish preparations, which seem to have met with a generally favourable response from workers as well as soldiers. There is no doubt that the event was meticulously organized by the Bolsheviks. However, in the small hours of 10 June the Congress of Soviets (which, it will be recalled, was in session in the capital) issued a declaration prohibiting all demonstrations of any kind for three days. There were also clear indications from army committees in the field that the units nearest the capital might intervene to disperse any demonstration by the garrison troops. (This was in spite of Kerensky's rather foolhardy declaration that no troops would ever, in any circumstances, be moved from the front to the capital.)

In the course of the morning of 10 June, the Central Committee, this time with Lenin's support, decided to call off the demonstration, and Bolshevik emissaries worked vigorously to persuade the marchers to stay in the barracks and factories. The fact that they were able to stop the marchers is certainly proof of their influence with some of the soldiers and workers, and particularly with the Red Guards, who by now were numbered in thousands. Nevertheless, the evidence of the contemporary press suggests that the majority of the garrison still accepted the authority of the Soviet rather than that of the Bolshevik Central Committee; and there is no doubt that the decision to call off the demonstration was a retreat, which caused anger in Bolshevik circles, especially in the Petersburg Committee and the Military Organization. The extent of the set-back is hard to assess. According to Sukhanov (the Internationalist, pro-Bolshevik chronicler of the revolution) he was told of detailed plans by the Bolsheviks to seize power on 10 June, but this seems inconsistent with Lenin's tactics as we know them, which were characterized by caution. Lenin must have been aware that the allegiance of the garrison to the Soviets was still strong, and that a majority of troops both in the capital and at the front close to Petrograd would oppose a *coup d'état* against the socialist Soviets.

Following upon its moral victory, the Congress of Soviets debated, with some heat, the policy which should be adopted towards the Bolsheviks in the light of what was generally assumed, by all except the Bolsheviks and their supporters, to be a frustrated conspiracy to overthrow the government. The demand for forcible measures against the Bolsheviks, including disarming the Red Guards, was strongly argued by the Menshevik leader, Tsereteli, by far the most impressive figure on the Soviet Executive Committee. This handsome, tall Georgian Social-Democrat, who had entered the coalition as Minister of Posts and Telegraphs, urged that having failed to seize power once, the Bolsheviks would, unless effectively stopped, try again, and that such an attempt could only play into the hands of counter-revolutionary forces. Although he won some support, the great majority of his fellow socialists were only prepared to go so far as to adopt a resolution against demonstrations called by any one party without the authority of the soviets — accompanied by pious exhortation to the Bolsheviks to behave like good democrats. The soviets thus failed to exploit their strength at a time when they might perhaps have hoped to do so with some success.

No doubt flushed with victory, the Soviet Congress decreed the holding of a peaceful demonstration on 18 June, confident that the support which they enjoyed in the capital would be clearly revealed. It proved a very unwise move. Whether due to the apathy of the supporters of the Soviet, or to intensive organization and propaganda by the Bolsheviks among soldiers and workers, who often had genuine cause for discontent, the demonstration, though relatively small, was characterized by slogans ('more placards than demonstrators', according to one comment) of obvious Bolshevik inspiration — such as 'All Power to the Soviets', or 'Down with the Ten Capitalist Ministers'. But some declarations of support for the government and for the war were also to be seen. The Anarchists, who alone carried arms, caused the only disturbance by effecting a jail-break. The government retaliated by evicting them from their headquarters and recapturing the freed prisoners, killing one of the anarchist leaders in the process. On the same day, 18 June, the military offensive began. It won an initial success, but it became apparent by the end of June that the campaign was a disaster for the Russian side (see Chapter 6).

Pressure for an immediate seizure of power continued among the more impatient Bolsheviks and Anarchists in the capital. The success of the demonstration of 18 June stimulated the more hot-headed. Support for immediate action was given by a conference of local Bolshevik military organizations held between 16 and 23 June. Some 26,000 Bolsheviks attended from 43 front and 17 rear units — actually a very small proportion of the total army. According to Podvoisky, the head of the Military Organization, Lenin told him on 18 June that power could not be captured by peaceful means, and that the proletariat must organize to seize control of government, if not in weeks 'then in any event in the near future'. However, in his speech to the conference on 20 June, Lenin stressed the need to fight for influence inside the soviets, and not to be provoked into premature action.

In the army, further impatience against the continuing offensive was aroused in garrison units where Bolsheviks predominated, especially the First Machine Gun Regiment. This regiment was ordered to supply 500 machine guns, and to reorganize so that two-thirds of its men could be moved to the front. Its members were restrained from rushing into action by the Petrograd Soviet and by Bolshevik leaders; but there is little doubt that, whatever the views of the more sober Bolshevik leaders, a substantial element within their Military Organization was raring for action in the days following the news of the offensive — one of the leaders of the Military Organization even claimed in 1922 that a plan for an armed movement involving 30,000 troops was worked out on 22 June. The official line of propaganda emanating from the Central Committee and the Military Organization, however, was to urge the soldiers and workers not to dissipate their strength in isolated actions, but to wait for the signal for the ultimate decisive move against the government.

When rebellion did break out in early July, its timing was influenced by the resignation on 2 July of the Kadet ministers from the cabinet, in protest against the policy pursued by the government in the Ukraine (see Chapter 4); but preparations for the armed overthrow of the government were actually made in the First Machine Gun Regiment the day before the resignations, if not earlier. It also seems clear that the troops received encouragement from members of the Bolshevik Military Organization. On 2 July the Organization urged the Central Committee to support the proposed 'insurrection', arguing that the First Machine Gun Regiment could easily overthrow the Provisional Government. The Central Committee refused, and ordered the Military Organization to discourage the rebellion, though how far they complied by trying to stop the preparations is another matter. The Anarchists were also much involved. A fiery anti-government rally, in which Trotsky among other leaders took part, was held on the afternoon of 2 July. By early on 3 July the temper of the First Machine Gun Regiment was at fever heat, and concrete plans for the overthrow of the government were prepared in the course of the morning. Emissaries were sent to a number of military units and to factories in the capital and in neighbouring districts like Kronstadt. Some of the troops were hostile, or at best neutral, but at least five regiments gave their support, as well as many factories. By midnight a sizeable force of soldiers and workers had mustered around the Tauride Palace, and were soon joined by 30,000 more from a large munitions factory, the Putilov works. In one way or another 100,000 troops were affected by the July events.

The soldiers' motive for revolt seems to have been the fear that they would be drafted to the front, though the Kronstadt sailors (who joined in the revolt next day) had a grievance of their own: the Provisional Government had attempted to secure some justice for the large number of officers whom the sailors had been keeping incarcerated in harsh conditions, in many cases without grounds. The Putilov workers believed that the 'capitalist' Provisional Government would not improve their wages. (These same workers had, on 14 May, approved of socialist participation in the government.) Over-riding all rational considerations were the envy and hatred which the revolution had unleashed in a politically ignorant people, conscious only of the hardships and humiliations which it had suffered for generations.

When the Central Executive Committee of the Soviets heard of the impending rebellion in the course of the afternoon, it issued a proclamation warning against armed demonstrations without orders from the Commander in Chief and stating that those who disobeyed would be treated as enemies of the revolution. But by seven that evening the first armed groups, with the machine gunners in the lead, had already appeared in the streets of Petrograd.

The Bolshevik version of the July insurrection, ever since Stalin's account at the end of July to the Sixth Bolshevik Congress, has been that the disturbances started 'spontaneously' against the wishes of the Central Committee, which was then forced to take over the lead of what became a mass revolt with overwhelming support in the capital. It was true that the plan for the rebellion started among the machine gunners, but it was also true that it was vigorously encouraged by rank and file Bolsheviks, and once the armed action in the streets had started it would have been politically dangerous for the Bolshevik leaders to wash their hands of it. The Central Committee and the Military Organization accordingly took over, and at 4 a.m. on 4 July issued a proclamation to the effect that the coalition government had collapsed (a reference to the resignation of the

Kadets) and that power must now pass to the soviets. Lenin, who was resting for a few days in Finland, approved the course adopted by the Central Committee on his return later that day. The story recounted by Sukhanov of a detailed plot to seize power at the beginning of July is open to doubt; but the assertion by Tsereteli sounds more convincing: that Lenin had hopes at the beginning of the July events that the Soviet would be forced to take power in view of the disarray of the coalition caused by the Kadet resignations, and that the Bolsheviks would soon after that succeed in ousting the socialists by their well-tried methods of intrigue.

The demonstrators, who numbered tens of thousands (not hundreds of thousands as Soviet historians maintain), engaged in pointless clashes, in which some four hundred were eventually to lose their lives. As the historian of the July days, Professor Alexander Rabinowitch, remarks, 'in all probability trigger-happy demonstrators, *provocateurs*, right-wing elements and quite often sheer confusion and panic were equally to blame' for the casualties. By the small hours of 4 July thousands of armed soldiers and workers had surrounded the Tauride Palace, where the Central Executive Committee of the Soviets was in session. The insurgents could easily have sacked the palace and arrested the members of the Executive, who were without military force to defend them, but they contented themselves with shouting slogans and threats. Some of the Putilov workers burst in to the palace, where one of them delivered a fiery speech about the treachery of the socialist ministers. Chkheidze, the Chairman of the Executive Committee, thrust into the orator's hand a copy of the committee's proclamation against armed demonstrations (made the previous day) and the crowd melted away.

This lack of decisiveness and determination characterized the events of 3-4 July, and belied the Bolshevik claim of overwhelming mass support and unrestrainable revolutionary ardour. Another feature of these days was the stream of lorries full of armed men racing up and down the streets of the capital, in a manner reminiscent of February; but the lorries and the faint-hearted assault on the Tauride Palace were only pale echoes of the days of the revolution, when virtually the entire population of the capital supported the infuriated crowds, in contrast to the hostility or indifference of the inhabitants of Petrograd on this occasion.

Disturbances and violence continued during 4 July. Bolshevik agitators maintained their activity in the morning, but with less success than on the day before, especially among the military. Attempts to organize demonstrations in Moscow and other provincial cities did not meet with much enthusiasm. On the other hand, the Commander in Chief of Petrograd was equally unsuccessful in bringing out any of the garrison troops for the defence of the government. There was firing on the demonstrators from rooftops and windows, presumably by anti-Bolshevik enthusiasts since the government and the Soviet had as yet no forces they could call on. The soldiers retaliated by storming the houses from which the shots had come, often lynching some of the occupants. In the course of the morning a large contingent of perhaps twenty thousand sailors arrived from Kronstadt and marched to the Kshesinskaia Mansion, the Bolshevik HQ, where they were addressed by Lenin and other leaders. (No record of Lenin's speech has been preserved.) Later in the morning tens of thousands of soldiers, sailors and workers marched on the Tauride Palace. Chernov, the most radical of the socialist ministers, came out and tried to reassure the mob, but met with a very rough reception. (It was on this occasion that the bizarre scene witnessed by Miliukov took place — an infuriated worker shaking his fist at Chernov, and shouting 'Take power, you son of a bitch, when it's given you!') Eventually Chernov was hauled down and thrust into a car. He was rescued from lynching in the nick of time by the courageous intervention of Trotsky.

The menacing behaviour of the demonstrators, as exemplified by this and other incidents, had a sobering effect on the Soviet socialists. Arguments by left-wingers like Martov that the Soviet should take power were rejected, and arrangements were set afoot to bring troops loyal to the government into the capital from the nearest points outside. (Units from the Fifth Army on the Northern Front, ten to fifteen thousand in all, arrived on 6 July.) Rumours that the soldiers were coming spread in the course of the afternoon and had an immediately sobering effect on the volatile Petrograd crowds. Even more impressive was the arrival around 1 a.m. on 5 July at the Tauride Palace of three guards regiments, with a band, and in full battle order. These were some of the regiments which had refused to come to defend the Soviet the day before. The defeat of the Bolsheviks was now evident to all.

Another factor which ensured the collapse of the July revolt was the making public by the Minister of Justice, Pereverzev, of evidence purporting to show that Lenin and several other Bolshevik leaders were German agents working to the orders of the German General Staff. The material on this issue had been in the hands of the Provisional Government for some time, but they did not wish it to be published since they feared that premature revelation would hamper their investigations. Pereverzev acted on his own initiative in making the details of the charge known inside one of the guards regiments, with striking effect on the mood of 'neutrality' maintained by it hitherto. The information available to the government was also published in summary form in a right-wing newspaper next morning, but rumours that the Bolsheviks had been established to be German agents had already swept the excitable city. There were spontaneous reactions against the Bolsheviks, some violent, and anti-semitic speeches were heard in the streets.

But the Bolshevik retreat was decided on before the charge of their complicity with the Germans became public knowledge. In the afternoon of 4 July, Lenin had already learned of the proposed revelation, and — a matter of equal importance — the firm reaction by the Provisional Government and the Executive Committee in sending for loyal troops. The Bolshevik leaders decided to call on the soldiers to return to their barracks and the instruction appeared the following day — on the back page of *Pravda*. Determined action by the Soviet socialists had, with comparative ease, defeated a rebellion which, even if support for it was slender in the capital and still more tenuous in the provinces, was at some stage probably regarded by Lenin as a first and vital step to Bolshevik power.

The evidence of Bolshevik contacts with the Germans published by Pereverzev was of dubious validity, though some of it was undoubtedly true. In particular, (as shown in the next chapter) official German documents which became available after the end of the Second World War establish beyond reasonable doubt that the Bolsheviks were in receipt of German instructions. The Provisional Government continued their investigation into Bolshevik contacts with the Germans in a rather desultory fashion, and it had not been completed by the time the Bolsheviks seized power.

Flushed with success, the socialist ministers now proceeded to take action against the Bolsheviks. At dawn on 5 July a detachment of soldiers was sent out by the Commander in Chief to the premises of *Pravda*, where they promptly wrecked the plant. All day long soldiers confiscated lorries in the city and carried out arrests. A large attacking force was mounted against Bolshevik headquarters, the Ksheshinskaia mansion, but the occupants evacuated it before the troops arrived. Some hotheads were in favour of attempting to organize further resistance or calling a general strike, but the leaders' more sober policy of capitulation prevailed in the end. The Kronstadt sailors voted to surrender, and were disarmed. The Anarchist headquarters were also cleared by troops.

On 6 July the Provisional Government ordered the arrest of leading Bolsheviks, and some, including Kamenev and Trotsky, were imprisoned. Many more, especially from among the members of the Military Organization, were arrested in the days that followed. Lenin and Zinoviev decided to seek refuge in hiding in Finland and not to stand trial, on the grounds that they had no chance of a fair hearing. This was widely interpreted outside Bolshevik ranks as an admission of guilt, and their long statement denying the charges of links with the Germans did little to allay suspicions. There was some criticism of the decision even in Bolshevik ranks.

It was also at this time, on 6 July, that Lenin persuaded his colleagues on the Bolshevik Central Committee that the slogan 'All Power to the Soviets' was now out of date, since they had clearly demonstrated their allegiance to the bourgeoisie. The slogan must now be 'All Power to the Working Class, led by the Bolshevik Party'. At the Sixth Congress of the Bolsheviks, held from 26 July to 3 August, which Lenin, still in hiding, did not attend, Stalin would have to explain the new policy of seizure of power by 'the armed people' to a somewhat bewildered audience.

As regards the garrison, the Provisional Government decided that units which had participated in the rebellion were to be disarmed and dispersed. The First Machine Gun Regiment was indeed deprived of its weapons, broken up, and its men sent to the front. Five other regiments were also to be completely disbanded and others to be partially dispersed according to a plan drawn up by the military authorities, but in the event the proposed action was never fully implemented. Government aims of depriving factories of the weapons stored for use by the Red Guards also proved completely ineffective. The Bolshevik press, after a short interruption, resumed publication. There is no doubt that the fortunes of the Bolsheviks declined as the result of the July defeat, but it was only a temporary set-back, and their organizations remained virtually intact.

The Provisional Government and the Soviet were probably only in part to blame for failure to deal decisively and finally with the mortal threat which Lenin's party presented to their very existence. They had, of course, left the matter rather late — it might have been wise to deal with the danger in June, as Tsereteli had urged — but Bolshevik strength derived from factors which by July were beyond the government's control: the anarchy released in February, and the economic decline for which that anarchy was largely responsible. Above all, there was the huge peasant army, whose longings for immediate grants of land had not been satisfied, and whose former discipline had been undermined by a popular revolution which made preservation of it no longer conceivable. Moreover, the soldiers' hopes for peace had been stimulated by the Soviet's constant urging of a settlement 'without annexations or contributions', which many of them interpreted as implying the prospect of an immediate peace. It was on the army that the Bolsheviks concentrated much of their activity, which will be discussed in the next chapter.

Meanwhile, the routing of the Bolsheviks had left unresolved the crisis caused by the resignation of the Kadet ministers. The socialist ministers, who believed that their policy in such matters as working out conditions of peace with the Allied Powers and measures on the land question and industrial relations had been mainly obstructed by the Kadet ministers, now saw a chance of moving forward. But their plans immediately came up against the unexpected opposition of Prince L'vov. The Prime Minister's main objection was to a proposal, supported by the socialists, for a prohibition of all transactions in land. This, in his view, would determine policy on the land in advance of the Constituent Assembly by, in effect, prejudging the question of expropriation of the landlords, since it would prevent them from safeguarding their property against ultimate confiscation. He also objected to other proposals, such as the declaration of Russia as a republic, and formal dissolution of the Duma and the State Council. The socialist ministers, including Chernov, were prepared to meet Prince L'vov on the issues of the republic and the Duma, but were adamant on the question of transactions in land. Prince L'vov resigned, and the premiership was offered to Kerensky, who readily accepted. He was warmly endorsed as Prime Minister by Prince L'vov in a statement on 9 July.

The problems which Kerensky faced in trying both to form a new cabinet and to devise an acceptable programme were considerable. On 8 July the government had published a declaration on future policy on industry and the land, but containing no reference to the proclamation of a republic or disbanding the Duma and the State Council. The intentions declared on industrial and land policy did not go nearly far enough to satisfy the peasants or the government's extremist critics, but they were radical enough to provoke a campaign in the 'bourgeois' press and to antagonize the Kadets and the industrialists. Indeed, as far back as March, the Kadet Minister of Trade and Industry in the first coalition cabinet, A.I. Konovalov, had resigned after barely a fortnight in office in protest against the way the government was yielding to workers' demands. He regarded this (as did his party as a whole) as an unjustified concession to one class which endangered the interests of the entire country, although he made it clear that he did not oppose higher taxation on profits (up to ninety per cent) and other measures affecting the industrialists.

On 12 July the law prohibiting transactions in land was agreed by the cabinet. At the same meeting, under the impact of the shock produced by the collapse of the army in the offensive, the death penalty was restored at the front. Prolonged negotiations for a new coalition were now embarked on with the aim of forming a national government which would reflect all the main interests in the country.

It proved a hopeless task. An attempt was made to bring in representatives of industry, but in a statement dated 19 July the Council of the All-Russian Union of Trade and Industry was severely critical of the government for its failure to safeguard liberty and citizens' rights, and expressed the view that only a radical break with the soviets could restore the health of Russia — a condition which no coalition Government could conceivably accept. As to the Kadets, they objected to Chernov's presence in the cabinet and refused to go along with the principles of policy outlined by the government, especially in its declaration of 8 July on industry and the land.

After a joint session on 21 July between the Provisional Government and the central committees of the main political parties (other than the Bolsheviks) it was eventually agreed that Kerensky should be allowed complete discretion to form a government — a promise that was in practice worth as much as the undertaking by the Executive Committee of the Soviet not to exercise control over the government. On 23 July, Kerensky formed a coalition cabinet in which eight socialists out-numbered seven 'bourgeois' representatives. But no real agreement had been achieved between the democratic forces in the country, and the cracks of dissent had merely been papered over.

Chapter Six

The Disruption of the Armed Forces

The collapse of the army and navy as a fighting force, which was the main factor ensuring the success of the Bolshevik insurrection, has been widely attributed to Order No. 1 (the eight-point order issued by the Petrograd Soviet to the garrison at the beginning of March). Certainly those within the Petrograd Soviet who had intended that Order No. 1 should become a means of disrupting the army, particularly the Bolsheviks, did all they could to ensure that copies of the document were distributed as widely as possible at the front, in spite of the fact that it applied only to the Petrograd garrison.

The Executive Committee of the Soviet was trying to pursue two ultimately irreconcilable aims — preserving the army as a force capable of prosecuting the war, and neutralizing it as a potential counter-revolutionary instrument. The committee was therefore alarmed by the widespread interpretation given to the order both by the garrison troops and at the front — that it permitted the election of officers. Accordingly, on 6 March, the Executive Committee issued Order No. 2. This stressed that Order No. 1 applied only to the garrison, and that it did not confer on the soldiers' committees (provided for by the order) the right to elect officers. However, it also added to the confusion by ordering that elections already completed must remain valid. The committees, it stated, were to be the authority in matters of public and political life (thus confirming that the army was recognized as a political organization) but in military matters commanders must be obeyed. Order No. 2 was vigorously opposed by the Bolsheviks in the Soviet, who regarded it as a capitulation to the Provisional Government.

Around the same time, the Minister of War, Guchkov, extended the abolition of the disciplinary restrictions enumerated in Order No. 1 to troops at the front, and set up a commission under General Polivanov to revise the laws of military service. (These provisions were embodied in Orders No. 114 and No. 115.) The death penalty, both in the rear and at the front, had been abolished by a decree of the Provisional Government on 12 March. In the army, the field courts martial were replaced by a kind of jury system for dealing with military offences, which was much exposed to outside pressure from the troops.

While it is obvious that all these moves could only serve to undermine the cohesion and discipline of the armed forces, it is open to doubt how far this can be laid solely at the door of Order No. 1. So far as the garrison troops were concerned, they were well aware of their political power, and determined to ensure that officers whom they regarded as hostile to the revolution should not be given the chance to hold them responsible for their acts of mutiny. In many cases Order No. 1 probably served merely as an excuse to sanction what was taking place without it. It is unlikely, for example, that the sailors' revolt in the Baltic Fleet, in which at least a hundred officers were murdered and hundreds were beaten up and arrested, needed Order No. 1 to inspire it. At the front, especially in areas closest to the capital, the settling of scores with unpopular officers was also a spontaneous process. Once the troops had sensed their power and immunity, they required no enactment to encourage them.

By the middle of March, if not before, the arrests of officers which were common in the rear had spread to the front. Thereafter they continued until the Bolshevik *coup d'état* of 25 October, and later. Pretexts varied. In many cases, reprisals were enacted by the soldiers against officers who tried to maintain discipline in the manner traditional before the revolution or indeed attempted to insist on obedience to orders at all. In other cases officers were removed for trying to stop the men displaying the red symbols of revolution. In the spy-mania which the Progessive Bloc leaders, among others, had fuelled by their speeches before the revolution, a German surname (of which there were many in Russia) was often a good enough reason for insisting on an officer's removal.

There were over eight million soldiers and officers on the long Russian front at the time of the revolution, with a further two million held in reserve in the rear. This manpower was distributed in fourteen armies, dispersed, from north to south, on the Northern, Western, South-Western, Roumanian and Caucasian Fronts. Strategically, the most important fronts were the South-Western and Roumanian, on which the offensive operations took place, and which took up over half of the total personnel. Politically, the most radicalized fronts were the Northern and Western.

The main revolutionary development among the fighting troops was the emergence of committees. Although a great impetus to this process was given by Orders No. 1 and No. 2, it seems to have started spontaneously even before these orders penetrated to the front. The Commander in Chief wisely bowed to a process that was inevitable, and on 11 March issued an instruction (no. 2137) to commanders of fronts to encourage the formation of committees and to ensure the participation of officers in them in an attempt to guide them along moderate lines. Things did not quite work out as General Alekseev intended. Nevertheless, right up to the Bolshevik take-over, the higher-level committees remained the only stabilizing influence in the army. They were for the most part dominated by Mensheviks and Socialist Revolutionaries, and argued the need to preserve discipline and to prosecute the war. Usually, they opposed fraternization with the enemy, which, encouraged by the Bolsheviks and by the Germans, proved to be one of the most potent means of destroying the soldiers' will to fight.

Many committees included both soldiers and officers, but there were also many composed only of soldiers, especially at the lower levels. Although predominantly Socialist Revolutionary in their majorities, many of them also showed signs of Bolshevik influence. Throughout the months leading up to October, soldiers' committees and soldier soviets, or soldier sections of local soviets in the garrisons, bombarded the government and soviet authorities in the capital with demands for a solution to the land question, without waiting for the Constituent Assembly. By October, their growing frustration had made them an easy prey to the promises of the Bolsheviks.

By this stage of the war, the officers were no longer the professional caste that they had once been: their numbers had been much diluted by wartime recruitment from lower social classes. Many of the new officers gave excellent service in the campaigns, and often their sympathy with the revolution made it easier for them to find rapport with the troops and in the committees: it is also true that there were recorded instances of cadre officers, who had survived the mass removals and arrests, who enjoyed the respect of their troops and were able to maintain authority. But the old Russian officer corps, which had demonstrated its potential for promoting commanders of ability, suffered in the early days of the revolution not only the assault of the committees (often undeserved) but also a drastic purge by the War Minister, Guchkov. About 150 officers were dismissed in the course of a few weeks, including 70 commanders of divisions. This purge, which was often motivated by demagogy rather than by reason, had the serious effect of lowering the already much shaken morale of the officers.

The stabilizing rôle of the committees was only relative: it stopped many of the worst excesses, but in the long run it could not prevent the rapid disintegration of the discipline and morale of the troops. Much has been written on the effects of Bolshevik undermining of the troops' morale, and it was indeed a powerful factor; but even

Menshevik and Social Revolutionary demands, in their propaganda for 'peace without annexations and contributions' (which became especially vocal after Miliukov's disastrous note to the Allied Powers on the subject of war aims) were sufficient to sap the will of the soldiers to fight. It was scarcely surprising that a politically naïve army of peasants, with their minds intent on what they regarded as their legitimate prize — the landlords' land — should have interpreted 'peace without annexations and contributions' as equivalent to 'immediate peace'.

There was, at the outset, no collapse of morale. Contrary to some predictions, especially by foreign observers, the Emperor's abdication did not cause dismay among the troops. However, there was delay in publicizing the manifesto of abdication, and that of the Grand Duke Michael which followed it, caused by arguments between Rodzianko, General Alekseev and the Grand Duke Nicholas (who remained Commander in Chief until 11 March). This period of delay, during which rumours reached many parts of the front, caused wild speculation and suspicion among the troops that their commanders were trying to deceive them. On 11 March General Alekseev, who was about to become Commander in Chief, reported that the overwhelming majority of units at the front (in contrast to those in the rear) were calm, and that their morale was good — though he spoke rather too soon when he stated that the front had not been beset by arrests of and attacks on the officers in the way that the garrisons had.

A summary of commanders' reports around this time on the Western Front was, on the whole, surprisingly optimistic: most of them, while recognizing that morale had been shaken by events, were confident that the army would be capable of going over to the attack in one or two months' time, while some even maintained that its spirits were unimpaired. This relative stability may have been due to the fact that during these early weeks after the revolution the front line troops looked to the Duma, and not to the Petrograd Soviet, as the legitimate government. There was also a determination, as Alekseev reported on 14 March, to bring the war to a victorious conclusion.

These judgments are to some extent confirmed by the accounts of a number of Duma members who paid visits to the front soon after the revolution and reported to the Provisional Government. But in their account of the last of these visits (to the South-Western Front in mid-April 1917) the delegates, while still confirming general support for the Duma, noted that morale had considerably deteriorated since their first visit immediately after the revolution. They believed this to be the result of intensive German propaganda. There was no will to fight for what was now widely believed to be a war in the interests of French and English capitalists. For the time being, indeed until well into April, the Soviet did not send representatives to the front: by then, largely under the influence of Miliukov's note and the resulting crisis, anarchy had spread. The troops looked to the Petrograd Soviet and its executive committee as the authority, instead of to the Provisional Government, which they now regarded as suspect and bourgeois.

As to the soldiers' committees, they were now in a difficult position. Most of them were dominated by Mensheviks and Socialist Revolutionaries, and the formation of a coalition government which included representatives of those parties made the committees consider it their duty to emphasize the preservation of discipline so as to make possible the government's defencist policy. This had the inevitable consequence of undermining their authority over the troops. The committees, especially at the lower levels, did their best to preserve their influence by voicing support both for the Petrograd Soviet and the Provisional Government.

By the beginning of May, General Brusilov, the Commander in Chief of the vital South-Western Front, reported at a GHQ Conference on morale in his command. He emphasized that the soldiers had lost faith in the government and that their whole allegiance was to the Soviet. He detailed a number of cases of refusal to obey orders, and attributed this breakdown of discipline to political, especially Bolshevik, agitation. Both Brusilov and the other front commanders, who supported his view of the situation, emphasized that one of the main problems was the relationship of troops and officers. The professional officers were hostile to the new developments and could find no common ground with the men; and even the new recruits to the officer corps who were sympathetic to the revolution clashed with the troops when they tried to enforce discipline. German intelligence information of the period supports this analysis.

The disruption of the army as a fighting force held a high priority among Lenin's aims after his arrival in Petrograd on 3 April 1917. His Theses, published immediately afterwards, it will be recalled, demanded 'a republic of soviets' and, among other things, 'the elimination of the army and police'. There should be the widest propagation 'in the army in the field' of the view that there could be no genuine democratic peace without the overthrow of capitalism. To this end, Lenin also advocated appeals for fraternization. Bolshevik military organizations were set up with feverish speed at the front and in the rear, and the Bolshevik military bureaux in Petrograd and

Moscow were soon receiving a flood of letters and visitors from the front. Many thousands, probably hundreds of thousands of newspapers and pamphlets were despatched to the soldiers, and propagandists worked on them systematically. The aim of all this activity was to destroy the army as a fighting force — to encourage desertion and refusal to obey orders or to fight, and to promote fraternization with the enemy. Lenin was primarily concerned to make a military offensive impossible, since he feared that a successful operation against the Germans would bring about a wave of patriotic fervour and make seizure of power by the Bolsheviks impossible. His main hope lay in dividing the rank and file troops from the defencist and anti-Bolshevik committees.

An equally important aspect of the Bolsheviks' policy, in which they were very successful, was winning over the Petrograd garrison, at least to a position of neutrality. Sometimes, as with the Kronstadt sailors and several regiments of infantry, they achieved enthusiastic support, and by mid-June they had made substantial headway with a large part of the garrison troops, who were primarily anxious to resist efforts to send them into the fighting lines. Even so, the Bolsheviks were unwilling at that date to proceed with their aim of seizing power, for fear that troops from the front be brought back to overthrow them.

Throughout the period of the Provisional Government, the strength of the Bolsheviks was less important in promoting their advance to power than the weakness of the government and the soviets. This was particularly evident over fraternization. If army commanders' reports from the fronts are to be trusted, German attempts at fraternization made no headway during March and April. Thereafter, in spite of determined opposition by the army committees, fraternization became widespread as the Provisional Government closed its eyes to open appeals for it by Bolshevik and pro-Bolshevik propagandists. The Bolsheviks denied any intention to disrupt the army's fighting capacity, but in fact fraternization was widely exploited by the Germans and Austrians both for gathering intelligence and for the recruitment of agents — as the evidence of their military archives establishes beyond doubt.

It was not only in advocacy of fraternization that German and Bolshevik propaganda were at one. The coinciding themes on the two sides — that the war was being prosecuted for the enrichment of the capitalists of Great Britain and France, or that seizures of power by the soviets and the overthrow of the Provisional Government were the only sure means of ending the war — naturally gave rise to a widespread belief that the Bolsheviks were German agents. (The government's abortive attempt to establish this charge against the Bolsheviks after the July rising has been referred to in Chapter 5.)

If German and Bolshevik policies were ever concerted, there is no evidence to bear it out, beyond the identity of aim — to put an end to the army as a fighting force. There is, however, strong evidence to suggest that the Bolsheviks received substantial financial support from the German government after April 1917. On the German side, archives of the Foreign Ministry, which became available for study after their defeat in the Second World War, leave no room for doubt that from 1915 onwards the Germans were seeking for a way to subsidize all Russian revolutionaries who opposed the war. Whether the money paid over for the purpose ever reached any actual agents cannot be stated for certain, but there is a very strong probability that substantial sums reached the Bolsheviks after March 1917. In a report to the Kaiser in December 1917, the German Foreign Minister claimed that it was not until the Bolsheviks had 'received from us a steady flow of funds through different channels and under different labels' that they were able to build up their propaganda effort. There is also supporting evidence on the Russian side. Much information, supported by very circumstantial evidence, appears in the memoirs of the head of counter-intelligence in the Provisional Government, and there are also some indications of financial transactions in Bolshevik sources.

According to the Provisional Government, money from German sources reached Lenin through a former Social Democrat, Parvus, the revolutionary name of an adventurer of unsavoury reputation who was at this point in Stockholm. Lenin's contacts with Parvus were alleged to be Haniecki, a Polish Social Democrat who was certainly close to Lenin, and Kozlovsky, an undistinguished Social Democrat in Petrograd. On two occasions Lenin expressly denied that he had ever had any financial dealings with either Haniecki or Kozlovsky, but these denials were untrue. Two of Lenin's published letters, written to Haniecki in April 1917 clearly show that there were money transactions with both men. ('We have received the money, 2,000 from Kozlovsky.' 'We have so far received . . . no money from you . . . . Be extremely careful and meticulous in your relations.') It should be added that 'special funds' are known, from Soviet sources, to have been placed at the disposal of a Bolshevik Central Committee Press Bureau headed by Molotov; and that at eight meetings in August and September 1917 the Bolshevik Central Committee discussed the 'complicated affairs' of Haniecki and Kozlovsky, though on each occasion a report of the discussion was omitted when the minutes were published in 1923. It may also be significant that it was Parvus who first discussed German proposals for peace with Karl Radek, the Bolshevik emissary in Stockholm, after the Bolsheviks had seized power.

However much Bolshevik propaganda, whether financed by the Germans or not, may have contributed to the collapse of the armed forces in 1917, other powerful factors were at work. The failure of the government to take, or appear to be taking, effective steps over the land question was bound to have repercussions in a largely peasant army, and there is ample evidence of the passionate interest the soldiers showed in it. Of the large number of deserters (which is referred to below) many were motivated by the desire to get back to their villages so as not to miss any sharing out of the landlords' estates that might take place.

The delay in convening the long-promised Constituent Assembly was another influential factor, in the army as elsewhere, in making the ultimate Bolshevik victory possible. Interest in elections to the Assembly was very widespread among the troops, and they looked to it, even after the Bolsheviks had seized power, as the body which would give them peace and land. Had the Constituent Assembly been brought into existence before the October coup, the army might have rallied around it, instead of backing the Bolsheviks. It is also possible that a Constituent Assembly which appeared to be taking resolute steps to inaugurate a land policy might have had a chance of persuading some of the soldiers to support the prosecution of the war.

Two other influential causes of disruption were the national question and the breakdown of supplies as the result of general economic collapse. Nationalist aspirations, unleashed by the revolution, reveal themselves in the ardent desire of troops of some of the main national minorities within the Russian Empire — Ukrainian, Lettish, Estonian and Caucasian, among others — to form their own national units. This desire was, in most cases, closely linked with ambitions to attain a federal or lesser degree of autonomy in their homeland, and to return there as soon as possible to effect redistribution of the land. For different reasons, (ideological in the case of the Mensheviks, for example, chauvinistic in the case of the Kadets) these ambitions were resisted by all the political parties, as well as by the General Staff on practical grounds. The result was that the creation of national units and formations was much obstructed, though in the end some Polish, Ukrainian, Lettish and Estonian national units did come into existence. How far the government lost an opportunity here of organizing, within the armed forces, a nucleus of units with good morale and with an incentive to fight for the future free Russia which the national minorities desired, is difficult to judge, and the experience of the Polish and Ukrainian military formations which did emerge does not offer much evidence.

The Bolsheviks, if usually less outspoken than the other parties, were equally opposed to these national aspirations, but they did succeed in winning over the help of the Lettish units on the Northern Front, on the vital approaches to the capital, primarily because of the failure of the Provisional Government to deal with the acute social and agrarian questions in what became Latvia.

The economic problems with which Russia was faced by 1917, after nearly three years of war, were inherited by the Provisional Government. They proved beyond its capacity to resolve. Disorganization of transport, lack of raw materials, the long duration of the war for which the underdeveloped Russian economy was unprepared, as well as the decline in productivity and manpower, had all taken their toll. At the end of June a special conference on supply for defence purposes, set up by the government, concluded that 'the state of industry is catastrophic.' Shortage of foreign currency made it difficult to continue to purchase supplies from the Allies, who were in any case increasingly reluctant to squander, as they saw it, vital materials on an army that was disintegrating. The national debt at 1 July 1917 had increased fivefold since 1 January 1914, and the Russian trade balance was over three billion gold roubles in deficit. The exchange value of the rouble had fallen drastically in the course of 1917, and there was galloping inflation.

Supplies to the army were alarmingly short, as figures based on official reports eloquently testify. Shells, clothing, horseshoes, indeed all necessities, fell below requirements by fifty or sixty per cent, and in some cases even more. Lack of food for the front, as well as for the civilian population, was by August 1917 stated by the Minister of Supplies to be 'getting worse every day. . . . The country is faced with the grim spectre of famine.' The peasants refused to sell their grain for worthless money, which in any case could not buy goods, since none were available. There was also, not surprisingly, a considerable drop in food production during the war; the average proportion of ablebodied males drafted into the army from the peasant households in fifty of Russia's *gubernii* was, according to a census taken in 1917, 47.8 per cent. By October many parts of the army literally faced starvation. During the first fortnight of October, the four European fronts received 20.3 per cent of their requirements of flour and grain, 36.6 per cent of cereals and beans, and 35.3 per cent of cattle fodder. Meat supplies were equally depleted: in some of the front armies they were down to one day's requirements or less.

The effect of this situation (which the Provisional Government admitted it was powerless to deal with) can easily be imagined. The demoralized troops were readily persuaded by Bolshevik claims that the passage of power to the soviets would ensure plenty to eat. There was mass desertion, and anarchical bands of soldiers plundered estates and trains carrying food.

By mid-April desertion had begun to be a serious problem. Peasant soldiers (as already pointed out) were mainly motivated by the apprehension that the land would be divided up in their home villages without them, and that they would miss their share. In this fear they were often encouraged by letters from home. In addition to desertion there was a marked rise in self-inflicted wounds and in sickness. By the autumn the forthcoming harvest gave a further impetus to would-be deserters; but quite apart from the concern of the soldier as peasant, there was an increasing urge to avoid the risk of fighting. The frequently quoted figure of two million deserters by October 1917 (a quarter of the total force at the front) may have been an exaggeration inspired by political motives, but there is no doubt that desertion took on mass proportions. The fact that by the end of October the shortfall of front establishments exceeded a million is eloquent enough proof of this.

The inadequacy of manpower led to pressure for the movement of garrison troops to the front. These demands were strongly resisted by the rear troops, with Bolshevik support, though there were some notable exceptions to the general trend. Moreover, when these soldiers, often demoralized by idleness and political indoctrination, did reach the front, their arrival soon had damaging effects on the morale of the others.

The decline in army morale alarmed both the Executive Committee of the Petrograd Soviet and the Provisional Government. Yet each was, for different reasons, inhibited from attempting to take really drastic steps to remedy the situation — assuming that there were steps to be taken that could have had a chance of success.

On 1 May, Guchkov resigned from the post of Minister of War, giving as his reason the fact that the Provisional Government did not exercise real authority. He was succeeded by Kerensky, who in July also succeeded Prince L'vov as Prime Minister. Kerensky was genuinely committed to fulfilling Russia's pledge to the Allies to start an offensive in support of their attack in the West, but he was a civilian who understood little of the factors which determine an army's morale, and he suffered from an excessive reliance on his powers of oratory — which could, indeed, achieve short-lived results when exercised on the troops. He was also a romantic socialist, whose sympathies lay with the men in their conflicts with their officers, of whose real or imagined counter-revolutionary ambitions he entertained a profound suspicion. He never lost sight of the fact that his real basis of support lay with the soldiers. The Executive Committee of the Petrograd Soviet (on which, as a member of it, Kerensky was necessarily dependent) was 'defencist' in the sense that it believed that the war had to be prosecuted until such time as efforts to conclude a fair peace had succeeded; but it fell increasingly under the domination of the Petrograd garrison and, moreover, for most of its existence was reluctant to take effective steps against one of the main causes of declining morale, the Bolsheviks, regarding them as extreme and unreasonable allies, but allies nonetheless.

Kerensky inaugurated his office as Minister of War by publishing Order No. 8, or the Declaration of Soldiers' Rights. This document had been prepared by the Polivanov commission, set up by Guchkov to revise the laws of military service, but Guchkov had refused to issue it. Kerensky, whether from a desire to curry favour with the troops, or from socialist sentiments, or because he realized it was too late to change the situation, now in effect gave legal recognition to the breakdown of discipline in the army. The general idealistic, if unrealistic, principle underlying the document was expressed in paragraph 8: 'Mutual relations of servicemen, while strictly maintaining military discipline, must be based on the feeling of dignity of citizens of free Russia and on mutual confidence, respect and courtesy.'

In some respects, such as the abolition of corporal punishment, or the provision that officers must be appointed by commanders, the order was, no doubt, above reproach. Kerensky also added to the Polivanov text a stipulation that commanders could, in combat conditions, take all measures, including force, against those who refused to carry out orders. But in other respects the order did real damage, most of all by allowing servicemen to join political organizations.

Around the same time, a conference in Petrograd of the Commander in Chief, the commanders of the fronts, the Provisional Government and the Executive Committee of the Soviet, painted a depressing picture of the state of the army at the front. According to the Commander in Chief, General Alekseev, the revolution, so far from bringing better morale, had brought the lowest instincts of self-preservation to the surface. Other commanders confirmed this, giving instance after instance of refusal to carry out military duties and of the prevalence of fraternization. General Brusilov, Commander of the South-Western Front, gave a similar, even more graphic, picture of soldiers refusing to fight because they were convinced that the Germans would not attack and that the war had become pointless. He also argued that the officers had suffered most: they had welcomed the revolution, 'but it turned out that liberty meant liberty only for the private soldier.'

The belief among the troops that they need not fear an enemy attack was the result of the skilful policy of the German High Command, which was well informed on the state of morale of the

Russian troops. Some military leaders wished to exploit this situation by an offensive designed to complete the collapse of the Russian army, but the government still placed its hopes on the conclusion of a separate peace. However, on 21 March the German forces carried out, as a reconnaissance operation, a strong attack on a post held by the Russian Third Army on the Western Front — with staggering results. In the course of one day, two Russian divisions suffered over a thousand casualties, and over ten thousand troops and nearly one hundred and fifty officers were taken prisoner — to the great astonishment of General Ludendorff. As a result, the German High Command forbade any further attacks on Russian positions, and intensified its propaganda campaign. (General Alekseev concluded from the disaster that the only hope of restoring the morale of the troops lay in going over to the offensive, and so informed the Minister of War on 30 March.)

The most notable fact about the commanders' reports on the morale of the troops on their fronts is that they show great variation between pessimism and optimism. For example, on 18 March the commanders of the five fronts had addressed a joint telegram to the Minister of War to the effect that the army was ready and willing to take the offensive. General Brusilov, in spite of his pessimism at the beginning of May, had two weeks earlier persuaded the Minister of War that he should be allowed to form shock battalions of volunteers from troops whose morale was unimpaired, for use as spearheads in an offensive. There were several reasons for these inconsistencies. One was probably the fact that commanders who were too pessimistic ran the risk of falling under suspicion as counter-revolutionaries. The other was that there were many units which did maintain their morale and patriotic fervour: the parting of the ways in the civil war was already discernible in nascent form.

General Brusilov's optimism was rewarded when he was appointed to succeed General Alekseev as Commander in Chief on 22 May with the launching of an offensive in mind. In November 1916, at a Conference of the Allies in Chantilly, it had been agreed that a joint offensive on the Western and Eastern fronts would be launched in an endeavour to break the Central Powers. The French assault began in April 1917, but there was no question of the Russian army's readiness to attack at that date, in spite of persistent pressure from the French. It was eventually decided that the Russian offensive would be launched in June. The ill-fated operation was preceded by weeks of debate — in the Soviet, in the press and by the committees at the front, who made every effort to raise the fighting spirit of the men. Kerensky himself toured the front, haranguing the troops dramatically.

He could usually raise ephemeral enthusiasm, but he had no answers to the problems that worried the soldiers, while the very process of allowing oratory and meetings to take the place of orders only served further to undermine discipline.

There can also be little doubt that the Russian plan was known to the Germans in all its details. One commander, General Denikin, later claimed that his motive for advising an offensive was the certainty that if the decision to attack were abandoned, this would immediately, in the lamentable lack of security that prevailed, become known to the enemy. German and Austrian divisions would then be withdrawn from the Eastern Front, and the position of Russia's Western Allies would be adversely affected.

The omens for success were disastrous. The decision to attack, so far as the commanders were concerned, was a counsel of despair. They knew the state of their armies — the lack of reserves, food and ammunition, and the spread of unrest and disease among the troops. But the government was in favour of an offensive, and in this it had the support of the socialists, though not, of course, of the Bolsheviks. One of the factors that gave rise to optimism was the lack of consistency in the attitude of the troops. As one army commander recorded, the same unit which accepted a Bolshevik resolution against the offensive one day would vote for a fiery resolution in favour of attack the next. Everyone was hoping for a miracle, and it did not happen.

The offensive was launched on 18 June by two armies of the South-Western front. The other army on that front, the Eighth, achieved a brilliant temporary success, but was forced to retreat by 11 July. The front as a whole lost over fourteen per cent of its manpower. Offensives on the Western and Northern fronts early in July ground to a halt after only a day or two of fighting, while on the Roumanian Front the troops were ordered to go over to the defensive before the attack was begun.

In general, this ill-fated campaign was characterized by two features: the courage, gallantry and self-sacrifice of the units which retained their morale, especially the shock brigades created by General Brusilov; and the refusal of those that were demoralized to support them or to follow them into battle. As General Alekseev had predicted, the institution of the shock brigades merely resulted in the sacrifice of some of the best Russian troops.

In spite of the failure of the offensive, Russia's allies had cause to be grateful, for the Germans and Austrians retained around 80 divisions on the Eastern Front until November and only moved 50 divisions and 5,000 guns to the Western Front after the Bolshevik take-over. For Great Britain and France, sore pressed on the Western Front, this was a significant relief, which helped to tide them over until American troops arrived in force in the spring and summer of 1918. The Provisional Government has often been reproached for failing to conclude a separate peace, but apart from the harm which this would have done to the Allied cause, it would have been in clear breach of an agreement between the Allied Powers, entered into at the outset of the war. If it was true that the Provisional Government did not show sufficient vigour in trying to defeat German efforts at subversion, in which the Bolsheviks played an important part, it was also true that they rejected all the clandestine peace feelers of the Central Powers. The socialists in the government were opposed to a separate peace as much as the 'bourgeois' ministers, though they were much more aggressive in the pursuit of a 'democratic' peace, without annexations or contributions. To this end, they attempted without success to organize a conference of socialist parties of all the belligerents. The Allied Powers understood little of the difficulties of the Provisional Government. They viewed the disintegration of Russian society with increasing alarm, but their demands for an offensive on the Eastern Front did little to help the situation; while their reluctance to discuss revision of war aims with Russia made the balancing act of Kerensky's government even more difficult.

The collapse at the front, as well as the attempted seizure of power by the Bolsheviks in July (see Chapter 5), emboldened the Provisional Government to yield to the insistent demands of the army leaders that steps should be taken to restore discipline among the troops. The measures taken came too late to be successful, and in any case did not tackle one of the main causes of disruption of morale, Bolshevik subversion at the front. They were also resisted by the Soviet. The socialists (and this included Kerensky, whose conversion to the need for military discipline was only temporary and far from consistent) were obsessed by the suspicion that the generals advocated military discipline only for the purposes of carrying out a counter-revolution. There is not a jot of evidence to support this fear, unless by counter-revolution is meant introduction of order in the rear and restoration of fighting capacity at the front. On 12 July the Provisional Government decreed the death penalty for offences such as desertion, flight from the battlefield, violence against officers, refusal to obey orders and the like, and 'military-revolutionary' courts were established, consisting of three officers and three soldiers. (The order was subsequently extended to the navy.) Some days later, the status of the military commissars assigned to the Commander in Chief, to Fronts and to Armies, who had been appointed some months before by the Petrograd Soviet, was redefined. Their tasks now, as agents of the Provisional Government, were to 'promote the reorganization of the army on democratic principles and the re-inforcement of its fighting capacity' (in that order) as well as 'to oppose any counter-revolutionary attempts'.

On 16 July a conference took place at Staff Headquarters, attended by ministers and chief commanders in the field. It was an emotional, not to say hysterical, occasion. The commanders painted an appalling picture of the collapse of discipline, but in essence they were demanding the impossible — that the clock be turned back, and that the effects of the revolution on the army be wiped out. In his concluding speech, Kerensky pointed out with some justice that to accede to the virtually unanimous demands of the generals would be to invite universal anarchy and massacre in the country. With one exception, no one paid any attention to the crucial question that was uppermost in the soldiers' minds — land. A firm and determined policy here might have done more to restore some kind of confidence and sanity among the troops than repressive measures: military discipline in the old sense was gone beyond recall.

That the new measures did not make much difference became evident when, on 19 August, the Germans broke through, and on 21 August captured Riga. As in June, the battle was characterized by the gallantry and heroism of some units and the abject cowardice and defeatism of others. The disbanding of units in Petrograd for despatch to the front had a particularly disorganizing influence on other troops with whom they mingled. As to the repeated Bolshevik complaints that they were subject to persecution at the front after July, the evidence does not bear this out. Their literature continued to reach the troops in abundance as before and the work of their agitators continued virtually unimpeded. The evidence of the archives available to us suggests that in many areas of the front Bolshevik propaganda and influence were intensified between the July disturbances and the Kornilov affair (described in the next chapter). It may indeed be doubted whether the belated measures of the Provisional Government changed anything at all.

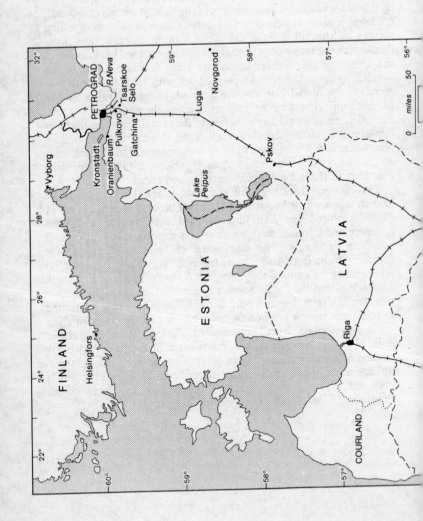

Chapter Seven

The Death-Throes of the Provisional Government

The last months of the Provisional Government were indeed pitiable. Anarchy mounted as unruly mobs roamed the country. Falling production and the breakdown in food supplies threatened economic disaster. The precarious coalitions of disparate elements, patched together on 23 July and again on 25 September in desperate attempts to form a semblance of strong government, lacked both authority and dignity. The collapse of the offensive of 18 June on which such great hopes had been placed, by none more than Kerensky, was a shattering blow, in the face of indisputable evidence that the main cause of defeat had been the demoralization of the troops. The demeanour of Kerensky at the conference which he held with commanders in the field on 16 July (mentioned in the last chapter) was that of a broken man, petulantly on the defensive against a series of devastating attacks.

Yet, whatever truth there may have been as a matter of history in the indictments launched by the assembled generals, especially those of the young General Denikin, commander of the Western Front, the remedies proposed would have amounted to nothing less than the disbanding of the entire Soviet system and a virtual return to the old régime — without the Tsar. General Kornilov alone, who had become commander of the South-Western Front after his clash with the Petrograd Soviet in April when his orders were countermanded by the Executive Committee, had suggested measures which, though stringent in their demand for discipline, had nevertheless recognized a restricted rôle for commissars and elected military committees. Two days later, on 18 July, he was appointed Commander in Chief, to replace General Brusilov. His commissar, Boris Savinkov, became deputy Minister of War to Kerensky.

Kornilov made his acceptance of the post dependent on Kerensky's agreeing to a series of stringent conditions. These included such matters as his complete independence in the matter of operations and appointments, and the extension of the death penalty (reintroduced at the front on 12 July) to offences by garrison troops. If Kerensky had second thoughts about the appointment, he was forced to compromise because Kornilov had the support of all those to the right of the Petrograd Soviet, and in particular the Kadets, with whom Kerensky was trying to cement a coalition. Kornilov, however, fully accepted that he was responsible to the government. On 3 August he came to Petrograd bearing his proposals in writing. These were apparently somewhat crude in form, and Filonenko, the commissar at Staff Headquarters, was entrusted with the task of editing the text. The substance of Kornilov's proposals was immediately leaked to the press and provoked a storm of protest from the moderate (as well as the extreme) left, which believed that discipline could be restored by persuasion and by a more sympathetic attitude of officers to the elected committees.

Kornilov came to Petrograd again on 10 August, colourfully protected by his Turkoman bodyguard, armed with machine guns (there had been rumours that an attempt on his life was planned). Kerensky was by now hostile to Kornilov, who aroused all his ever-present suspicion of counter-revolution. Open support for the general, which was voiced in the strongest terms in right-wing circles, could only have served to fire the Prime Minister's doubts.On the other hand, Kornilov had ample reason for despising Kerensky: he had refused on this occasion to let him address the full cabinet (had indeed tried to stop his visit) and at a meeting with the cabinet on 3 August had warned him not to be precise in discussing military dispositions for fear of leakage to the enemy. This incident had profoundly shocked the general who, not unnaturally, drew the inference that German intelligence had penetrated the cabinet. But the evidence suggests that at this stage Kornilov still had reason to hope that he could reach agreement with the government, and that Kerensky accepted the necessity of putting through, if need be by force, measures for the restoration of discipline at the front and in the rear which the Soviet could be expected to resist.

Meanwhile, a conference of a great variety of bodies of the moderate left and of the centre and right of the political spectrum, including ministers and public figures, was drawing near. This gathering, known as the State Conference, had been convened by Kerensky to mobilize support for the second coalition, and met in the Bolshoi Theatre in Moscow on 12 August. Some 2,500 delegates represented the soviets, the provincial and town local government bodies, trade union and professional organizations, the cooperatives, the banks, the industrialists, learned societies, religious and national groups, and the army and navy — among others. Its deliberations led to no practical conclusions, but they were revealing of the condition of the country and of the antagonism which divided the moderate left (there were virtually no representatives of the extreme left) from the liberal centre and the industrial right.

Kerensky, who dominated the proceedings, indulged his powers of oratory to the full, without contributing much of substance to the solution of the national crisis. His main message was that the government would resolutely defend the revolutionary order both against left extremists — a reference to the Bolshevik July insurrection — and against a military coup — a reference to the military commanders' demands for drastic measures to restore discipline in the army and in the country for which right-wing circles had been displaying enthusiasm for some time.

The socialist Minister of the Interior described Russia as 'on the edge of disaster': the multiplicity of authorities throughout the country precluded any united government will, while private, sectional interests acted to the detriment of the common good. The Minister of Trade and Industry spoke of facts familiar to all: the catastrophic state of food supply, and the fall in production, which he attributed both to anarchy among the workers and to the decline in the condition of industrial plant. He ended by calling for sacrifices from both the workers and the industrialists. The Minister of Finance painted an equally dismal picture and gave notice of the heavy taxes that it was now, if somewhat belatedly, *proposed* to levy on the wealthy. The most surprising part of his speech was the disclosure of the enormous sums which the network of land and supply committees cost the government. No other minister spoke.

In the long debates which followed, the socialists (there appear to have been no Bolsheviks present, or at any rate given the opportunity to speak) in the main blamed the industrialists for their high profits and lack of cooperation, while the industrialists blamed the state of the country on the anarchical behaviour of the workers. There were some extreme statements made, attacking the soviets at home and the committees in the army in the field. Both the Chairman of the Petrograd Soviet, Chkheidze, and the Menshevik leader, Tsereteli, made responsible speeches stressing the need for all sections of society to sink their private interests in the common good, for the avoidance of violence in industry and on the land, and for the achievements of the revolution to be safeguarded by the government in close cooperation with the Soviets and the army committees.

Tsereteli was probably expressing the view of the overwhelming majority present when he deplored any attacks on the democratic order, whether from the left or the right, and called for support from all the delegates present in the theatre. But this was a gathering of the most responsible sections of the country. Its deliberations could have had little effect on the anarchy which was rampant in the rear and at the front; nor, for that matter, on the Bolsheviks who were riding to power in its wake, and who had already roundly condemned the State Conference as 'counter-revolutionary'. They had indeed successfully brought a large number of Moscow's workers out on strike when it opened.

On 9 August a conference then meeting in Moscow of several hundred public men — leaders of business, agriculture, industry, the professions and the army, and liberal and conservative political figures — had pledged its confidence and hopes in Kornilov. On 14 August the general made a dramatic appearance at the State Conference. His train, protected by his Turkoman bodyguard, was met by conservative and liberal leaders, officers, cadets, and ladies who strewed flowers. His arrival in the theatre was greeted by a wild ovation from the delegates on the right side, and stony silence on the left. His speech was moderate. He described the breakdown of morale in the army in the recent offensive, which had caused him, as commander on the South-Western front, to resort to the death penalty some days before it was enacted by the government. Much more was now needed to restore discipline. The prestige of officers must be raised. Committees and commissars should be retained, but their responsibilities clearly limited. Discipline must be restored in industry in order to ensure supplies. It was not so much the content of the speech that aroused ever-latent suspicions in socialist bosoms of a military dictatorship in the offing, as the fact that centre and right delegates at the conference treated the Commander in Chief as the destined saviour of the country. In spite of any apprehension he may have felt, Kerensky recognized that the measures proposed by Kornilov for dealing with anarchy on the home front would have to be implemented, even if this involved a break with the Soviet. On 17 August he instructed his deputy, Savinkov, to draft the necessary decrees.

Following the Moscow State Conference, Kornilov proceeded to transfer a considerable number of troops from the front to positions around Petrograd. Riga fell to the Germans on 21 August, and the government decided to put Petrograd Military District under the Commander in Chief's jurisdiction. The forces moved were mainly the Third Cavalry Corps, commanded by General Krymov, with the Savage Division of ferocious Caucasians attached to it. There were good military reasons for these dispositions, in view of the relative proximity of Riga to the capital. There were also political reasons. A reaction could be expected to the new stringent decrees that were being prepared. There were, moreover, persistent rumours of an imminent Bolshevik rising, timed for 27 August, the semi-anniversary of the revolution.

On 23 August Savinkov arrived at Staff HQ with instructions from Kerensky. On 24 August he approved the troop movements ordered by Kornilov, though there is a conflict of evidence on one important point. Savinkov recalled that Kornilov agreed to rescind the order to the Savage Division and to remove General Krymov from command of the Third Corps, while Kornilov maintained that he merely noted the request without agreeing to it, simply promising to do his best to comply. Kornilov accepted without demur the proposal that his command of the Petrograd Military District should not include troops in the city itself. It was also agreed that he should notify Savinkov by coded telegram on 27 August that the troops would mass on Petrograd on the 28th, and request that martial law be proclaimed on the 29th. These matters were all discussed on 24 August, in the presence of Kerensky's brother-in-law, Colonel Baranovsky, Chief of Operations in the Ministry of War. It would certainly appear from the full accounts of this conference which we possess that Kornilov would have been left with the impression that Kerensky was now prepared, if need be in defiance of the Soviet, to adopt the drastic measures considered necessary by his Commander in Chief.

At the discussions with Savinkov, Kornilov was critical of Kerensky for his vacillation and indecision, but pledged his support for him and expressed the view (which he had already voiced to Kerensky himself on 3 August) that 'as the generally acknowledged leader of the democratic parties, he should remain at the head of the Provisional Government.' Krymov was given orders to move on Petrograd on receipt of information of a Bolshevik rising, and drafted an order to his corps to impose strict martial law on entering the capital. Further movement of troops on Petrograd went ahead, and the pre-arranged telegram was despatched to Savinkov in the small hours of 27 August. Everything suggested a concerted plan between the government and Staff HQ, and that Kerensky had, however reluctantly, accepted the necessity of strong military support for the government against Bolshevik, or socialist, opposition. Indeed, on 26 August he had promised Savinkov that he would sign the stringent new decrees on discipline that same day. But something happened which, in his mind at any rate, justified him in going back on his undertaking.

On 22 August one V.N. L'vov, who had been Procurator of the Holy Synod in the first coalition cabinet but had been dropped by Kerensky from the second, had come to see the Prime Minister. He spoke mysteriously of 'certain groups' and offered to sound them out with a view to forming a strong national government. L'vov later maintained that he was given full authority to conduct negotiations, and that Kerensky expressed his willingness to stand down. Kerensky says that he suspected a conspiracy and used L'vov as a method of reconnaissance. L'vov's version is corroborated to some extent by Kerensky's own account fifty years later (though not in his earlier versions) that he told L'vov, when authorizing him to enter into discussion with the 'certain groups', that 'I am interested in forming a solidly based government, not in hanging on to power myself.' However, there seems little doubt that in the conversations at GHQ which took place after his meeting with Kerensky, L'vov grossly exaggerated his authority. His account of his talk with Kornilov, which he relayed to Kerensky on 26 August, and Kerensky's interpretation of it, proved to be of vital consequence for the future history of Russia. There are three versions of it: Kerensky's, in several variants, the first just after the meeting with L'vov; L'vov's, written in 1920; and Kornilov's deposition, written on 1 or 2 September 1917 for the Special Commission of Investigation, set up by Kerensky on 29 August.*

According to Kerensky, L'vov's message to him from Kornilov was in the form of an ultimatum: that 'the continuance of the Provisional Government in power could no longer be permitted'; that martial law must be declared in Petrograd; that all ministers should resign until a cabinet had been formed by the Commander in Chief, to whom all powers should be transferred; and that Kerensky and Savinkov should go straightaway to Staff GHQ at Mogilev where the portfolio of Minister of Justice in the new cabinet awaited Kerensky.

L'vov's version, written in exile after Kerensky had published his account, is in substance the same. Kornilov said that a Bolshevik rising was imminent, and Kerensky's life was in danger. Power must be transferred to the Commander in Chief. Kerensky, for his own safety, should come at once to Staff GHQ. The account is, however, embellished with dramatic detail, mainly concerning the influence on Kornilov of his orderly, Zavoiko. We are told of a proclamation prepared by Zavoiko for the army, promising around twenty-two acres of land to every soldier, and of a hint by him that Kerensky would be murdered when he got to GHQ. However, in his very first version, given during the preliminary interrogation immediately after his arrest on 27 August, L'vov denied that he had transmitted Kornilov's proposals in the form of an ultimatum, and maintained that the final decision had been left to the Provisional Government.

Kornilov deposed that L'vov, whom he had never before met, came as an avowed emissary from Kerensky. Kornilov told L'vov that a Bolshevik coup was being prepared in Petrograd and that Kerensky should come to GHQ, where he would guarantee his safety. L'vov

*Published in part in 1917, but first made available in full by Dr G. Katkov in 1980 in *The Kornilov Affair* — an illuminating study to which I am much indebted.

told him that Kerensky would be prepared either to leave the government or to stay with Kornilov's support. Kornilov expressed his conviction that the only solution for the state of the country was proclamation of martial law and the establishment of a dictatorship — and that he would subordinate himself to Kerensky or to any other dictator. He would not refuse the dictatorship himself, if he were offered it. The substance of this version of the conversation is confirmed by the account in the memoirs of Kornilov's Chief of Staff, General Lukomsky, of what Kornilov told him immediately after L'vov's visit.

It is important to recall, when considering Kerensky's reaction to L'vov's visit, that troop movements on Petrograd and the imposition of martial law had been agreed on his behalf by his deputy, Savinkov, and by the Chief of Operations at the Ministry of War at their meeting with General Kornilov at GHQ only two days before. The question of strengthening the government had possibly also been raised at some earlier date, though indefinitely enough for Kerensky to have believed that he would end up as the dictator. The stringent measures first proposed by Kornilov on 3 August were, as Kerensky had promised Savinkov, to be laid for endorsement before the cabinet that very night. Yet Kerensky's histrionic reaction on 26 August was that of a man who is suddenly, to his astonishment, faced with a plot to depose him. Having persuaded himself of the fact of an 'ultimatum', he devised what he intended as a trap for Kornilov. He arranged a 'conversation' with him on the Hughes apparatus. The official transcript of this conversation is the only document of which we have an indisputably authentic record. Here is the substance of it.

Kerensky: Good day, General. V.N. L'vov and Kerensky at the apparatus.* We beg you to confirm the statement that Kerensky is to act according to the communication made to him by Vladimir Nikolaevich [L'vov].

Kornilov: . . . Confirming again the description of the present situation of the country and the army as it appears to me which I requested V.N. to convey to you, I declare again that the events of the past days and of those that I can see coming imperatively demand a definite decision in the shortest possible time.

Kerensky: I, Vladimir Nikolaevich, ask you whether it is necessary to act on that definite decision which you asked me to communicate privately to Kerensky . . . .

Kornilov: Yes, I confirm that I asked you to convey to Alexander Feodorovich my urgent plea that he should come to Mogilev.

---

*This is untrue. L'vov was intended to be present but did not turn up, so Kerensky pretended that he was there.

Kerensky: I, Alexander Feodorovich, understand your answer as confirmation of the words conveyed to me by V.N. To do that and leave here today is impossible. I hope to depart tomorrow. Is it necessary for Savinkov to go?

Kornilov: I beg earnestly that Boris Viktorovich should come with you. What I said to V.N. refers in equal degree to Savinkov . . . . Believe me, only my recognition of the responsibility of the moment makes me so persistent in my request . . . .

Kerensky: Goodbye. We shall soon see each other.

Kornilov: Goodbye.

One can imagine that Kornilov lived to regret that he had not asked Kerensky what it was that he, Kornilov, was supposed to have communicated through L'vov.

Kerensky was evidently satisfied that this conversation offered proof of treason by Kornilov, with the complicity of L'vov. L'vov was arrested when he arrived at Kerensky's apartments at the Winter Palace (where the Prime Minister had installed himself some time before) and Kerensky then interrupted a meeting of the Cabinet, which was discussing the Savinkov/Kornilov decrees, with an announcement of Kornilov's 'treason', as established by the Hughes apparatus record. The decrees were now forgotten — Kerensky had perhaps found a way of avoiding a decision to break with the Soviet which he had never really had the courage to face.

Even before going to the meeting, if Savinkov is right in his recollection, Kerensky had sent a curt telegram to Kornilov in his name alone, dismissing him from office and ordering him to Petrograd. Kerensky did not tell his ministers that he had done this. He persuaded a somewhat suspicious and reluctant cabinet to let him form a new, more streamlined, government, and the ministers dutifully tendered their resignations though, in the confused days which followed, some of them continued to exercise their functions.

The telegram to Kornilov, which arrived in the early hours of 27 August, ordered him to yield his post to General Lukomsky. But Lukomsky refused: 'It is too late to halt an operation started with your approval . . . . In order to save Russia you must go along with Kornilov . . . . Kornilov's dismissal would bring horrors the likes of which Russia has never seen . . . .' Lukomsky had good reason, according to his own account, for being dumbfounded. After the conversation on the Hughes apparatus he had found Kornilov well satisfied, working on the composition of a new cabinet 'to have it ready for the arrival of Kerensky and Savinkov, and to come to full agreement with them'. He added that he would be glad if he were freed of the necessity of being the dictator. He also sent telegrams to Rodzianko, Prince L'vov and Miliukov, inviting them to come to

GHQ on 29 August, the day Kerensky and Savinkov had said they would arrive. On receipt of the telegram of dismissal (which bears no official number and was in any case of dubious validity, since the change of the Commander in Chief required the authority of the full cabinet) Kornilov, as he told the Special Commission of Investigation, decided that the government had succumbed to the Soviet and that he would not relinquish his command without further investigation. He so informed Savinkov in the afternoon.

In the evening Kornilov received a copy of the statement issued by Kerensky (published in the press on the next day, 28 August) which accused the Commander in Chief of presenting him with an ultimatum to surrender all power to him, asserted that this demand was part of an attempt by 'certain circles' to put an end to the achievements of the revolution, and ordered Kornilov to surrender his office. It also placed Petrograd under martial law. Provincial Commissars were at the same time instructed to combat local counter-revolution.

Kornilov then, again to quote his own evidence, 'decided to act openly to bring pressure to bear on the Provisional Government to force it' to expel the traitors from the ranks of the cabinet and to form a 'strong, stable government'. With this in view, he ordered General Krymov, commander of the Third Cavalry Corps, to continue to move his troops around the capital.

That night Kornilov issued an intemperate reply to Kerensky's statement, branding its first part as a 'lie', accusing the Provisional Government of acting in harmony with the German General Staff, and calling dramatically on the Russian people to save the 'dying motherland'. If the reaction of Kerensky to L'vov's fateful visit on 26 August can be explained by loss of nerve, hysteria, deceit or misunderstanding, Kornilov's action on 28 August was certainly rebellion. Kerensky's immediate reply was to despatch a telegram to the managers of all railway lines in the rear and at the front ordering them, in the name of the Provisional Government, not to obey orders from General Kornilov, 'who has betrayed his country, and openly risen against the government'. On 29 August Kerensky issued an order to the Petrograd garrison, accusing Kornilov of treachery, as made evident by his removal of troops from the front thus 'weakening its resistance' against the Germans, and of intending to march the armed forces on the capital to create a 'fratricidal war'. On the same day the Soviet Executive Committee described General Kornilov's revolt as aimed at restoring the old régime and depriving the people of land and liberty. To this end, it went on, he was ready to open the front and betray his country. It appealed to the troops to obey only the orders of the Provisional Government. These views were echoed in the socialist press on 29 August.

In the initial stages of the conflict Kornilov seemed certain of success. Many commanders in the field expressed their solidarity with him. On 28 August the representative of the Ministry of Foreign Affairs at GHQ foretold overwhelming support for Kornilov and urged Kerensky to come to an agreement with him in order to avert civil war. Prices on the stock exchange shot up. The Union of Officers sent telegrams to all military headquarters urging them to rally to Kornilov. But Kornilov made no move to come to Petrograd. In the event, the rebellion collapsed almost without a shot being fired.

The defeat of Kornilov was due to the rapid and determined rallying of forces in the country in defence of the achievements of the revolution which Kerensky had persuaded them were threatened. By morning of 28 August news of the advance of the Third Cavalry Corps reached the session of the Central Executive Committee of the Soviets (now, since June, the principal soviet authority), which was debating the future of the Provisional Government. The committee pledged full support to Kerensky, and a flood of directives to impede the movement of counter-revolutionary forces was issued to army committees, provincial soviets, postal and railway workers and the garrison. A Committee for Struggle Against the Counter-Revolution was set up, including three Mensheviks, three Socialist Revolutionaries and three Bolsheviks. (The rôle of the Bolsheviks in the wake of the Kornilov affair is dealt with in the next chapter.)

The Committee for Struggle Against the Counter-Revolution was supported by literally hundreds of other committees throughout the country which sprang up with surprising rapidity, by labour organizations, army and naval committees, postal and railway workers, the Petrograd garrison (with the exception of the Cossack troops and the military cadets) and the Baltic Fleet. This *levée en masse*, which better than anything else symbolized the complete impotence of the Provisional Government and its apparatus, now engaged in feverish activity. Arms and ammunition were distributed in the garrison, steps taken to ensure food supplies, communications disrupted in the face of the advance of the Third Cavalry Corps, and emissaries despatched to harangue the rebel troops. Factory workers enrolled in the 'Red Guard', the Bolshevik-controlled force which, ostensibly suppressed since the July days, was now revived and grew rapidly.

A fever of resistance to counter-revolution swept the country. But it is doubtful if a real threat of dismantling the entire régime established after the fall of the Tsar ever existed — unless Kerensky's abortive attempts to reach agreement with Kornilov on countering the power of the Soviets can be described as counter-revolution. No significant elements in the country favoured restoration of the monarchy. Kornilov, the son of a Cossack peasant, was an outspoken critic of the Tsar. There is nothing to suggest that he ever had political ambitions. His main concern, like that of his fellow generals, was the desperate need to restore discipline in the army and in the rear which supplied it.

Those, and there were many, whose sympathies lay with Kornilov, at any rate up to the time when he embarked on open rebellion, lay low. The surrender of the Third Cavalry Corps and of the Savage Division was swift and bloodless. The troops were engaged by literally thousands of agitators and local workmen and peasants who, with surprising ease, won them over. The soldiers had been sent into action for the purpose of putting down a Bolshevik insurrection against the Provisional Government; when they discovered that they were in fact being used to lay siege to that government, they were above all anxious to display their loyalty by refusing to advance. General Krymov, on receipt of assurances that he would not be arrested, came to the Winter Palace at Kerensky's request. According to his own lights, he had obeyed his superior officer's orders in what he had every reason to believe was action concerted with the government. Accused of prevarication by Kerensky in a heated interview, he walked out of the palace and shot himself. He left a note for Kornilov which has never been made public.

Efforts have been made over the years, especially by Kerensky, to establish that there was a counter-revolutionary conspiracy, headed by Kornilov, to depose the Provisional Government and establish a military dictatorship. Unless he was acting a part with skilful duplicity, the facts presented in the preceding pages suggest that, until 28 August when Kornilov decided to 'act openly' to force the government's hand, he had reason to suppose that he was acting with the authority of the government and that measures to modify and strengthen its rule would be agreed with Kerensky. On the other hand there is ample evidence that, for months before the events of August, sections of Russian society, which blamed the anarchy in the country and the collapse of the army on the soviets and on the socialists, hoped for a military dictatorship which would put an end to them and restore order. By August this view was shared by a majority of the Kadet party and by important groups like the All-Russian Union of Trade and Industry and the Union of Landowners. But while there is no doubt that the Kadets would have welcomed a dictatorship headed by Kornilov when once it had been established, a recent historian of the party in 1917 concludes that most of them felt that 'dictatorial efforts could not succeed unless both the cabinet and the Soviet acquiesced voluntarily', which ruled out conspiracy.*

*William G. Rosenberg, *The Liberals in the Russian Revolution.*

There were, however, both military and civilian centres of conspiracy, which tried to exert pressure on Kornilov. The military ones included the Union of Saint George Cavaliers in Petrograd, and the Union of Officers of the Army and Navy, which maintained a Central Committee at Staff GHQ in Mogilev. There were two main civilian organizations. One, the Society for the Economic Rehabilitation of Russia, was founded as early as April 1917 by prominent industrialists, whose main aim was anti-Bolshevik propaganda. On 14 August (according to memoirs published in 1937) members of this society met Kornilov on his train after the State Conference and decided to give him funds required for an impending operation against political extremists which, in agreement with Kerensky, he was planning to undertake. At no time was there any suggestion of acting against Kerensky. The industrialists believed that the reason why the funds could not be supplied by the government was that reports of this would immediately leak to the Bolsheviks.

Also among the right-wing civilian organizations was one calling itself the Republican Centre which included a Military Section consisting of representatives of many military organizations. Two Ministry of War aides, including Kerensky's brother-in-law, Baranovsky, were members of this committee. According to Kornilov's Chief of Staff, a delegation from the Republican Centre visited Kornilov at Mogilev a few days after his return from the State Conference in Moscow, and told him about their organization and their plans for the defence of Petrograd against the Bolsheviks. They said they were short of officers, and Kornilov agreed to arrange for officers from the Union of Officers in Mogilev to be sent to Petrograd. 'It was agreed . . . that, in case of a rising of the Bolsheviks . . . this organization should step forward and occupy' the headquarters of the Soviet, and 'try to arrest the Bolshevik leaders.' It was shortly after this that the movement of troops on Petrograd was agreed with Kerensky's deputy, Savinkov. Not a jot of evidence has appeared since 1917 to suggest that Kornilov ever conspired to overthrow the Provisional Government.

During 28 August, while the fall of Petrograd to the Third Cavalry Corps seemed imminent, there was considerable pressure on Kerensky from the Kadet members of his cabinet (strictly, former members, since they had resigned the day before) to come to some agreement with Kornilov. To this end Kerensky was urged to yield power to General Alekseev as dictator, or at least to include him in a reformed government. At one stage Kerensky seemed inclined to yield, but by 29 August, with the defeat of Kornilov now evident, there was no longer any question of Kerensky's diluting his power. The order to the garrison accusing Kornilov of treachery was released, and a proclamation was issued claiming that virtually the entire army was loyal to the Provisional Government, except for General Denikin, who had been 'detained at his headquarters'. On the same day an Extraordinary Commission was set up, headed by the Chief Prosecutor of the Navy, Shablovsky, to investigate the case of Kornilov and his accomplices. The commission had not concluded its investigations by the time the Provisional Government was over-thrown, and only some portions of its materials have been published.

Having resisted the pressure from his Kadet ministers, Kerensky did in fact offer the post of Chief of Staff to Alekseev, who accepted reluctantly, hoping to prevent any excessive measures against officers who had supported Kornilov. Alekseev arranged with Kerensky that he would endeavour to settle the conflict with Kornilov as peaceably as possible, and satisfied himself after referring to GHQ that there was no intention there of offering any kind of resistance, unless they were attacked. He accordingly set out for Mogilev. To his astonish-ment he discovered on his way to GHQ that Kerensky had ordered a detachment of troops to move on Mogilev. According to General Alekseev, both Kerensky and his new War Minister 'had invented' a threat of violence by Kornilov, prompted by fear. After a series of heated conversations with Kerensky and his aide, Baranovsky, Alekseev succeeded in halting the military force within a short distance of Mogilev.

Kornilov and his Chief of Staff, Lukomsky, and five other officers, offered no resistance to arrest. When the Commission of In-vestigation arrived at GHQ they arranged for the transfer of the officers to a Catholic monastery near Mogilev, where they remained in reasonable comfort (amidst continued clamours from the left for their execution) until after the Bolshevik seizure of power on 25 October. Shablovsky then succeeded in ordering their release before the Bolsheviks had time to lay hands on them, and they emerged to take an active part in building the 'White' Army. Kornilov was killed in action early in the civil war.

Alekseev was as astonished as had been Shablovsky to discover on arriving in Mogilev that the movement of troops on Petrograd had taken place by arrangement with the Provisional Government. He did not stay long as Chief of Staff. He resigned within little more than a week, on 9 September. In a newspaper interview he gave as his reasons the unfair treatment meted out to Kornilov and the breakdown of discipline and morale in the army, which he was powerless to remedy.

After dismissing Kornilov, Kerensky himself assumed the position of Commander in Chief, which meant in effect that the army was left without a head. Bolshevik propaganda was now much intensified. Arrests and murders of officers on the flimsiest suspicion of sympathy with Kornilov became widespread and were actively encouraged by the Bolsheviks. On 30 August Lenin wrote from his exile to the Central Committee that every effort must now be made by Bolshevik propagandists to encourage the soldiers 'to beat up the generals and officers who have expressed support for Kornilov'. The, mostly young, officers who replaced them, and who were put forward by the committees primarily for their loyalty to the revolution, were either incapable of exercising command or made no attempt to resist any of the soldiers' demands. One of the marked consequences of Kornilov's failed attempt was a great increase in fraternization at the front. This was much encouraged both by the Bolsheviks and the Germans — the propaganda on both sides was strikingly similar. The military committees did their best to discourage fraternization, but in many cases this merely aroused the fury of the soldiers and led to re-elections which resulted in more compliant bodies.

Kerensky was anxious to reconstruct a coalition government, which would include the Kadets. He was, however, faced with considerable opposition from the 'democratic forces'. As an interim measure, on 1 September, he formed a Directory of five — the four, apart from himself, were the Minister for Foreign Affairs, the new Minister of War, General Verkhovsky (an unbalanced man of strong left-wing views), a Minister of the Navy, and an undistinguished Menshevik Minister of Posts and Telegraphs. At the same time he proclaimed Russia a Republic — a popular move, but one which plainly usurped the province of the Constituent Assembly.

The Central Executive Committee of the Soviets, together with the equivalent committee for the peasant soviets, decided that a 'congress of all democratic organizations' must be convoked. This would decide on the future form of the government. So far as Petrograd and the areas around the capital were concerned, there is no doubt what the sentiments of workers, soldiers and peasants were. These became evident from the innumerable resolutions passed at the time, many of them of Bolshevik and pro-Bolshevik inspiration. These political statements, which have been studied by a recent historian of the revolution, Alexander Rabinowitch, demanded harsh treatment of Kornilov and his supporters, refused to collaborate in any form with the propertied classes and called for the creation of some kind of exclusively socialist government which would put an end to the war.* There is, however, no reason to suppose that these

*See *The Bolsheviks Come to Power*, pp. 154-159.

views were as widely held in similar sections of society in the provinces.

The Democratic Conference met in Petrograd on 14 September. It provided Kerensky with a platform for one of his last displays of oratory which, in spite of severe heckling, won him a prolonged standing ovation at the end. In practical terms the gathering decided nothing: its vote on the proposed coalition was too close to give Kerensky any kind of mandate. In the end, the Praesidium of the Conference adopted a compromise resolution proposed by Tsereteli: the government to be formed would be responsible and accountable to an institution designed to sit permanently until the Constituent Assembly met. This 'Provisional Council of the Russian Republic' must consist predominantly of democratic elements. This body, usually known as the Pre-Parliament, met on 7 October, and was in session when the Provisional Government was overthrown. Meanwhile, the third, and last, coalition was announced on 25 September. It was a blend of socialists, non-party members, and four Kadets.

In spite of the standing ovation, the Kornilov affair seriously reduced Kerensky's support in the country. The right wing and centre regarded him as having betrayed Kornilov and the country, through either cowardice or ambition for power. The socialist left, much encouraged by Bolshevik propaganda, was deeply suspicious that until the very last moment he had been involved in a conspiracy against 'democracy'. The real winners in the affair were the Bolsheviks, whose fortunes, after their decline in July, rose rapidly. On the whole, their supporters wished for the rough democratic system provided by the socialist soviets. Few of them realized that the Bolsheviks' real aim was a one-party autocracy.

Chapter Eight

The Bolsheviks Take Power

The effect of the repressive measures which the Provisional Government adopted against the Bolsheviks after their attempted insurrection in the early days of July proved very short-lived. Bolsheviks did, it is true, remain in gaol, some until after the Kornilov affair, some even until after the Bolshevik revolution. Nevertheless, and although Lenin remained in hiding until October, the party was able to maintain its cohesion and to hold its Sixth Congress. As shown in Chapter 6, Bolshevik influence in the army increased after July.

Even more significant was the attitude of the local soviets. Detailed questionnaires filled in by delegates to the Sixth Bolshevik Congress (26 July to 3 August) showed that the overwhelming majority of local soviets had reacted with hostility to the Bolsheviks in early July; but a study of these soviets' mood in the aftermath of the July rising, made by Professor Rabinowitch, the most recent historian of 1917, shows that their primary concern was not to condemn or defend the Bolsheviks. It was, he says, 'with such matters as the government's effort to disarm workers and to transfer radicalized soldiers from the capital, the reinstitution of capital punishment at the front, the apparently indiscriminate attacks on the left, and the resurgence of the extreme right'. All this was perceived by 'almost every district soviet' as a threat to the revolution. Even before the Kornilov events, on 18 August, the Petrograd Soviet adopted a resolution against only four votes (one of them Tsereteli's) protesting against the death penalty at the front, and against the arrest of Bolsheviks — and this was a soviet which still had a socialist majority.

In spite of these encouraging signs, Lenin had, as far back as 10 July, decided that counter-revolution had by now established itself in power so firmly, with the help of the Mensheviks and Socialist Revolutionaries who dominated the soviets, that 'all hopes for the peaceful development of the Russian revolution have finally disappeared'. The slogan of transfer of power to the soviets was now out of date, and the 'aim of the struggle', Lenin wrote, 'can only be the passage of power to the proletariat, supported by the poorest peasantry'.

These views were reflected in the resolution adopted by the Sixth Congress, though Stalin (in the absence of Lenin in hiding in Finland and of Trotsky in prison) had some difficulty in persuading the delegates to agree to it. The resolution accused the socialist leaders of rescuing the bourgeois Provisional Government by entering into a coalition in April, and of sinking even lower to the extent of supporting the counter-revolutionary policy of the bourgeoisie and its military supporters. Peaceful transition of power to the soviets had become impossible, and the 'revolutionary proletariat', without yielding to provocation by the bourgeoisie and engaging in a 'premature battle', must, 'when conditions are favourable', take power.

Just after the congress, Lenin refined his doctrine by arguing that, without preliminary seizure of power by 'the proletariat', the Constituent Assembly would either never be summoned or, if it were, would be rigged by the counter-revolutionaries and would be nothing but a powerless talking shop. Meanwhile, as the questionnaires to the delegates showed, in the overwhelming majority of the 162 party organization districts represented at the Sixth Congress, only a minuscule proportion of the local proletariat was enrolled in the Bolshevik party.

The branding of the socialist parties as supporters of counter-revolution had long preceded the Kornilov affair at the end of August. But the events of 26 and 27 August, as presented to the public by Kerensky, offered the Bolsheviks what they regarded as irrefutable proof that the coalition of the socialists with the middle-class parties had led straight to counter-revolution, as they had always maintained it would. Lenin's reaction to the Kornilov events was that they were quite unexpected, and demanded a reconsideration of tactics. In a letter to the Central Committee on 30 August, he argued that it would be quite wrong, in the light of what had happened, to support either Kerensky or the defence of Russia. He called for the arrest of Miliukov and Rodzianko, the dispersal of the Duma and land for the peasants, and he urged the soldiers to beat up their officers, and the like. Above all, any solidarity with or support of the government must be avoided. Immediate peace proposals should be made to the Germans.

It would not seem that this advice was taken seriously by the other party leaders. For one thing they were well aware, as Lenin apparently was not, that, in the capital at any rate, the support in the garrison and the factories was not for some abstraction called 'the armed proletariat' (which in practice could only mean the party which claimed to speak for it, that is to say the Bolsheviks) but for the

Soviet. This was particularly evident in the flood of political resolutions adopted in Petrograd in the course of September. It was possibly under the impact of this mass mood that on 1 September Lenin wrote an article entitled 'On Compromises' in which he suggested that the socialists should break with the bourgeois parties and form a government, allowing the Bolsheviks full political freedom. In return, the Bolsheviks would revert to their former policy of support for soviet power. In a postscript two days later, ostensibly written in the light of the news of the formation of Kerensky's temporary government, known as the Directory, Lenin maintained that the suggested compromise had been overtaken by events. But even a socialist so far to the left as the Menshevik Sukhanov regarded the move as a ploy whereby Lenin hoped the Bolsheviks would oust the socialists from the soviets by one means or another when once they had won full freedom of action. In the course of the next ten days Lenin continued to urge the idea of the 'compromise': union with the socialists could ensure free competition in elections and would produce a stable government. Above all, if the socialists broke with the bourgeois parties, it would make a civil war impossible: the middle classes would not venture to oppose the united people. But soviet power, he argued, did not mean a cabinet formed of the majority in the Soviet: it meant 'radically remaking the entire state power apparatus' and replacing it with 'the organized and armed majority of the people'.

Lenin's apparent support for a peaceful course of action evoked considerable sympathy in the Central Committee of the party — the Petersburg Committee was, as usual, more radically inclined. But meanwhile the Bolsheviks had been gaining political successes. For the first time Bolshevik resolutions won majorities in the Petrograd and Moscow Soviets — on 31 August and 5 September respectively. The effect of these results seems to have been to drive any thought of a deal with the socialists from Lenin's mind (if he had ever genuinely intended one). On 15 September the Central Committee was faced with two letters from Lenin. The first, which was also sent to the Petersburg and Moscow committees, opened with the startling sentence: 'Having obtained a majority in the Soviets of Worker and Soldier Deputies of both capital cities, the Bolsheviks can and must take state power into their hands.' The government, he maintained (without any foundation in fact), was about to surrender Petrograd and conclude a separate peace: only the Bolsheviks could prevent this by organizing armed insurrection in Petrograd and Moscow. 'It is necessary to consider how to agitate for this without stating it in the press.' It was naïve to wait for a 'formal' (inverted commas in the original) Bolshevik majority.

The second article, 'Marxism and Insurrection', claimed to distinguish between insurrection considered as an art, according to Marx, and a *putsch*. A proper, marxist insurrection had to be based on a leading class — not on either a conspiracy or a party. Secondly, it must be related to a popular revolutionary upsurge. And thirdly, it must take place at a moment when the activity of the leading sections of the people is at its highest, as well as the hesitation of the enemies and 'weak half-friends' of revolution. All these conditions, according to Lenin, were now present in Russia. If, after seizing power, the Bolsheviks' offer of peace without annexations or contributions were rejected, then they would become 'defencists' and save Petrograd by conducting a 'really revolutionary' war.

Lenin ended his analysis with an appeal not to lose a moment, but to organize a staff for insurrection, send the most trustworthy regiments to the most important points, seize the Peter and Paul fortress, arrest the general staff and the government, send reliable detachments to neutralize the Savage Division and the military cadets, mobilize the armed workers for a last desperate battle, immediately seize the telephone and telegraph, and so forth. It is difficult to believe that a programme of this ineptitude could ever have emanated from Lenin. All the evidence which accumulated in the coming weeks went to show that, when they were not indifferent, workers and soldiers overwhelmingly supported a soviet government of all socialist parties, and that an openly Bolshevik-led insurrection of the kind Lenin proposed could well have met with real resistance — as it had in July. In the Central Committee on 15 September his demand found no supporters. There was even some feeling that all records of his suggestions should be destroyed. In the end the vote to preserve one copy of Lenin's letters was six to four, with six abstentions.

The Bolsheviks were at that date participating in the Democratic Conference which, as mentioned in the last chapter, had been convoked by the Central Executive Committee of the Soviets and which met on 14 September. Lenin's letters demanded that the Bolshevik delegation should abandon the conference and proceed straightaway to the more useful work of haranguing the workers. However, far from leaving, the Bolsheviks took part in the debates and made proposals. Kamenev, among the most 'parliamentary' of Bolsheviks, proposed that a government should be formed at the conference, consisting exclusively of the 'democratic' elements represented there — that is, the socialists and the Bolsheviks. This, together with Trotsky's subsequent demand for a popular government which would have the support of the soviets, showed Lenin that his appeals had been rejected. On 21 September, in spite of the fact that a new coalition government including Kadets was already in process of formation, the Bolshevik Central Committee decided by 9 votes to 8 to take part in the Council of the Republic, or Pre-Parliament, which was due to meet shortly, but agreed to reconsider the decision in a fuller meeting. This hastily convened gathering, almost as large as a party congress, and as representative, which met the same day, voted 77 to 50 to participate in the Pre-Parliament.

On 23 September, the Central Executive Committee of the Soviets was persuaded by the Bolsheviks to hold a meeting with delegates to the Democratic Conference at which it was agreed to convene an All-Russian Congress of Soviets in Petrograd on 20 October.

Another important step forward by the 'Soviet' factions in the Bolshevik party was the election on 25 September of a Bolshevik-dominated Praesidium of the Petrograd Soviet, with Trotsky as its chairman. (His introductory speech included the promise that 'the arm of the Praesidium will never be used to stifle a minority.') From this time on, all indications point to the fact that Trotsky was resolutely pursuing a plan for a Bolshevik seizure of power which would be linked to the forthcoming Congress of Soviets. It was in furtherance of this policy that on 7 October, when the Pre-Parliament met, Trotsky staged a noisy walk-out on behalf of the Bolsheviks: the decision to participate, taken on 21 September by what had in effect been a party congress, had been unceremoniously over-ruled by the Central Committee on 5 October. Trotsky accused the new 'bourgeois' government of fomenting civil war, strangling the revolution and the Constituent Assembly, and preparing to surrender Petrograd. He ended his harangue amid violent and abrasive interjections, by calling for 'All Power to the Soviets'.

Trotsky's conversion to boycott of the Pre-Parliament may have been the result of Lenin's intensive, at times almost hysterical, campaign to win the Central Committee over to his point of view. In a letter to I.T. Smil'ga, after moving to Vyborg from Helsingfors, he complained that the Bolsheviks only passed resolutions, instead of preparing their armed force for the overthrow of Kerensky. He urged Smil'ga (who was chairman of the Executive Committee of the soviet of soldiers and workers of the Finland district) to form a secret committee to mobilize the forces in Finland for support of the insurrection. He also urged him to copy his letter and transmit it to the Petrograd and Moscow Bolsheviks. On 29 September, a few days later, Lenin sent an article to the Central Committee, most of which was intended for publication but which also contained some passages for private distribution to the Petersburg and Moscow committees. He alleged that there was a tendency in the Central Committee to wait for the forthcoming Soviet Congress before taking action, and to oppose immediate insurrection. Such a policy was a disgrace, it was 'complete idiocy' and 'complete treason'. A letter on similar lines was circulated among the Bolsheviks of Moscow and Petrograd on 1 October. On 7 October, having exacted permission to do so from the Central Committee, Lenin took up illegal residence on the outskirts of Petrograd.

Lenin's appeals found a ready response in the militant sections of the Moscow and Petersburg Committees. The dissemination of his views, for which the Central Committee had not hitherto shown much enthusiasm, also made it more difficult for the party leaders to resist the mounting pressure for action. The decision of the Central Committee on 3 October to authorize Lenin's move was probably the first indication of the changing mood. The resolution to boycott the Pre-Parliament, taken on 5 October against only one dissenting vote, was a clear indication of the new left trend.

On 10 October, the Central Committee met in Sukhanov's flat (in his absence) to take a momentous decision. Lenin appeared in disguise — clean-shaven, and with a wig on his bald pate. It was a small gathering, since only twelve of the full number were there. Lenin complained of resistance to the idea of insurrection in the past five or six weeks. Yet all circumstances were now in its favour since, unlike the position in July, the majority was behind the Bolsheviks. The peasants were united in their demand for land. It was senseless to wait for the Constituent Assembly, 'which clearly will not be on our side'. The main opposition came from Kamenev and Zinoviev, who alone opposed the resolution adopted: this recognized that 'armed insurrection is inevitable' and that the time for it was ripe, and called on all party organizations to take this into account in formulating their practical decisions.

Kamenev and Zinoviev explained their position in a long letter addressed to the main party organizations and committees. The gist of their argument was that an insurrection at the present time would be suppressed by the bourgeoisie, with disastrous consequences for the revolution. It was not true that either the majority of the Russian people or the international proletariat was behind the Bolsheviks. There was no stomach for insurrection in the garrison, and the Provisional Government had the support of considerable forces. The proper course was to prepare, and press, for elections to the Constituent Assembly in which the Bolsheviks could win as much as a third of the votes. Besides, Bolshevik influence was growing in the soviets, and the forthcoming Congress of Soviets would lay the foundation for truly revolutionary soviet power of all democratic parties. Kamenev and Zinoviev envisaged an ultimate parliamentary victory: either 'our opponents will have to yield to us at every step, or we shall form "a governing bloc" together with the Left Socialist Revolutionaries and non-party peasants to carry out our programme.' Lenin's accusation that the two leaders published their letter in a non-Bolshevik left-wing newspaper was untrue, but the document was widely gossiped about — as were all party affairs — and, to Lenin's fury, the gist of it did appear on 17 October.

Lenin now insisted that a long article which he had intended as a private rebuttal of Zinoviev's and Kamenev's arguments should be published. It appeared in three instalments in the main Bolshevik newspaper between 19 and 21 October, although on 20 October the Central Committee refused to accept Lenin's almost hysterical demand that Kamenev and Zinoviev should be expelled from the party.

The intention of the Bolsheviks, or at all events of Lenin, to mount an insurrection must have been plain for all to see, and rumours of an impending Bolshevik rising flooded the newspapers. It is unlikely that the general tension in the capital in the ten days which preceded the taking of power was much relieved by statements such as that of Trotsky on 18 October that no armed rising had been ordered by the Bolsheviks, but that the forthcoming Congress of Soviets would be stoutly defended against all counter-revolutionary attempts on it.

The Central Committee resolutions of 10 October, which approved of insurrection 'in principle' but without setting a date or deciding on practical measures, could hardly have satisfied Lenin, who remained in hiding on the outskirts of Petrograd, maintaining contact with the party by messengers as best he could. He had little success in shifting the party from its overall conviction that a soviet bid for power must await the general Congress of Soviets due to meet shortly. His urgent insistence that a Congress of Soviets of the Northern Region should take the initiative to overthrow the government when it met from 11 to 13 October found little support. The Petersburg Committee, usually the most militant element in the party, showed at a meeting on 15 October that it felt considerable doubt about any attempt at an armed rising, and voted for the creation of a soviet government at the forthcoming congress. Presumably the arguments of Kamenev and Zinoviev, as well as some other influential leaders, that it would be dangerous to rise independently of the congress were having their effect. Besides, reports presented to this meeting showed that in the Petrograd region a positive response to a Bolshevik call for insurrection could only be expected in a few districts: the majority were either not prepared to come out, or were only ready to answer a call from the Petrograd Soviet.

On 16 October, an extended meeting of the Bolshevik Central Committee took place, at which representatives were present from the Executive Committee and Military Organization of the Petrograd Soviet, as well as from trade unions, factory committees and others. Lenin attended this meeting and spoke in support of insurrection. The general impression conveyed by the local reports presented at this meeting on the mood in Petrograd was certainly not one of enthusiasm. In the end, a resolution proposed by Lenin was adopted by 20 votes to 2, with 3 abstentions. This reaffirmed the decision of 10 October, called for support for an armed insurrection and expressed 'full certainty that the Central Committee and the Petersburg Soviet will in good time indicate the most favourable moment and the most appropriate methods of attack'. This formula did not preclude what Trotsky and many others in the party wished for — a seizure of power timed to coincide with the forthcoming congress. The following day, the Central Executive Committee (on which socialists predominated) postponed this congress from 20 until 25 October, to allow more time for preparations.

How did Petrograd react during those last days before 25 October, while the intentions of the Bolsheviks were becoming ever more evident? In general, the socialist parties had no illusions left about the Bolsheviks, knowing after what had happened in July that they were capable of armed insurrection. They were not convinced by the Bolsheviks' repeated claims that they were merely organizing defence against counter-revolution or attacks on the Soviet Congress, nor yet that the government, by its disastrous policies, was forcing the masses to rise. But the socialists persuaded themselves that any armed demonstration would founder against the sound sense of the workers and the garrison — though apprehensions were expressed on some occasions that such irresponsible adventurism could lead to bloodshed, and even civil war. On 17 October the (socialist) Central Executive Committee of the Soviets published an appeal which spoke of 'dark forces' which were trying to provoke excesses in order to crush the revolution, but did not mention the Bolsheviks. (Plekhanov commented acidly: 'Hail Lenin, the semi-leninists salute you!') Some socialists on the right of their parties called for resolute and determined action against the Bolsheviks.

There seems to have been some secret discussion in right-wing circles, but nothing was resolved or planned — the failure of the forces of 'counter-revolution' at the moment when they could most be expected to surface is the best comment on the chimerical nature of this much-publicized threat in Bolshevik and socialist circles. The Kadets were by then a spent force, although they cooperated in the

Pre-Parliament, having entered the third coalition government, and placed their hopes on the Constituent Assembly.

The Pre-Parliament met, in the presence of foreign ambassadors, on 7 October — the Duma and State Council having finally been dissolved by decree the day before. The lack of unity or sense of urgency which the Pre-Parliament displayed in the few weeks of its existence give little grounds for supposing that, had there been no insurrection, it would have accomplished much. A list of draft laws submitted to it by the government on 19 October contained no reference to land or to public order — two of the most critical questions facing the country.

On 20 October, in secret session, the Minister of War, General Verkhovsky, delivered a sensational speech. With the aid of facts and figures he sought to show that the armed forces had reached the stage of demoralization and exhaustion which made it impossible for them to continue as a fighting force. His picture did not differ substantially from that described in Chapter 6, which is largely based on evidence of the archives, and it was later confirmed by a military intelligence report from GHQ for the period 15-30 October which, while not claiming to portray the situation in every unit of the five fronts, gave a vivid picture of the extent of the disintegration where it had been recorded. The Cossack troops alone had preserved full discipline and fighting capacity. In other units, orders were not being obeyed and officers were being humiliated and insulted. The desire for peace 'at all costs' was so strong that both the committees and the Provisional Government had lost the confidence of the troops.

General Verkhovsky predicted that the Bolsheviks would before long take action to exploit the advantage which they had gained by advocating peace. It was essential to cut the ground from under their feet by entering into negotiations with the Allies and persuading them to bring the war to an end. The effect of negotiations for peace would bring an upsurge of morale in the army, which would then be available as a force against anarchy in the country.

The speech caused great excitement in the chamber, and immediately reached the press in the garbled form of a proposal to conclude a secret separate peace with the Germans. The government and Verkhovsky denied this, the newspaper which had published the report was closed down, and the Minister of War was unceremoniously despatched on sick leave. But the harm to the government had already been done.

All available evidence points to two facts. First, the Provisional Government, though well aware that a Bolshevik attack was imminent, believed, or persuaded itself, that it would fail ·ignominiously, and that the forces available to the government were adequate to repel it. Secondly, no steps were taken to ensure that the forces of defence were strong enough. According to the memoirs of several witnesses, including the British Ambassador, in the course of the last days before the Bolshevik attack Kerensky repeatedly expressed the view that his forces were adequate to meet any assault. He even hinted in private that he hoped the Bolsheviks would take up arms so that he could crush them once and for all. His complete confidence is confirmed in the record of a teleprinter 'conversation' with the Chief of Staff in the night of 21-22 October. Kerensky may well have relied on what he was told by Colonel Polkovnikov, the Commander of the Petrcgrad forces. Between 14 and 17 October this officer repeatedly asserted both in public and in private that the garrison supported the Provisional Government and would not rise against it, but that all necessary measures had been taken should any disorders occur.

To understand the way in which the Bolsheviks took power it is necessary to go back a few weeks, to the time when the government made known its intention to move some troops of the Petrograd Garrison to the Northern Front. It is probable that the initiative in this matter came from the politicians: General Cheremisov, the Commander of the Northern Front, does not seem to have been too anxious to add anarchical and demoralized troops to his command, though he went along with government policy. Nothing could have been more calculated to alienate the garrison, nor to provide better propaganda for the Bolsheviks, who were already trumpeting the supposed, but untrue, intention of the government to evacuate and surrender Petrograd. The socialists were also disturbed by what they regarded as a sinister move, and on 9 October proposed the setting up of a special committee to consider defence needs and military plans. Trotsky immediately seized on this opportunity, and persuaded the Petrograd Soviet to accept his alternative proposal to create a 'revolutionary defence committee' which would take steps to arm the workers and ensure the defence of Petrograd against attacks which were being 'openly prepared by . . . Kornilovites'.

Thus arose the Military Revolutionary Committee (MRC). This preponderantly Bolshevik body, with Lazimir, an eighteen-year-old Left Socialist Revolutionary as its nominal chairman, became the staff for the organization of the insurrection. When on 16 October the Bolshevik Central Committee set up a 'Military Revolutionary Centre' of five, including Stalin, this was expressly stated to form a part of the 'Soviet Revolutionary Committee', nor did it thereafter function as a separate entity. This 'Centre' has figured prominently in Soviet histories of the Bolshevik revolution as proof that it was Stalin, and not Trotsky, who played the major part in its organization, because Trotsky was not one of the five members. In fact, Trotsky, as Chairman of the Petrograd Soviet, virtually controlled the MRC, and thus the members of the Centre who were a part of it.

The MRC was formally constituted on 20 October, but in the preceding two or three days it organized a conference of representatives of most units of the garrison in order to get a clear picture of the mood of the troops. Fifteen of the eighteen representatives who made reports expressed lack of support for the government and demanded transfer of power to the soviets. They did not, however, evince any enthusiasm for armed action, and about half of those who supported soviet power said, or implied, that they would come out only if summoned by the Petrograd Soviet. In spite of such evidence, Lenin, at a secret conference in his hiding place, refused to listen to leading MRC members who urged that more time was needed for preparations. He repeatedly stressed the urgency of overthrowing the government before the Congress of Soviets met on 25 October, so as to prevent Kerensky from summoning loyal troops from the front.

Almost the first act of the MRC was to appoint Bolshevik commissars to garrison units and ammunition stores, for the purpose of 'taking the necessary defensive measures'. In the night of 21-22 October, delegates of the MRC informed the Military Commander of Petrograd that henceforth only orders signed by the MRC were valid. Polkovnikov threatened the delegates with arrest, but did not carry out his threat, and indeed dissuaded Kerensky from attempting to do so. He did later send an ultimatum demanding that the statement of 21-22 October be rescinded, and there is some evidence that his order was complied with. This was on the insistence of the Left Socialist Revolutionary members of the MRC who, before they agreed to join it had demanded that it should issue a declaration that its purpose was not seizure of power.

A system of permanent liaison with all garrison units was set up, through commissars appointed by the MRC. So far as available information goes, these commissars experienced no difficulty in asserting the authority of the Petrograd Soviet in whose name they acted. On 23 October, the MRC published a proclamation to all citizens of Petrograd conferring full authority on the commissars whose orders in areas under their jurisdiction were to be paramount — all in the interests of defence against counter-revolution. A long report to the Petrograd Soviet on the same day claimed control over all military units and depots, over the issue of ammunition and over the Peter and Paul fortress. Stores of weapons and bullets were accumulated in the course of these days by the authority of the MRC.

There was no cut-and-dried plan of insurrection. Everything points to the fact that seizure of power was improvised around events as they developed, with the meeting of the Congress of Soviets in mind, and under the frenetic direction of Trotsky. As late as 24 October a hastily convened meeting of the Central Committee was still making last-minute arrangements for such matters as contacts with the post, telegraph and railway, for food supplies and for monitoring the actions of the government. Right to the end Trotsky maintained the pretence that all actions of the MRC were taken in defence of the Congress of Soviets against the Kornilovites. Even on the afternoon of 24 October he denied that any armed conflict was intended, insisting that the forthcoming congress must decide the issue of government.

By this time Kerensky had at last been goaded into an act which enabled the Bolsheviks to respond, ostensibly to put down counter-revolution: during the night of 23 to 24 October, a force of military cadets had raided, closed down and occupied the two main Bolshevik newspapers. Kerensky was also rumoured to have ordered loyal troops to the capital from the front. A company from one of the most revolutionary regiments was despatched by the MRC to reopen the newspaper offices, which it did without difficulty. Fiery proclamations were issued, calling for defence against 'counter-revolution'.

All the evidence suggests that when the crisis came the great majority of units of the Petrograd garrison did not support the government but simply remained neutral. As the incompetent Colonel Polkovnikov reported on the morning of 25 October, 'the government had no troops at its disposal.' The Cossack units rejected its call for support, leaving the government with only a few hundred women soldiers and around two thousand military cadets on its side. The Bolsheviks, on the other hand, could count on several regiments to carry out their orders. Units of the Baltic Fleet also supported them (some eight thousand sailors from Kronstadt took part in the take-over in Petrograd and in the fighting against the forces mustered by Kerensky). In addition, they had the Red Guards to call on, although their morale could not always be relied on.

In the event, the Bolshevik take-over was almost bloodless: in contrast with what had happened in February, nothing could have been less like a city in the throes of revolution than Petrograd on 25 October. Crowds of well-dressed people thronged the streets in the evening. Theatres and restaurants were open, and at the opera, Shaliapin sang in *Boris Godunov*. The principal stations and services had all been taken over by the morning of 25 October without a shot being fired. There was much discussion about arresting the ministers of the Provisional Government, and a detailed plan is said to have been worked out — Lenin, who arrived secretly in Petrograd around 2 a.m. on 25 October, vehemently insisted that the ministers should be deposed before the Congress of Soviets met in the afternoon. In his last letter to the Central Committee, written on the evening of 24 October and delivered by messenger, he had urged immediate seizure of power, and the arrest of the ministers without waiting for next day. It was not important who seized power, the MRC 'or some other organization'. To delay was 'like unto death'. In the end, the ministers were not made prisoner until the small hours of 26 October.

The delay in taking action against the government (which was probably due to uncertainty about the amount of support that would be offered by the troops) did not prevent Lenin from issuing a proclamation at 10 a.m. on 25 October to the effect that the Provisional Government had been overthrown, that all power had passed to the Petrograd Soviet in the form of the MRC, and that land, peace and a soviet government were now assured. The MRC also issued a proclamation claiming, untruthfully, complete control in the capital and throughout the land. In the afternoon the Petrograd Soviet met to hear brief declarations from Lenin (greeted by an ovation) and Trotsky, announcing the birth of a soviet government. The few Mensheviks present refused to associate themselves with what they described as a 'conspiracy'.

The Second All-Russian Congress of Soviets opened its proceedings at 10.40 p.m. This hastily convened gathering had little claim to speak for all the soviets of Russia. For one thing, the rural soviets were virtually unrepresented, since the peasant Central Executive had voted on 27 September not to send delegates to the capital. The two hundred soldiers at the congress represented scarcely half of the armed forces. In many instances the army committees did not have time to meet in order to elect delegates: there were repeated instances (recorded in Soviet sources) where the more radical committees at lower levels succeeded in securing election of Bolshevik delegates before the army committees could act. Soviet archives record many instances of resolutions at all levels in the army, protesting against the summoning of the congress before the Constituent Assembly had met. The haste in preparing the congress also meant that only a part of the total number of local soviets sent delegates to it. In fact, the Bolsheviks benefited from the lack of confidence which the socialists had felt in the congress. Even so, according to incomplete records, the Bolsheviks only had a majority with the support of the Left Socialist Revolutionaries — 300 out of

670 delegates were Bolsheviks, almost half of the 193 Socialist Revolutionaries were now 'Left', 68 were Mensheviks, 14 were Menshevik Internationalists, and the remainder belonged to small groups or were unaffiliated.

Trotsky's tactics of ensuring that seizure of power by the effectively Bolshevik MRC should be made to appear as an assumption of power by the soviets had been successful — even if not in the way that Trotsky had planned, and in the Petrograd Soviet, not in the congress. But the subsequent take-over in the congress was unexpectedly made easy by the socialist parties. Whatever the private intentions of Lenin, Trotsky and a few other leaders may have been, the great majority of the party expected 'soviet government' to mean a coalition of the Bolshevik and socialist parties, without the hated bourgeoisie. In a referendum taken among delegates to the congress, the great majority declared for 'All Power to the Soviets', or 'a coalition of all parties without the Kadets'. A proposal by the Internationalist Martov to deal first with the formation of a government of all socialist parties in order to avoid bloodshed was greeted with loud applause, was accepted by the Bolsheviks and adopted unanimously. But representatives of the socialists now declared that their two parties (the Socialist Revolutionaries and the Mensheviks) refused to be associated with an armed conspiracy which was a violation of soviet democracy and which threatened civil war, and announced that they were leaving the congress. After they had gone, to the accompaniment of cat-calls, Martov renewed his appeal. But Trotsky was now able to make short shrift of it by refusing association with 'miserable bankrupts . . . who are destined . . . for the waste-paper basket of history'.

The most significant act of the congress that morning was the adoption of a manifesto drafted by Lenin proclaiming that the soviet government would at once propose 'a democratic peace to all nations'; and would 'safeguard the transfer without compensation of all land . . . to the peasant committees'. At 5 a.m. on 26 October the truncated congress voted itself into power, against only two dissenting votes and twelve absentions. But in the days that followed the question of coalition proved to be far from resolved.

The congress also elected an all-Bolshevik 'Council of People's Commissars', headed by Lenin. This council, *Sovnarkom*, was to become the real government of the country in the early years.[*]

On 24 October Kerensky, in the last speech which he was destined to make in Russia, discoursed to the Pre-Parliament in an emotional

[*] Eight LSRs joined it on 26 November but the coalition lasted only three months.

manner on the misdeeds of the Bolsheviks, who had brought Petrograd to a state of insurrection. He called for full support from the Pre-Parliament for resolute defensive action against the rebellious 'rabble'. His speech was rapturously received, with ovations in the middle and at the end of it, from all except the Internationalists, who, headed by Martov, remained stubbornly seated. The enthusiasm was deceptive: not only the Internationalists but the socialists and others were sceptical about the possibility of resisting the Bolshevik-led movement by military means, even if they were available. In the end, a resolution proposed by all the socialists present was passed by 123 votes to 102, with 26 abstentions. This called for the transfer of land to the land committees, urged the Allies to enter into peace negotiations and proposed the creation of a committee of public safety from 'organs of the revolutionary democracy' to act in concert with the government. It was probably much too late for this policy to succeed, even if it was wise enough in its intention of cutting support from under the Bolsheviks' feet at the eleventh hour. When Dan and other socialists later urged Kerensky to accept their proposed course of action, the Prime Minister, 'worn out and exhausted' and wounded by the failure of the Pre-Parliament to support him, declared that the government 'had no need of admonitions'.

By 9 a.m. on 25 October Kerensky was convinced that the only hope lay in mobilizing the support of loyal troops at the front. By 11 a.m. he had succeeded in borrowing an escort car from the American Embassy, and sped off to the front, preceded by a Renault flying the US flag. Around the same time, a single commissar of the MRC entered the Mariinsky Palace where a few members of the Pre-Parliament were gathered, and ordered the palace to be cleared. The delegates left under protest.

By 6.30 p.m. on 25 October a battleship and several cruisers, including the *Aurora*, had reached Petrograd from Kronstadt and were anchored with their guns trained on targets in the city. An ultimatum was now delivered to the Petrograd General Staff, demanding surrender and threatening otherwise to destroy the Winter Palace as well as their own building. The officers attempted without success to obtain instructions from the government inside the Winter Palace, and escaped. By 7.40, with only one officer left inside it, the General Staff building was occupied by MRC forces.

The Provisional Government inside the Winter Palace was presided over by Konovalov, in the absence of Kerensky. At 8.30 p.m. it received an ultimatum calling for surrender of its members, under threat of bombardment of the palace by *Aurora* and by the guns of the Peter and Paul fortress. In spite of the fact that the twenty minutes allowed for surrender had long expired, it was only at 9.40 p.m. that the *Aurora* was ordered to fire — and discharged one blank shell. The main effect of this was to accelerate the thinning out of the cadet defenders of the palace, who had already begun to dwindle. The women soldiers, who had formed part of its defence force, also left before the palace was invaded. At 11 p.m. some live shells were fired, and the palace was slightly damaged.

Inside the palace, the ministers waited for the end without much possibility, with their minimal defences, of doing anything to avert it. After receiving the ultimatum, they had managed to send out a radio-telegram 'To All, All, All', explaining that they had refused to surrender and had put themselves under the protection of the people and the army. The story of the dramatic storming of the Winter Palace, popular with Soviet historians and in the cinema, is a myth. At around 2 a.m. on 26 October, a small detachment of troops, followed by an unruly crowd and led by two members of the MRC, entered the palace. The remaining officer cadets were, apparently, prepared to resist, but were ordered to surrender by the ministers. In the end, the total casualties were three officer cadets wounded. The members of the cabinet, who narrowly escaped being lynched by the crowd which was enraged at Kerensky's absence, were placed under arrest and taken to the Peter and Paul Fortress. There was some looting inside the palace.

'It makes one's head go round,' Lenin is reported to have said to Trotsky (in German, for some reason) when it was all over. It had been surprisingly, unbelievably easy.

Chapter Nine

The Bolsheviks Consolidate

The task of consolidating Bolshevik power after 25 October fell to the Military Revolutionary Committee (MRC) which had held its first meeting on 20 October. It acted in the name, and with the authority, of the Petrograd Soviet, which had set it up. It included, apart from leading Bolshevik members of the Soviet, delegates from (among others) the Baltic fleet, the factory committees and the military committees. Its total membership grew to 82, of whom 53 were Bolsheviks. A rota of permanent representatives from every unit in the garrison was instituted on 23 October.

The MRC was thus not wholly Bolshevik in composition, and the Bolsheviks had to be circumspect for a time in dealing with colleagues who were still under the delusion that power was to pass to the Soviet, and not the Bolsheviks. The Left Socialist Revolutionaries, as was mentioned in the previous chapter, had only agreed to join the MRC on 24 October after it had issued a statement that 'contrary to all kinds of rumours' the MRC declares that it exists 'in no way for the purpose of preparing and putting into effect a seizure of power, but exclusively for the defence of the interests of the Petrograd garrison and democracy' against counter-revolution. Despite all this, the three volumes of minutes and records of the MRC show beyond any doubt that its main activity during almost two months of existence was precisely the consolidation of Bolshevik control over as much of the country as could be achieved. Nor is there any question about Bolshevik domination of the MRC, through such prominent figures as Trotsky, Stalin and Sverdlov, and the future *Cheka* leaders Dzerzhinsky, Latsis and Peters. Lenin also intervened at times in the MRC, though his activity was mainly centred in the Council of People's Commissars (*Sovnarkom*).

The daily meetings of the MRC were sometimes quite stormy. Delegates from the armed forces and other organizations expressed concern that the Constituent Assembly should be summoned, and not impeded, and there were occasional protests about Bolshevik actions against freedom of the press.

The immediate concern of the MRC was the appointment of Bolshevik commissars to all the military units and every other kind of institution in the capital, to cities and districts throughout the country, and to the army at the front. Hundreds of such commissars were appointed — three hundred in October alone, some of them, it will be recalled, before 25 October. The commissars seem to have had little difficulty in establishing their authority in the garrison units. The troops in Petrograd had a strong vested interest in maintaining in power the party which was pledged to resist any attempt to move them to the front, and which, moreover, was extremely unlikely to call them to account for past acts of mutiny. The ambition of the soldiers was, in the main, to get back home as soon as possible and deal with the question of the land. They were also anxious not to be involved in fighting a civil war, and this gave rise in the first weeks to pressure from the garrison for the formation of a coalition government, which the Bolsheviks (as will be seen) skilfully outmanoeuvred. That the Bolsheviks were aware that the garrison as a whole was 'neutral' rather than pro-Bolshevik is evident from the fact that the guarding of their headquarters, Smolny, was entrusted to picked pro-Bolshevik Lettish troops brought from the Northern Front.

There was also resistance in some institutions, like the State Bank, to the MRC commissars, as there was to the new Bolshevik People's Commissars in some of the ministries. This mainly took the form of refusal by the civil servants concerned to cooperate. Their attempt to stop the Bolshevik onslaught (in spite of some organization and finance behind it) had little chance of success, and was broken by arrests, dismissals, threats of dismissals and of confiscation of property. The last incident — in the Ministry of Trade — took place as late as 26 November, and some passive resistance continued until 1918.

For the first two months of Bolshevik power, the Petrograd MRC was the main organ for public order and security in the capital, and struggle against counter-revolution was from the start laid down as its responsibility. (There were MRCs with similar functions in Moscow and in other cities.) An investigatory commission came into being in the first few days, and a Central Military Revolutionary Court was set up on 12 November, for trial of those handed over by the commission. Nine days later, on Dzerzhinsky's suggestion, a Committee for Struggle Against the Counter-Revolution was created, the forerunner of the *Cheka* which was to emerge in December (see Chapter 12). The commission broke up one real, but not very large or effective, counter-revolutionary organization, headed by the monarchist Purishkevich, whose members played a part in an ineffective rising of the military cadets at the end of October.

During these first weeks there was a spate of house-searches, confiscations and arrests — on one day a hundred arrest warrants were issued. In addition to actions ordered by the MRC, there were numerous cases of violence by self-appointed bandit-revolutionaries, including some lynchings. It is fair to say that the MRC does appear to have tried to stop such excesses and to punish the offenders, but there were no executions.

One of the endemic problems was drunkenness, and the disorder that it brought in its train. Much of the energy of the MRC was devoted to providing adequate guards for the huge stores of wine and spirits in the Winter Palace and elsewhere. Some stocks were sold to Sweden and much alcoholic liquor was pumped into the drains — to the great dismay of passers-by. Stringent measures against drunkenness were enacted on 27 November: a special commissar had been appointed the day before, but he fell into disgrace within a few days.

The actions of the MRC from the outset bore many of the marks which were to distinguish future Bolshevik policy. 'Does not Lenin's government, as the Romanov government did, seize and drag off to prison all those who think differently?' wrote Maxim Gorky on 7 November. The statement is exaggerated so far as the Bolsheviks were concerned, and very unfair on the old régime, but it was typical of the attitude of anti-Bolshevik socialists on the extreme left. The socialist members of the cabinet arrested on 26 October were soon released, but the non-socialists were kept in prison.

On 26 October, at a night session of the City Duma (the elected municipal council), an All-Russian Committee for Salvation of the Country and the Revolution was set up. It consisted of the Praesidium of the Pre-Parliament, representatives of the Mensheviks and the Socialist Revolutionaries (who controlled it), together with representatives from the old, socialist, Central Executive Committee, the railway, post and telegraph unions, and others. It appealed to the population not to carry out the orders of the usurpers, and promised to form a new Provisional Government to act until the Constituent Assembly met.

The Committee of Salvation was far from determined on military action to overthrow the Bolsheviks. The mood in the capital in these early days was characterized by the prevalent belief that the Bolsheviks could not last, and this view was shared by all shades of political opinion from socialists to Kadets. A gathering of Kadet intellectuals on 28 October prophesied the end of Bolshevik power in from two weeks to a few months. On 29 October the main Socialist-Revolutionary newspaper gave the Bolsheviks a couple of days, while the Menshevik organ foretold that the Bolsheviks would recoil in horror from what they had done. In view of this imminent collapse of Bolshevik rule, as they saw it, the most urgent task facing the Committee of Salvation was the creation of an all-socialist government in order to prevent civil war should troops move on the capital to overthrow the Bolsheviks. Ever present, too, was the fear of counter-revolution, with wild and totally unfounded rumours of an impending onslaught by General Kaledin, well known for his opposition to the Bolsheviks and to soviet power. There was also considerable opposition to Kerensky personally — still Commander in Chief and now endeavouring to muster a force for the recapture of Petrograd — and to the entire Provisional Government, whose members were for the most part in prison.

While fearful of civil war and counter-revolution if it should encourage military action against the Bolsheviks, the Committee of Salvation apparently did not scruple to organize an insurrection of military cadets in the capital. The rising, on Sunday 29 October, was not only badly planned but premature, its hastiness prompted by suspicion that the MRC had knowledge of the plan — as indeed it had. The Committee of Salvation, and Colonel Polkovnikov, who was in charge of the operation, were convinced that forces under Kerensky's overall command would come to their aid. The officer cadets, whom none of the garrison troops supported and who were reinforced only by some officers from Purishkevich's organization, were easily overcome, with great brutality and heavy casualties.

Meanwhile, in Pskov, the headquarters of the Northern Front, Kerensky was having difficulty in mustering an anti-Bolshevik force. He subsequently blamed his failure on what he alleged were the pro-Bolshevik sentiments of General Cheremisov, the front commander. Cheremisov was not pro-Bolshevik, but he certainly disapproved of using troops to resolve what he regarded as a political squabble. He considered the appointment by Kerensky of a Kadet politician, Kishkin, to take charge of the defence of Petrograd as a grave mistake; and he persuaded Kerensky, who was in a state of nervous collapse, to countermand the order to move on the capital which had been issued to squadrons of the Savage Division, under the command of General Krasnov. These were the only units which it had been proved possible to induce to support Kerensky and the Provisional Government, and reluctantly at that. Although the order to move was restored by Kerensky when he recovered, the delay may have done some harm.

The Cossack squadrons occupied Gatchina without resistance on 27 October, and Tsarskoe Selo on the following day. But on 30 October, in an attempt to move on the capital, Krasnov's Cossacks were defeated, near the observatory at Pulkovo, by a greatly superior

Bolshevik force, in which a few thousand sailors formed the resolute element; the Red Guard and the garrison troops employed in the engagement proved unreliable. In spite of lurid propaganda about Kerensky's intentions to restore the monarchy and the rule of the landlords, the Bolsheviks had difficulty in persuading the factory workers of Petrograd to support them.

The reluctance of the army to engage in any kind of fighting was considerably enhanced by the publication on 27 October of the decrees of the Congress of Soviets on peace and on land: the former proposed immediate negotiations to secure a democratic peace, the latter, an essentially Socialist-Revolutionary proposal, remote from the established Bolshevik policy of nationalization, abolished private property in land but provided for the distribution of it to peasants according to their needs. Another order of the congress, the abolition of the death penalty at the front imposed by Kerensky in June, was also well received in the armed forces.

After the defeat of 30 October, Gatchina became the scene of complicated intrigues by the various factions anxious to secure peace based on a new government — with or without the Bolsheviks, with or without Kerensky. The final blow to the Bolsheviks' opponents was dealt by the MRC. The Bolsheviks, under pressure from eight regiments of the garrison and representatives of some other organizations, such as the socialist committee of the railway workers' union *Vikzhel* (which could threaten to halt the railways), had been induced to despatch a delegation from the MRC, headed by the People's Commissar for the Navy, Dybenko, to discuss armistice terms. The meeting took place at Gatchina on 1 November. In his memoirs Dybenko frankly admits that his aim was to use the talks as cover for the seizure of the staff HQ at Gatchina by his sailors, and the arrest of Krasnov and Kerensky. The terms agreed included the surrender of Lenin and Trotsky to stand trial on charges of treason, and of Kerensky to be arraigned on unspecified accusations.

The staff and Krasnov were indeed captured shortly after this mock armistice, although Krasnov was released on a verbal promise that he would not further oppose the Bolsheviks. (He went south and played an active part on the White side.) Kerensky, however, warned of the impending betrayal being discussed on the floor below him in the palace which housed the staff of the anti-Bolshevik forces, succeeded in escaping, disguised as a sailor.

There are those who argue that with proper leadership an effective anti-Bolshevik force could have been organized in the north-west. As it was, this was rendered impossible by Kerensky's unpopularity, by the army's general hostility to embarking on a civil war, and by the ambivalent attitude, for fear of counter-revolution, of the socialists on the Committee of Salvation. At a meeting of the old socialist Central Executive Committee of the Soviet on 12 November, Tsereteli argued that the main task of democracy was not to combat the Bolsheviks, but to save the revolution from the bourgeoisie, which was only waiting to liquidate the Bolshevik rising by shooting down the proletariat. 'We must prepare a retreat for the Bolsheviks when they begin to disintegrate.' It was easy enough for the Bolsheviks to triumph against so misguided an opposition, which failed to perceive that the overthrow of the Bolsheviks was the only way to avert a civil war.

In the early period of the Bolshevik rule, the two indisputable leaders of the victorious party, Lenin and Trotsky, were borne along by the conviction that what had happened in Russia was only a step towards the glorious future — world socialism. Events that occurred inside the country were seen by them as of minor, transient importance, insignificant set-backs in the triumphant march of history which they had been destined to initiate. One of these negligible hitches, from Lenin's point of view, was the question of an all-socialist coalition government, and the resulting dissensions in the Central Committee of the party. Demands for such a government were voiced by those who interpreted soviet power to mean just that, and were not persuaded by the Bolshevik argument that the socialists had had their chance and had rejected it at the Second Congress. Many of the army delegates who thronged the MRC also called for socialist participation. The most pressing demand was made by the socialist-dominated *Vikzhel*, in the Central Executive Committee. (As elected by the Second Congress on 26 October this was overwhelmingly Bolshevik and Left Socialist Revolutionary, and included neither Mensheviks nor the Socialist Revolutionaries from the mainstream party.) *Vikzhel* delegates were also sent off to persuade Kerensky to compromise.

In face of this pressure, with the military opposition as yet undefeated and the ultimate issue of power in considerable doubt, there was a move for compromise within the Bolshevik Central Committee. On 29 October a meeting of eleven of its members, which significantly did not include Lenin or Trotsky, agreed that 'the Central Committee recognize as necessary the widening of the base of the government and the possible alteration of its composition'; but only a minority of four, including Kamenev, voted for the inclusion of all socialist parties as essential. However, Kamenev was deputed that same night as one of the three Bolshevik delegates to a conference of representatives of all the socialist parties convened by *Vikzhel*. A commission was set up which adopted a resolution, in which the

Bolsheviks concurred, calling for an immediate cessation of hostilities between Kerensky's forces and the new régime. Further meetings of the conference were held, and in the night of 31 October to 1 November Kamenev and the other Bolshevik delegates (there was one from the Central Executive Committee) agreed to the setting up of a 'People's Council' to which a more representative government would be responsible. Moreover they did not demur at the suggestion that Lenin and Trotsky should be excluded from the new cabinet. While these meetings were going on, strong demands for an end to fighting and a socialist coalition were being voiced in factories throughout the capital. According to one account, the meeting was enlivened by a worker delegation which expressed the view that Lenin, Trotsky and Kerensky should all be hanged on the same tree.

At this point Lenin, whose absence from the meeting of the Central Committee of 29 October could hardly have been accidental, intervened. On 1 November a stormy meeting of eleven Central Committee members and eleven other prominent Bolsheviks took place to hear reports from Kamenev and other Bolshevik delegates to the *Vikzhel* conference. Their conduct was attacked by Trotsky, Dzerzhinsky and especially Lenin, who contended that Kamenev's policy must be stopped at once. There should be no talks with *Vikzhel*, which had no mass support; the important thing was to send troops to Moscow. At a later stage he added that the whole point of the discussions with *Vikzhel* had been to win time, 'as a diplomatic cover for military operations'. (This was with reference to the threat by *Vikzhel* to stop troop movements. A detachment of sailors was, in fact, sent to Moscow.)

Lenin's view was not shared by the meeting as a whole, and a resolution to put an end to the discussions on coalition was defeated. But this was a tactical decision only, since the resolution adopted stressed that the purpose of taking part in the discussions was to expose the 'insubstantial' nature of the whole idea of coalition and to bring the question to an end. That the minority were still not satisfied became evident at a further meeting of the Central Committee on the same day, which opened with Lenin's proposal (for reasons which are unclear) to expel the People's Commissar for Enlightenment, Lunacharsky. This was defeated, but Lenin continued his attack in intemperate terms against Kamenev and Zinoviev, whom he accused of 'treason' and of causing a split. Loud applause greeted Lunacharsky's remark that the result of such tactics by Lenin would be that one man would be left in the party — the dictator. Trotsky interpreted this as an expression of feeling against himself as well as Lenin.

On 2 November five Bolsheviks, headed by Zinoviev and Kamenev, voted against a resolution in the Central Executive Committee of the Soviets which demanded that Lenin and Trotsky must be included in any government. On the following day Lenin drew up a declaration which demanded, on pain of expulsion, submission to the majority view of the Central Committee on coalition. Each member of the Central Committee was summoned into the presence and faced with a request to sign: ten signed at once — including Lenin's hard core, Trotsky, Stalin and Dzerzhinsky. Five, headed by Zinoviev and Kamenev, refused. The remaining six were probably absent from Petrograd and would have signed if requested, from what is known of their views.

The revolt of the five Central Committee members was, however, motivated by another question as well as that of coalition. This was the issue of freedom of the press, which was accepted social democratic policy, to which even Lenin had paid lip service. In an article published in mid-September 1917, he had argued that when once the soviets were in power it would be possible to institute a just press law under which the government, and then all political parties, large and small, would receive allocations of paper in proportion to their size. On 28 October a decree by the Central Executive Committee of the Soviets which conferred power on the MRC to close down newspapers which were openly seditious aroused no opposition because it was stated to be temporary only, while the emergency lasted. (Nine leading newspapers were in fact closed down as early as 28 October.) But on 4 November a proposal by the Bolsheviks in the Central Executive Committee to assume the power to confiscate all newspaper presses and, if need be, suspend liberal and even socialist papers, aroused a storm of opposition from some Bolsheviks and from the Left Socialist Revolutionaries. The five dissident Central Committee members then resigned. This was followed by the resignation of four People's Commissars and five other leaders. In a declaration, to which two further commissars (including Shliapnikov) adhered, without resigning, they repudiated 'the preservation in power of a purely Bolshevik government by means of terror'. The Left Socialist Revolutionaries supported them by resigning from the MRC — but, with typical inconsistency, remained in the Central Executive Committee.

The revolt did not last long. The dissident Bolsheviks had committed themselves too far to an insurrection of which they had not foreseen the consequences. They included no leader of the stature necessary to challenge Lenin and Trotsky. Lenin was not far wrong in dismissing the rebellion as that of some 'isolated intellectuals' whom the workers would not follow. The rebels eventually recanted when faced with the threat of expulsion. The *Vikzhel* conference on coalition petered out at a meeting on 7 November, which the Bolsheviks did not bother to attend: by that date the armed resistance of Kerensky had been defeated and Moscow was in Bolshevik hands. In January, after intensive propaganda among railway workers and in defiance of the vote of a railwaymen's congress, the Bolsheviks succeeded in replacing the socialist *Vikzhel* by a new pro-Bolshevik railway committee.

The Bolsheviks could now ignore the real socialists. It seemed clear that they were not prepared to set up armed resistance to the Bolsheviks, and indeed their ambiguous attitude to the use of force as members of the Committee of Salvation had probably helped to ensure the defeat of Krasnov's Cossacks. As to popular opinion, the surge in favour of a coalition government among the workers in the Petrograd factories subsided with the end of military action in the north-west and of the immediate threat of civil war.

There was, however, one body of socialists which the Bolsheviks needed to use. The left wing of the Socialist Revolutionaries had been drawn to the Bolsheviks through its opposition to the war and to the 'defencist' policy of many of the party's leaders. Its adherents had, however, been reluctant to break with their party, and their emergence as a separate entity only came at the Second Congress of Soviets when the left delegates, who formed a good part of the Socialist Revolutionaries, refused to walk out of the congress and were expelled from the party by its Central Committee. For the time being, the Bolsheviks needed them to maintain the fiction that they were anxious to set up a coalition, and that it was the socialists who had rejected it. In particular, the vast peasantry supported the Socialist Revolutionary Party, so that there was considerable value in an alliance with a portion of it which, though pro-Bolshevik, still regarded itself as Socialist-Revolutionary. For a while the LSR maintained a policy of 'isolating Lenin' and forming a coalition with the more moderate Bolshevik leaders, but as time went on it became obvious that there was no future in this tactic.

Between 18 November and 12 December, agreement was reached for seven LSRs to enter the Council of People's Commissars, *Sovnarkom.* Romantic, inconsistent, poorly led and inexperienced, they did not live long to enjoy the fruits of their betrayal of their leaders and fellow socialists. They were no match for Lenin, who, to their surprise, had suddenly adopted their peasant programme and incorporated it in the decree on the land. What for Lenin was a temporary, tactical manoeuvre was for them an ideal and a principle: the clash of the LSR with the Bolsheviks over the peasants was not long delayed (see Chapter 10). During the short tenure of the LSR People's Commissar for Justice, Steinberg, there was constant conflict between him and the Bolsheviks on the issue of terror. The final break came after Lenin accepted the Central Powers' annexationist peace terms (see Chapter 11).

There remained the Constituent Assembly as the hope of the democratic opponents of the Bolsheviks. The election was held on 12 November, the date arranged by the Provisional Government. To the last, Bolshevik propaganda had been insistent that only they would ensure the summoning of the Constituent Assembly and prevent the Provisional Government from frustrating this great event in Russia's history. In announcing victory on 25 October, the MRC promised to convene the Assembly without delay. On the following day in the Soviet Congress, Lenin declared that 'Even if the peasants should return a Socialist Revolutionary majority to the Constituent Assembly we shall say, so be it . . . . We must leave full creative freedom to the popular masses.' A few weeks later, in the Central Executive Committee, Lenin spoke in support of a decree which conferred on the voters in the election to the Assembly the right of recalling delegates and replacing them, arguing that this would ensure the peaceful transfer of power from one party to another. All this was very different from what Lenin was saying in private, according to several accounts.

The Bolsheviks could hope for a substantial vote in Petrograd and in the parts of the army in the field which were heavily under their influence, such as the Northern and Western Fronts. The Mensheviks and Kadets, as they realized themselves, had lost so much influence as a result of Bolshevik propaganda, and particularly through the decrees on peace and on land, that their overall chances in the election were very slender. The victors were certain to be the Socialist Revolutionaries, the traditional party which the peasants knew and which they accepted, without much understanding of political issues, as the party that for years had promised them land. The pro-Bolshevik LSRs were not likely to affect the issue — in spite of Lenin's subsequent argument that the date of the election had not provided time for the new party to present itself to the electors. The evidence suggests that even where the left wing was able to put forward its own list of candidates, it did not achieve success against the traditional party.

At one time, Lenin considered postponing the election, but was dissuaded on the grounds that the Bolsheviks were still too weak to flout the popular mood. Hints of force were heard in Bolshevik speeches as the election approached — on 8 November, one of the leaders of the Petersburg Committee spoke of the possibility of a 'third revolution' if the Assembly should prove to have an anti-

Bolshevik majority — but the elections went ahead without the Bolsheviks being able to do very much about rigging the results. Professor Radkey, in his survey of the evidence on the voting, concluded that 'although a good many voters were subjected to intimidation in one form or another, the vast majority of the electorate freely exercised the right of suffrage .... It was far from being a model election; but it certainly was not a farce.'

Forty-one million votes were recorded, of which the Bolsheviks polled under one quarter. There were two million votes for the Kadets, two million unclassified and some seven and a half million for national minority parties. The remainder — over twenty million in all — went to socialists of all kinds, the Socialist Revolutionaries securing over fifteen million. Thus, three-quarters of the country did not vote for the Bolsheviks, and half the country voted for socialism and against Bolshevism. Of the 707 delegates elected, 175 were Bolsheviks, 370 Socialist Revolutionaries, 40 LSRs, 16 Mensheviks and 17 Kadets. The Bolsheviks had a majority in the industrial centres, and polled about half the votes in the army — significantly, as Lenin noted some years later, in the units which were closest to the two capital cities on the Northern and Western Fronts. The Socialist Revolutionaries had a slight majority on the South-Western Front, and overwhelming majorities on the Roumanian and Caucasian Fronts. The Bolsheviks were supported by some of the peasants in uniform, but not by those in the villages. The overwhelmingly anti-Bolshevik composition of the Assembly was already evident by the beginning of December.

When the sad remnants of the Provisional Government issued, from their hiding place, a summons for the Constituent Assembly to meet on the appointed day of 28 November, the Bolsheviks responded with an all-out attack on the Kadet Party and by closing down newspapers which had published the appeal. On 28 November, a decree of *Sovnarkom* ordered the arrest and trial of all leading Kadets, 'being the party of the people's enemies', and enjoined special vigilance over the party as a whole. This proved a signal for action against Kadets in many cities. In Petrograd, a number of leading Kadets were arrested when they attempted to take their seats in the Constituent Assembly on the day fixed for its opening by the underground Provisional Government, namely 28 November. Two Kadet ministers under arrest in hospital were lynched on the day of the opening of the Constituent Assembly. An enquiry ordered by Lenin established that the guilt for the murder lay with certain sailors of the Baltic fleet, but no further steps were taken. On 23 November, the members of the All-Russian Commission for Elections to the Constituent Assembly, both Kadet and SR, had been arrested.

An attempt at a show trial of Countess Panina in the new Military Revolutionary Court badly misfired. The Countess, a prominent Kadet, had long been famous for her benevolent work for the poor of Petersburg, and her trial (for withholding 93,000 roubles in the Ministry of Education, on the grounds that the Bolsheviks were usurpers) outraged the Petrograd workers, who held meetings and flooded *Sovnarkom* and the MRC with demands for her release. She was convicted, but freed soon afterwards.

There were still a number of leaders within the Bolshevik party who retained something of their social democratic traditions and were troubled by the idea of forcibly dispersing a freely elected popular body, on which the hopes of all revolutionaries had centred for generations. There were signs of what Lenin described as 'constitutional illusions' in the bureau* of the Bolshevik 'fraction' of the Constituent Assembly which, curiously enough in view of his past 'hard' record, were shared by Stalin. Lenin had even less difficulty in dealing with these rebels than he had had at the beginning of November with the Central Committee dissidents. The bureau was, on Lenin's proposal, dissolved on 11 December, and his 'Theses on the Constituent Assembly' were unanimously adopted by the 'fraction' a few days later. These did not expressly threaten armed dispersal of the Assembly, but did assert that 'any attempt to . . . consider the question of the Constituent Assembly from a formal, legalistic point of view . . . is a betrayal of the cause of the proletariat.' At the same time, a garrison meeting adopted a resolution that the slogan 'All Power to the Constituent Assembly' was counter-revolutionary. Some of the LSRs were also uneasy about the betrayal of the age-old party ideal, but they drew comfort from persuading themselves, as one of their leaders put it, that there had never been anything finer than the soviets, and one must therefore not flinch from dispersing the Assembly.

The Assembly opened in Petrograd on 5 January 1918. The Bolsheviks had prepared for it a long 'Declaration of the Rights of the Toiling and Exploited Peoples', embodying the legislation of the Congress of Soviets on land, peace and workers' control of industry. The point of this Declaration lay in the statement that the Assembly 'admits that it has no powers beyond working out some of the fundamental problems of reorganizing society on a socialistic basis'. By a vote of 237 to 146 the Assembly rejected this act of abdication of power, whereupon the Bolsheviks withdrew, followed by the LSR.

In the Council of People's Commissars the Bolsheviks argued for the immediate dissolution of the Assembly, while the LSR members urged that either there should be new elections or a revolutionary

*The bureau, elected on 2 December, was a steering committee of the fraction.

convention should be formed consisting of the left-wing elements in the Assembly. However, in the Central Executive Committee, to which the question was referred, the only opposition to the Bolsheviks' proposal came from a small group of Menshevik Internationalists who had joined the Central Executive Committee after the Bolshevik coalition with the LSR. When one of them courageously denounced 'socialist banners reddened with proletarian blood' — a reference to the dispersal by the Red Guard of a worker demonstration on 5 January, which resulted in nine dead and twenty-two wounded — he was shouted down. Only two Bolsheviks voted against the resolution. On 6 January, the Red Guards refused to admit the delegates to the adjourned session of the Assembly (which had spent the rest of the previous day debating the future of Russia) and the meeting did not take place.

It was the end of the Constituent Assembly. Its dispersal caused little stir in the country and was reported to have been treated with indifference in the army. The Socialist Revolutionaries had resolved, shortly after the Bolshevik seizure of power, to defend the Constituent Assembly with all the force they could muster. When the time came, two guards regiments were prepared to join a demonstration in support of the Assembly, on condition that they could parade with arms. Two guards regiments might have been a formidable counterpart to the forces available to the Bolsheviks, but the Socialist Revolutionary Central Committee refused to accept their condition. In the result, a second unarmed worker demonstration was fired on by the Red Guards, causing a hundred casualties.

Events had moved fast since 25 October. In the eyes of a population of which only a small minority understood the meaning of democratic government, the popular decrees on land and peace had already pre-empted the Constituent Assembly. At the Third Soviet Congress, which met soon after the Constituent Assembly, 'to pass sentence' on it, as Zinoviev expressed it, the Bolsheviks and LSRs had secured an overwhelming majority. Over half of the soviets which sent delegates had been re-elected in November or December, and all but ten had ousted 'kulaks', 'officers' and 'bourgeois elements' as a preliminary to the elections. Out of 419 delegates, 377 voted their approval of the Bolshevik and LSR withdrawal from the Assembly. The choice for both the liberals and the socialists now lay between acquiescence in Bolshevik rule, with minimal prospects of constitutional opposition, and civil war.

Chapter Ten

The Bolshevik Take-Over Outside the Capital

The full story of the Bolshevik take-over in provincial Russia has not been told.* Without access to local archives, information has to be sought in the press, in memoirs, and in the documents published in the Soviet Union. But the latter are for the most part selective and geared to portray the 'triumphant march of Bolshevism', which is very different from what happened. (An exception is offered by the well-edited minutes of the Petrograd Military Revolutionary Committee; and recently some scholarly Soviet monographs have also appeared.) In many cases, information is lacking on such essential questions as the extent of Bolshevik control before October, the break-down of the population, the disposition of military forces, the stocks of food available, and the like. The sketch that follows will deal with the urban soviets by regions, with the military forces, Moscow, the peasants, and some of the main national areas.

In general, the Bolsheviks eventually assumed power by putting the local soviet in control, but in the process the soviets were transformed. The balance of influence within them shifted from the full meeting to the small executive; parties other than the Bolsheviks and (initially) the LSR were for the most part expelled; and local soviets were subjected to increasing central and regional control. In some cases, the Bolsheviks enjoyed extensive local support, which often increased as the land and peace decrees of the Congress of Soviets became known. Where they did, and where re-election of a non-Bolshevik soviet was not likely to produce a Bolshevik majority, they had resort to force in the shape of the Red Guards or of neighbouring pro-Bolshevik troops. Considerable tactical skill was shown in such manoeuvres as releasing arrested Bolsheviks in time to swell the vote; ensuring open voting at any congresses, and threatening to publish the names of those who did not vote for the Bolsheviks, thus exposing them to violence from pro-Bolshevik

---

*Admirable pioneering work has, however, been done by Professor John Keep in his recent book *The Russian Revolution* and some research is being conducted under the direction of Professor Alexander Rabinowitch.

soldiers; or amalgamating worker and soldier soviets where this was likely to increase the pro-Bolshevik majority, as was usually the case.

Although there was a great variety of patterns from place to place, there were certain features which recurred frequently. The socialists, when defeated in the re-elections to the soviet, usually did not stay on to fight but abandoned the field by walking out. Where force was used to disband the socialist opposition, it was often met by loyalist forces, usually of officers and of officer cadets, with resulting casualties. In the autumn of 1917, many Bolsheviks still understood 'soviet' power to mean a coalition of all socialists opposed to the Provisional Government and were willing to collaborate and compromise. This policy was deeply resented by the fanatics in the party, whether from the centre or local, who stood for uncompromising war on the socialists and encouraged cruelty and excesses. Before long, they had set the tone for Bolshevik rule throughout provincial Russia. There is ample evidence of the important support provided to the Bolsheviks by the LSR.

The Bolsheviks in the cities were organized in nearly three hundred town committees — some substantial, some quite small. Forty of them had separate military committees. At a lower level, the Bolsheviks were enrolled in the largely anarchic factory committees and the Red Guards (the latter are discussed later in the chapter). In some soviets, the Bolsheviks had won a majority before October — mostly after the Kornilov débâcle — but even when they were in the minority, their greater discipline gave them an advantage. There is no evidence that any rising throughout the country was planned or organized from the centre, though the impetus to a Bolshevik take-over was usually given by the news from Petrograd, and there were many cases where emissaries were sent out from the capital. The haphazard way in which the Bolsheviks came to power in the provinces suggests that there, as in the capital, it was not so much that the Bolsheviks won as that the Provisional Government and the socialists lost. If the government had taken some measures to defend the cities, and if the socialist Central Executive Committee of the Soviets had taken effective steps to offer support to the anti-Bolshevik socialists in soviets throughout the country, a Bolshevik victory might not have been so easy.

Professor Keep discerns three main patterns of take-over — though there were, of course, many variants. If the Bolsheviks already controlled the soviet, they set up a revolutionary committee (MRC) which, with the help of the Red Guards, would assume power. The socialists would be expelled or, more usually, would walk out. If the soviet was in the hands of moderates, then the revolutionary committee would be formed with the support of rank and file

Bolsheviks and would demand a re-election of the soviet. Where the socialists were more resolute, they would form a committee of public safety to resist the Bolsheviks, and conflict would ensue. In the third type of case, where the local Bolsheviks were of a moderate disposition and willing to collaborate with the public safety committee, external pressure from extremists would be applied. With the aid of such revolutionary committees, set up to counteract non-Bolshevik soviets, often in conjunction with pro-Bolshevik soldiers in the local garrison, power was seized in the course of three and a half months in 263 centres, according to a recent Soviet source.

In the north-western region, in close proximity to the Northern Front, the Bolsheviks found a ready response. The soldiers were largely pro-Bolshevik, and the commanders were above all anxious that their troops should not be dragged into civil war, thus exposing the front. Further from the front line there was some opposition. In Novgorod, for example, conflict arose between the neutral executive committee of the soviet and the Bolshevik and LSR MRC. The MRC eventually won by force.

In the central industrial region the transfer of power was generally smooth. The Bolsheviks had made substantial headway before October — in Ivanovo-Voznesensk, for instance, the centre of the textile industry, they already had an 82 per cent majority in August. In Kineshma, for once, the moderates did not walk out, and for a time, until the Bolsheviks used force, there was a joint socialist-Bolshevik government.

In the Urals, the Bolsheviks had a majority in most of the soviets, but a number of towns stood out for some time. In Ekaterinburg (now Sverdlovsk), the Bolsheviks controlled the soviet, but agreed to a coalition régime. They were in a minority for a month until incited to turn on the socialists by a senior emissary from the centre. In Perm', where the Bolsheviks controlled the city government (the municipal duma) and the Mensheviks the soviet, the local Bolsheviks were also in favour of coalition, but were eventually overridden by 'hard' Bolsheviks. In Zlatoust, the moderates managed to hold out until 18 March 1918, when they were overpowered by military force.

The pattern varied in the cities on the Volga. In Kazan', the Bolsheviks took over with the aid of the garrison. In Nizhnii Novgorod, the moderates set up a strong salvation committee, but walked out in protest after a rigged re-election of the soviet. The municipal duma kept up resistance to the soviet until the end of January 1918. In Samara, even though the Bolsheviks were the strongest force in the soviet, the deputies had to be swamped with factory committee members before they would elect a revolutionary committee and vote support for Petrograd. For a time, the garrison was able to insist on the inclusion of Bolsheviks on the revolutionary committee. In Saratov, after the soviet had been packed with trade union and factory committee members, the moderates walked out, and there were clashes with some casualties. The victory of the Bolsheviks was due, as in many places elsewhere, to the dominant position which the local soviet had acquired and to the fact that a demand for soviet power was identified with a call for an all-socialist government without 'bourgeois' participation.* In practice, where revolutionary committees were set up, the Bolsheviks predominated over the LSRs by as many as five to one.

In the central agricultural region, to quote Professor Keep, 'the general picture is one of the Bolsheviks and their allies relying on the garrisons and segments of the civilian force sympathetic to their cause, building up their strength until they could overawe the soviets and the mixed committees they set up.' Some of these soviets 'were unreliable instruments, likely at any moment to surrender to the "petty-bourgeois vacillations" characteristic of the peasantry and those who spoke in their name.'

In Siberia, where there were no landlords and there was no land-hunger, the main advantage which the Bolsheviks usually enjoyed was absent, and they did not achieve power until the spring of 1918. There was armed resistance by officer cadets in Irkutsk. In Blagoveshchensk, in the Far East, cadets actually overthrew the Bolshevik-controlled soviet. The Bolsheviks regained control with the help of troops, and there were a thousand casualties. In general it may be observed that two factors facilitated the ultimate triumph of the Bolshevik-controlled MRCs. One was the usual practice of the socialist portion of a soviet to walk out and abandon contest when defeated in re-elections. The other was the fact that the Provisional Government had failed to organize an effective system of administration in the provinces.

The Bolshevik victory in Moscow took more time than in Petrograd. We owe our knowledge of events there to the historian S. Mel'gunov, a moderate socialist eye-witness, who laboured (in Russian) to disentangle truth from fiction in available accounts. It is clear that no preparation for the Moscow take-over was made in Petrograd: the decision by the Moscow Soviet, which had a Bolshevik majority, to set up an MRC for the seizure of power was only taken on 25 October, after receiving news of events in Petrograd. Unlike its Petrograd prototype, the Moscow MRC was not a homogeneously radical body: it included three out of seven members who remained

---

*The case of Saratov has been examined by Professor Donald J. Raleigh in a most illuminating forthcoming study, which I have had the privilege of reading.

on it with the express intention of minimizing the consequences of a Bolshevik adventure.

Although the fighting, in which there may have been as many as a thousand casualties, lasted until 3 November, there was little stomach for it on either side. The Socialist Revolutionary Committee of Public Salvation was, above all, anxious to prevent bloodshed. It was, moreover, convinced that the Bolsheviks had no chance of surviving in power, and at no stage showed any determination to overthrow them. It was also inhibited throughout by fear that civil conflict would play into the hands of counter-revolution, and placed all its hopes on the Constituent Assembly. The MRC in turn was anxious to compromise, and was only driven into battle by pressure from extremists in the suburban party organizations. The capitulation by the socialists was due in part to their loss of morale, and in part to the fact that the military forces of the commander of the city, which consisted mainly of officers and officer cadets, had virtually run out of ammunition. They were also heavily out-numbered. The majority of the 15,000 officers in the city remained neutral. The MRC, in addition to the Red Guard and other armed workers, had artillery at its disposal and was reinforced by the arrival of sailors and Red Guards from Petrograd. The terms of surrender agreed on 2 November were generous with respect to the treatment of the cadets and other combatants, but they were not, in the event, observed by the Bolsheviks, who were under pressure from extremists.

It soon became clear that the soviet power established by the Bolsheviks in the provinces was, like that which emerged in the capital, little more than a cloak for Communist Party rule. (The Bolsheviks called themselves 'Communists' after their Seventh Congress in March 1918.) From the start, the Communists proved masters at manipulating elections to the soviets in such a way as to ensure substantial majorities for themselves. The date of balloting would be announced at the last minute, so as to give their opponents no time for preparation. Hostile deputies would be recalled, or their candidature prevented, since the soviets were being constantly warned not to allow 'enemies of the soviet régime' to gain influence inside them. The election of any candidate could, moreover, be annulled by the next higher soviet. Voting was invariably by show of hands, and in the presence of Communist officials. Soviets could also be swamped with sympathizers from the trade unions or the Red Army. Besides, the composition of the soviet as a whole mattered increasingly less as effective power passed to its executive committee. By 1918 these executive committees were already over 83 per cent Communist in the provincial soviets.

This ascendancy of the party in the soviets was never denied, but rather theoretically justified by the Communist leaders. In 1920, Zinoviev stressed that 'without the iron dictatorship of the party' soviet power would not have lasted three weeks, let alone three years. In 1923, Trotsky, answering the charge that the Communists had set up the dictatorship of the party in place of the dictatorship of the soviets, claimed that the party had given the soviets the opportunity to transform themselves 'from shapeless parliaments of labour into an apparatus for the domination of labour'. He failed to point out that the 'shapeless parliaments' which had thus been transformed had once been genuine, self-governing worker organizations. Lenin was never tired of stressing that soviet power was a 'million' times more democratic than the bourgeois democratic system, because it enabled the working masses to 'participate in the management of the worker and peasant state'. But, as Trotsky pointed out in 1923, the soviets did not exist in order to 'mirror the majority statically', but in order to 'build it dynamically'. This was the task of the party. As the Eighth Congress of the party resolved in March 1919: 'The Communist Party makes a special effort to put into effect its Programme and unrestricted leadership in the state institutions of today, the soviets . . . . The Russian Communist Party must win for itself, through practical, daily selfless work in the soviets and through the occupation of all soviet posts with its best and most loyal members, undivided domination in the soviets, and the practical control over their entire work.'

However, not a word of all this appeared in the Constitution of the RSFSR (the Russian Soviet Federal Socialist Republic) which was adopted by a congress of soviets on 10 July 1918, and the Communist Party was not mentioned in it. The aim of the constitution was to provide a permanent framework of government to take the place of the new system which the defunct Constituent Assembly had been originally intended to supply. The constitution purported to vest plenary power in the soviets, as embodied in an All-Russian Congress, and in a Central Executive Committee between congresses. But it left the powers of *Sovnarkom*, which had already become the real power, in the state vague in relation to the soviets. The dictatorship of the proletariat and the poorer peasantry was stated to be temporary, but while it lasted certain restrictions were to apply: the franchise was weighted in favour of the cities and against the villages; and certain groups, such as priests, merchants, employers of labour or those living on unearned income, were denied the vote altogether.

At the outset, in October 1917, the Bolsheviks were faced with the fact that, in the armed forces at the front, the great majority of the unit and formation committees, especially at the higher levels, were socialist in composition. This presented a potential danger to the kind of power that Lenin contemplated, one that left no room for the participation in government of the two main socialist parties. It was therefore essential to mobilize, as soon as possible, the rank and file support which was expected to be generated by the decrees on land and on peace. It is difficult to get a clear picture of the mood of the soldiers in the field when the news of events in Petrograd reached them. To many, certainly, the decrees meant that the war was over and that what mattered was to get back to the villages to see about the allocation of land. Desertion increased, the bands of marauders which roamed the country swelled. Hundreds, if not thousands, of soldiers' delegations were despatched to the capital to ascertain the latest news.

Nevertheless, a recent study of soldiers' letters and other material in Soviet archives suggests that there may have been some more sophisticated political attitudes at the front than is commonly believed. For one thing, there was a very widespread view that what had happened was only the first step, and that it was essential for the Constituent Assembly to meet as soon as possible to ensure distribution of the landlords' land and to make certain that peace would really be concluded. Among the delegates from the front there were many who voiced a demand for an all-socialist government which mirrored the multi-party pattern of the soviets. There was frequent condemnation of any policy leading to civil war. Both openly anti-Bolshevik and fully pro-Bolshevik sentiments were expressed, and demands were voiced for improvement of material conditions.

Bolshevik efforts to neutralize the potentially hostile committees and officers were made immediately — in some instances even before 25 October. Hundreds of emissaries were sent off to the front, either as commissars with authority from the MRC, or with instructions to set up local military revolutionary committees. The aim in both cases was to ensure, as soon as possible, the election of new, pro-Bolshevik committees, and to elect new officers. The success of the operation varied from front to front. On the Caucasian front, for example, the Bolsheviks had not succeeded in establishing control by the time of its collapse in 1918. On the Roumanian and South-Western Fronts, the situation was complicated by the existence of the Ukrainian Rada as a political influence. On the former front, the Bolsheviks, who were not numerous, made comparatively little headway, in spite of support in some units for their peace policy: the prevalent mood was against them and all hopes were placed on the Constituent Assembly. When the Bolsheviks tried to achieve control by setting up pro-Bolshevik committees by force, their efforts were frustrated by the determined action of the Commander in Chief, on whose life an unsuccessful attempt had been made.

But success was achieved on the two fronts which were the most important because of their proximity to the capital — the Northern and the Western. There was some difficulty at first in securing control on the Northern Front, which was reported to be equally divided for and against the Bolsheviks; but their victory was never in doubt, according to reports from the front, since the issue of peace proved the decisive one within a matter of weeks. On the Western Front, victory over the socialists was swift. The Bolsheviks could rely on the support of the great majority of the garrisons. They were also able to swell the ranks of their supporters at army conferences and meetings by releasing the soldiers who had been imprisoned in the last months of the Provisional Government for refusal to obey orders and other breaches of military discipline.

The Bolsheviks could often not rely on more than the neutrality of the garrison troops, and the importance of the Red Guard in helping them to achieve victory in the capital and in the provinces will have to be noted. This force, formed by the Bolsheviks in the factories, had been authorized by the Provisional Government when it had been thrown into a panic by the Kornilov affair. The effect of this, though probably not intended, was to provide the Bolsheviks with a private army. They had, in fact, set up the Red Guard long before it had been legitimized, ostensibly for the purpose of defending the factories — according to German information it numbered twenty-five thousand by May 1917. From the Bolshevik point of view, the Red Guards offered the further advantage of helping to disrupt industry, since the factory owners were obliged to provide their wages. Apart from this, they were valuable as a means of terrorizing the industrialists into making concessions, which they could not afford — thus contributing to the economic ruination of the country. The Provisional Government did not even heed the warning of the July Days, when the Red Guards were used as an insurgent force. Intense efforts to seize weapons, indeed whole arsenals, were successfully made by the Bolsheviks in the weeks preceding 25 October. By the time the capture of power was effected, the Red Guards were numbered in thousands in many areas throughout the country. Although the exact figures cannot be known, their strength in the capital has been estimated at between 32,000 and 40,000, and in Moscow at 30,000.

One of the peculiarities of Russia in 1917 was the existence in some places of Bolshevik or extreme radical 'islands', in which the writ of the Provisional Government either did not run, or was only partially effective. Here, Bolshevik assumption of power in October presented little difficulty. Two examples may be mentioned. In Tsaritsyn on the Volga, two factors contributed to radical sentiment: a large industrial working population which faced increasing hardships, and a sizeable garrison with strong anti-war sentiments, particularly among the substantial proportion of wounded evacuated from the front who were anxious not to be sent back. Growing radicalism among the soldiers and workers, and the lynching of an officer at a Bolshevik-sponsored demonstration on 22 May, led to demands for action to suppress extremism in the city. A military detachment was despatched from Kazan', but the excessive measures taken by its commander drove the socialists into union with the Bolsheviks, and the alliance was further cemented by fears of counter-revolution, engendered during the days of the Kornilov affair. When the detachment was eventually recalled, power fell into Bolshevik hands, many weeks before their victory in Petrograd.

The naval base of Kronstadt, situated on an island in the Finnish Gulf about twenty miles from Petrograd, had had a strong revolutionary tradition before 1917. The fall of the monarchy in 1917 was accompanied by savage excesses, in which fifty-one officers were murdered and some two hundred and eighty imprisoned without trial in conditions of hardship. (The Provisional Government, after much effort, succeeded in securing their transfer to Petrograd for trial.) From the start, Kronstadt claimed to put into effect soviet power, and was able to assert against both the Provisional Government and the Petrograd Soviet the independent authority of its own local soviet — in spite of occasional face-saving compromises. Its socialist enemies, not inappropriately, branded the naval base as the 'Kronstadt Republic'. The Bolsheviks did not have a majority on this soviet, which for the most part was run by a coalition between the Socialist Revolutionaries and a small left-wing party known as the Maximalists, though the Socialist Revolutionaries approximated more to the LSR than to the party of Chernov.

A particular feature of political life in Kronstadt was the daily popular meeting in Anchor Square, which seemed to dominate the soviet in what became a rough form of direct democracy. From the start, by a large majority of its soviet, and certainly in Anchor Square, Kronstadt repudiated the entry, after May 1917, of the Petrograd socialist leaders into the Provisional Government. The sailors regarded themselves as the vanguard of soviet democracy, and as the model for what they believed should apply in the whole of Russia.

The sailors were always available whenever force was needed to bolster an attempt to instal soviet power. They were resolutely behind the insurrection at the beginning of July 1917, and may have played a part in forcing the Bolshevik Central Committee into trying to lead it. Their rôle in consolidating Bolshevik power in October and November 1917 may well have been decisive. There was uneasiness in Kronstadt that the rising in October had resulted in Bolshevik power and not in the kind of soviet power the sailors stood for, but the position was accepted by the great majority in the local soviet. At first, the Bolshevik victory made little difference in Kronstadt, and it was not until June 1918 that the Communists (as they had become) achieved a majority in the soviet. The communist system was eventually fully installed. The soviet then became a façade for central party decisions, the Anchor Square meetings were abolished, except for well-organized special occasions, the authority of commissars replaced the committee system, and officers were nominated without regard to the wishes of the rank and file. The revolt of the crew of the *Petropavlovsk* on 28 February 1921 (considered in Chapter 12) showed that the old libertarian spirit had not been killed.*

In the face of the peasant longing for land as the prize of 'soviet power' Lenin had taken over the LSR agrarian programme as the basis for the Decree on Land adopted by the Second Congress. This abolished the landowners' property without compensation, and placed their estates at the disposal of land committees and peasant soviets until the Constituent Assembly met. This was merely a tactical move, however. In theory and in practice the Bolsheviks were opposed to an agriculture based on proprietory small-holdings. They looked to class war in the villages for their future policy, and hoped by that means to mobilize the landless for a crusade against the better-off peasants in alliance with, and for the ultimate benefit of, the proletariat. (No doubt this is what Lenin meant when he told his wife that 'we must find a little handle which will enable us to sew up in our own fashion the populist idea of socialization.') The LSR, on the other hand, were genuine, populist egalitarians, they had some support among the better-off peasants, and their view corresponded much more to the realities of village aspirations.

When, in 1918, redistribution of land took place, the Bolsheviks were little able to affect it, and the principle discernible in the rough and ready operation was that of egalitarianism. Of course, socialists of all kinds had for centuries kept up the myth that if once the land were taken from the landlords and divided up there would be abundance for all. Precise calculations are difficult, since conditions

*Tsaritsyn and Kronstadt have been studied respectively by Professor Donald J. Raleigh of the University of Hawaii (in the *Slavic Review*, No 2, 1981) and Professor Israel Getzler of the Hebrew University, Jerusalem (in his recent book, *Kronstadt, 1917-1921*).

varied across the country, but data for twenty-nine provinces show an average increase per person of 0.39 *dessiatines*, or 1 to 1.5 per household (a *dessiatine* is equivalent to 2.7 acres, or 1.09 hectares). One marked effect of the repartition of land was the strengthening of the traditional village commune, which was to remain the principal peasant organization until collectivization in 1929.

Bolshevik policy of a centralized economy alone was bound, sooner or later, to lead to conflict with the peasant small-holders. As it was, the clash was accelerated by the acute food crisis, which the Bolsheviks inherited. They had formulated no policy, beyond slogans, to deal with it. The failure of other methods to produce more than very modest results strengthened the voices of those, notably Lenin, who had urged compulsion from the start. This led to the setting up of the 'committees of the poor', organized in the villages by emissaries from the towns, who stimulated class war and practised what was in effect ruthless expropriation of produce. (They were allowed to retain a proportion of the requisitioned food as an incentive.) The methods seem to have been successful for a time in procuring surplus grain: the ultimate price paid was the antagonism between the towns and the villages which was to perturb Lenin so much in 1922-23 (see Chapter 13). The policy of instigating bitter class war in the villages also helped to aggravate the breach between the LSR and the Communists.

But in 1917 harmony between the two factions was still high. On 10 November, the long awaited Second All-Russian Congress of peasant deputies met in Petrograd. It was about equally divided between the Bolsheviks and their new LSR allies, and the traditional Socialist Revolutionary party, led by Chernov. The LSR leader was a firebrand ex-terrorist, Maria Spiridonova, who enjoyed great popularity. The main support for the LSR came from the soldier deputies (1 for 20,000); the peasant deputies (1 for 150,000) had been comparatively little affected by the war and stayed with their traditional SR champions. The open conflict between the rival groups resulted in virtual pandemonium. In the end the congress split up and the two groups met separately. Soon afterwards the Bolsheviks and their allies forcibly evicted the SRs from the premises in which they had ensconced themselves. A new Executive Committee was elected by the left wing alone, and this ostensibly 'peasant', but in reality 'soldier', body merged with the existing Central Executive Committee of Workers' and Soldiers' Deputies of the Soviets.

The losers in this unedifying battle were the peasants, whose champions were divested of their right to speak for them. Notionally the LSR acquired this right from the moderate SR; in practice the LSR were to prove powerless to resist the Bolsheviks in the months to come, where the interests of the peasants demanded it, though, while they were able to do so, they battled as well as they could in a position that more experienced politicians would have recognized as hopeless from the start. In 1917 the LSR betrayed the Socialist Revolutionary party of which they were still members, but they did so in the full conviction that its leaders were contaminated with counter-revolution by their participation in the Provisional Government coalition and by their efforts to resist the Bolshevik seizure of power. In November 1917, with signs apparent of the forthcoming SR victory in elections to the Constituent Assembly, the LSR believed that by siding with the Bolsheviks, and thereby sacrificing the Constituent Assembly, they were serving the cause of democracy and exalting the rôle of the soviets. Presumably they did not, according to their own lights, betray the peasants, though this was the result.

Before long, Bolshevik subjugation of the villages began. The setting up of the 'committees of the poor' was an important phase, but the Bolsheviks also set out to devise means of weaning the peasants from Socialist Revolutionary control. The historian of the Socialist Revolutionaries, Professor Radkey, has shown in a detailed study based on Soviet sources how the peasant soviets were Bolshevized during the last months of 1917 in three major areas: White Russia, the central industrial region around Moscow, and even in the traditional Socialist Revolutionary stronghold, the 'black earth' and Volga regions. Re-election of soviets and fusion of peasant with worker and soldier soviets, in some cases with the aid of naked force, was the method normally used. The soldiers everywhere, desperate for peace and convinced that only the Bolsheviks would bring it to them, played a big part.

But in 1918 rural soviets were generally a weak reed to rely on: they had little authority in the villages. The Bolsheviks therefore sought to rely on methods which were more in accord with their traditional style. Fusion of rural and urban soviets was one device, but other ways of control from the centre were improvised and new, more amenable organs created at the local level. One of the main means of gaining control was by the despatch of 'commissars', or of humbler 'instructors' or 'agitators' — many of them demobilized soldiers returning to their villages. (The overall total of these emissaries has been put at 47,530.) These soldiers were carefully instructed in the art of Bolshevizing their villages on return. Their influence was certainly considerable, but their primitive approach often antagonized the peasants who, at any rate before the 'committees of the poor' had emerged, were inclined to favour the Bolsheviks, who sanctioned their seizures of the land. In addition to the rough and ready committees, the communists had laid the foundations of a mechanism of control in the villages by the end of 1918. With 97,000 rural cadres grouped in 7,370 organizations, a good start had been made. In the rural soviet executive committees, Communists (and a few sympathizers) predominated. These rural Communists had more in common with the officials at the centre than with the peasants from whose midst they had sprung. Their administration was a far cry from the kind of peasant self-government that the LSR once persuaded themselves they were helping to institute.

The extension of Bolshevik power in the provinces after October 1917 was considerably complicated in those areas of Russia inhabited by non-Russians. Russian marxists had been much preoccupied over the question of the policy that should be pursued, after the overthrow of the monarchy, towards minorities of non-Russian nationality. Orthodoxy demanded that class should prevail over nationalities — marxists should not pander to what would, under socialism, become a relic of the past. Lenin, for whom questions of doctrine were always subordinated to the interests of the revolution, realized very early (certainly by 1913) that nationalism would prove too valuable a disruptive force in the Russian empire for the Bolsheviks to reject it. In the teeth of opposition from his more doctrinaire colleagues, he insisted on the right of full political self-determination for any minority in the Empire that desired it. He also rejected any form of autonomy within a federal structure, which was what the minorities mostly wanted, offering them instead (or appearing to offer them) a more extreme form of independence which they were not demanding and which in most cases was inappropriate to their needs. The offer of 'free self-determination, up to and including separation from Russia and the formation of independent states' was published by the new government on 2 November. But the matter was not so simple. Even before the revolution, Lenin made it clear that, while separation was to be offered, that did not mean it would be encouraged, and in the long run it was only a stage towards 'a rapprochement, even a merging of nations, but on a truly democratic basis . . . which is unthinkable without the freedom of secession'.

Lenin's doctrine was of value in helping on the disintegration of Russia in 1917. By 1918, with the outbreak of the civil war, many important minority areas were outside the jurisdiction of the new régime. Their reintegration into Russia only became a real consideration after victory in the civil war in 1920, and by then Lenin's ingenious mind had discovered a way of offering self-determination and at the same time refusing it. This took place in March 1919 when the Eighth Party Congress debated and adopted the party programme. The formulation agreed left it open to the Communists to use promises of independence to attract the sympathies of the population in areas where they were still trying to come to power; but it did not impede their efforts to overcome nationalist opposition where they were already in control. It also provided them with theoretical justification for reincorporating any territory lost during the Civil War on the strength of a decision by the local Communist party, however small and unpopular it might be. The programme proclaimed the right to political secession of all nations, but 'as to the question who is the bearer of the nation's will to separate', the Communist party would have to take into consideration 'the level of historical development on which a given nation stands'. In other words, where a nation was deemed backward, its 'vanguard' would decide for it. A 'federalist unification of states', such as the one adopted in 1918 by the Constitution of the RSFSR, was proposed 'as one of the transitional forms on the way to full unity'. In July 1920, at the Second Congress of the *Comintern*, Lenin explained that 'backward peoples' in general could progress to socialism without going through the capitalist phase, given 'systematic propaganda' by 'the victorious proletariat', and aid from the Soviet government. This was the method used by the Soviet government among its own 'backward' minority peoples.

In many of the areas where minority nations lived, developments became interwoven with the last phase of the war with the Central Powers and with the civil war, and will be looked at in the next chapter. Here, we shall look briefly at the immediate impact of the October take-over in some of the major non-Russian territories.

When the end of the Provisional Government was imminent, its relations with the growing nationalist forces in the Ukraine were near to breaking point (as was related in Chapter 4). This led to a rapprochement between the Rada and the Bolsheviks, and for a time uneasy power-sharing prevailed, with the Rada and the secretariat ruling Kiev and some of the countryside west of the Dnieper, and Bolshevik-dominated soviets ruling the other towns. Conflict soon broke out: the Rada, which on 6 November proclaimed the Ukraine a People's Republic and a component part of the Russian federation, refused to convene an All-Ukrainian Congress of Soviets, as the Bolsheviks wished, for fear that it would be dominated by the city soviets. The Rada now tried to work for a moderate socialist Russian government, which would lead to a federal union with an autonomous Ukraine. It won the support of several cities, but not Kharkov, which became the centre of Bolshevik power in the Ukraine, and where the Bolsheviks (unlike those in Kiev) were extremely hostile to the Rada.

Relations between Petrograd and Kiev, good at first, worsened towards the end of November. *Sovnarkom* was mainly concerned with Ukrainian activities at the front — both the encouragement of the movement of Ukrainian units and formations to the Ukraine, and the Rada's relations with a potential counter-revolutionary force, the Don Cossacks, led by Ataman Kaledin. The Rada in turn took repressive measures against the Bolsheviks in Kiev, suspecting them of plotting a coup. In spite of this, hostilities did not break out until 5 January 1918, when a force directed from Kharkov, consisting of pro-Bolshevik Ukrainian troops and reinforcements from the north went into the attack. These men, commanded by a maniacal sadist, wrought havoc in the cities which they captured, and entered Kiev on 26 January. The new government rested on bayonets, with no popular support. The situation was further complicated by bitter hostility between the Kharkov and the Kiev Bolsheviks, which reached the stage of two separate Bolshevik Ukraines being proclaimed. The question was temporarily resolved when the Germans, at the request of the Rada, occupied the Ukraine, and the Bolsheviks had to flee for safety.

Another important non-Russian area, the muslim borderlands, remained largely cut off from the new soviet government until 1919, but Bolshevik policy was formed during this period of isolation. Sensitivity towards Islamic people was a central issue for Lenin and played a major rôle in converting him to support for self-determination, because of the importance he attributed to national movements among colonial peoples generally. Greater efforts were therefore made to win support for the Bolsheviks among muslims than elsewhere in the former empire, while at the same time insisting on political subordination to Moscow. The Bolsheviks failed in 1917 to win the support of the Muslim Constituent Assembly and Executive Council which had come into existence. Stalin, as People's Commissar for Nationalities, did however succeed in setting up a pro-Bolshevik Muslim Committee, which soon lost all traces of independence.

In the Volga-Ural region, the Bashkirs, who had sided with the Whites, were induced by promises of independence to come over to the Communist side. The failure to honour the undertaking led to a Bashkir rebellion in 1920, and military conquest of the country. A Tatar republic came into being without conflict in 1920, though roots of future dissension were present in the nationalist, pan-Islamic ambitions of the local Communists, which were for the time being tolerated in Moscow.

Three further small autonomous regions were established in the area shortly afterwards. In Central Asia, the Kirghiz Republic, later to be divided into separate Kazakh and Kirghiz Republics, was established in 1920. The promises of autonomy were not kept, and there was friction between the mainly Russian officials and the native nationalists, which only the famine of 1921 prevented from breaking out in rebellion.

The question of the Crimea, closely interwoven with the civil war, is discussed briefly in the next chapter, and the complex story of the establishment of Soviet rule in the Caucasus also belongs to the history of that period.

For the muslim inhabitants of Russia the foundations of policy were laid in the early years of Soviet rule: on the one hand, complete political control, centralized in Moscow, coupled with the repression of all native institutions which did not recognize soviet paramount authority; on the other hand, an effort to win muslim sympathies by concessions which did not jeopardize power. Russian communists engaged in administering muslim areas were constantly enjoined to have strict regard for native susceptibilities.*

*There is an excellent account of Communist policy towards non-Russian nationals in R. Pipes, *The Formation of the Soviet Union.*

Chapter Eleven

Civil War

Since promises of peace had been the main factor in ensuring victory for the Bolsheviks, it was essential for them to act speedily to bring the war to an end, especially in view of their extremely precarious hold on power. The new government sent appeals to the Allied Powers to open peace negotiations with Germany, but these appeals were ignored. The Bolsheviks therefore turned to the Russian army.

At the time of the Bolshevik take-over the effective Commander in Chief (nominally Kerensky was Commander in Chief) was General N.N. Dukhonin, a loyal supporter of the Provisional Government who had tried without success to come to its aid by moving troops to the capital. When he eventually refused to carry out an instruction from the new government to offer an immediate armistice and to open up peace negotiations, he was dismissed, but ordered to remain at his post until his successor, Krylenko, a Bolshevik lawyer, with some slight military experience, should arrive at GHQ.

Krylenko proceeded slowly to GHQ, removing on his way generals who refused to enter into armistice talks. On 9 November, Lenin broadcast* to the soldiers and sailors: 'The question of peace is in your hands. Do not let the counter-revolutionary generals wreck the great cause of peace.' On 20 November, Krylenko reached GHQ, at Mogilev, with a detachment of sailors. They captured the staff headquarters without meeting any resistance. Dukhonin was arrested, and Krylenko failed to prevent a crowd of soldiers, sailors and peasants from beating him to death.

Negotiations with the Central Powers were opened on 20 November, and an armistice signed on 2 December. The Allied Powers rejected an invitation to participate in the discussions, the USA, which was at first inclined to accept the proposal, being dissuaded from doing so by Great Britain and France. Peace talks opened at Brest-Litovsk on 9 December. The Central Powers were represented by the German and Austrian Foreign Ministers and by

---

*Radio propaganda played an important part in the Bolsheviks' rise to power.

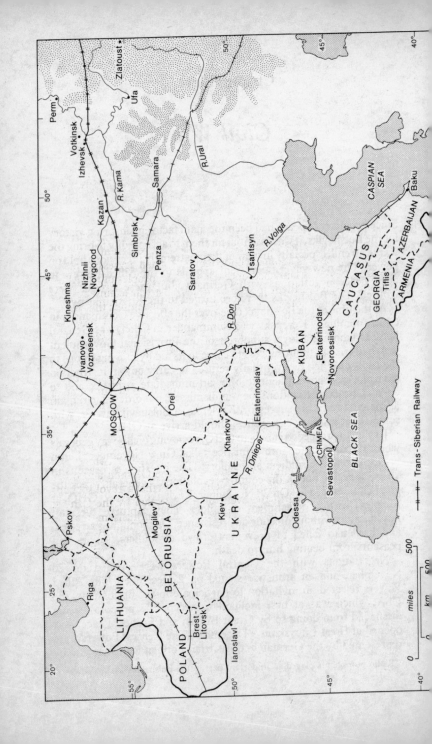

General Max Hoffmann, representing the German Supreme Command, who proved by far the toughest negotiator. The Russian team was headed by A.A. Ioffe. The Russians were above all anxious, presumably for political reasons, to ensure that the peace terms should not include any right of annexation of the territories occupied by the Central Powers — mainly Poland, Lithuania and the Baltic province of Courland. Germany and Austria appeared to accept these conditions, until General Hoffmann privately explained to Ioffe that 'self-determination' as interpreted by Germany did not extend to the Baltic territories and Poland: these areas had already withdrawn from Russia, and should they choose to unite with Germany that could not be considered annexation.

In Petrograd, meanwhile, at a joint meeting of the Central Executive Committee of the Soviet and army representatives, an LSR resolution was adopted condemning German aggressive plans, and an appeal was launched once again to the peoples of the Allied Powers, calling on them to stop an imperialist war against revolutionary Russia. A note to the Central Powers condemned their peace terms: the latter replied by withdrawing their original proposal. Lenin now sent Trotsky to Brest-Litovsk in place of Ioffe, with instructions to delay negotiations for as long as possible. He had meanwhile discovered that the army units which were still in a condition to fight were anti-Bolshevik, and he may have suspected (as was the case) that the Germans were contemplating a resumption of hostilities with a view to bringing down the Bolshevik régime. Negotiations were interrupted on 5 January: two days later, in a series of theses, Lenin argued that the German terms must be accepted, however annexationist. The proposal raised a storm not only among the LSR, but throughout the entire Bolshevik party, which had accepted seriously Lenin's assurances that the German and other proletariats were on the verge of revolution, and that a 'revolutionary war' would be waged in the event of the rejection by the Central Powers of just peace terms. However, the enthusiasm for the unrealistic revolutionary war, in the absence of an army with which to fight it, soon died down. At a meeting of the Central Committee on 9 January, only two supported revolutionary war: the great majority voted for Trotsky's rather futile proposal to declare the war at an end, but refuse to accept annexationist peace terms. A declaration to this effect was made on 10 February* and the Russians broke off their negotiations with the Germans.

On 18 February the Germans, who were not taken in by rhetoric, resumed their attack. As they had foreseen, the Bolsheviks were forced to sue for peace for fear that if they attempted resistance they

---

*New style: old style was abolished on 1 February.

would be overthrown by the anti-Bolshevik elements of the army. An onerous peace was eventually signed on 3 March. In addition to Poland and the Baltic regions, Russia lost 27 per cent of her sown area, 26 per cent of her population, a third of her average crops, three-quarters of her iron and steel, and 26 per cent of her railway network. These harsh terms produced a short-lived revolt in the communist party, but it soon succumbed to a *fait accompli* and the treaty was ratified.

The LSR reaction was more permanent. Relations between the romantic and unrealistic LSR and the Bolsheviks were already near breaking point even before the Treaty of Brest-Litovsk. As a peasant party they had been antagonized by the Bolshevik policy of forcible requisitioning of village produce. As participants in the security police, the *Vecheka*, they had constantly harassed that body and in February had actually succeeded in setting up an enquiry into charges of corruption. The peace treaty with Germany proved the last straw. The LSR voted against ratification in March, and resigned from *Sovnarkom*. Their demands for a revolutionary war grew ever louder, and they suspected the Communists of making secret concessions to the Germans even greater than those contained in the treaty. Their tempers were roused to a fever when the new German ambassador, von Mirbach, arrived in Moscow (now the country's capital), and on 6 July he was murdered in his embassy by the LSR Bliumkin, with the connivance of some other members of his party. A few Communists were kept under arrest for a short time, and a small LSR detachment seized the telegraph office. Some days later, the C-in-C on the Volga front declared war on the Germans, but was immediately killed. The LSR revolt was insignificant, but it provided Lenin wih an excuse to put an end to an ill-matched political partnership. Physical reprisals were very moderate — in general the Communists hoped, with good reason, that they could eventually attract many LSRs to their side.* The LSR even retained the theoretical right to sit in the soviets provided they repudiated the July affair. But in practice (with Lenin's written encouragement in one instance) they were driven by arbitrary action from soviets to which they had been elected.

The summer of 1918 was, for many reasons, the low ebb of Communist fortunes. The troops of the Central Powers, in some cases taking advantage of invitations from anti-Communists, spread deep into Russia. The independence of the Ukraine had been

---

*It is also very probable that Mirbach's murder was, at the least, not unwelcome to the Communists, since he was associated with an anti-Bolshevik orientation which was growing up in the German Foreign Office, as Dr G. Katkov argued in 1962 in an important paper.

recognized by the Central Powers at Brest-Litovsk, and a separate peace concluded on 9 February. Kiev had been occupied by Soviet troops the day before, but on 2 March the German army drove them out and restored the Rada, though not for long: on 28 April, the Rada was driven from office and a puppet régime installed which was to last until the German troops departed from Russia in December 1918.

On the Don, a Soviet government had been installed at the end of February 1918, but was under constant attacks from anti-Communist Cossacks who, under General Krasnov, attempted to enlist German aid in order to form an independent Don-Caucasian Union. The German army was in control of the Donets coal basin. In the Caucasus, it occupied Tiflis at the invitation of the Georgian government which had declared the country independent on 26 May. German forces also occupied the Crimea, capturing Sevastopol on 30 April. All Russian first-line battleships had left three days earlier for Novorossiisk, a Black Sea port then in Communist hands, and the Germans demanded their return. The Communists ordered them back to Sevastopol, but the sailors scuttled them on the way — according to one source in response to a secret instruction from *Sovnarkom*.

In Finland, the setting up of a Communist régime in part of the country had led to a civil war. By the terms of the Treaty of Brest-Litovsk, Soviet forces had been withdrawn from Finland, and German intervention soon determined the issue of the civil war in favour of the White side.

On top of all this, by the summer of 1918 the Communists were faced with intervention by forces of the Allied Powers (discussed below) and the Russian anti-Communist military assault was also proving successful. In the south, an army which had been forming under General Denikin — the Russian Volunteer Army — captured Ekaterinodar and the port of Novorossiisk. In the north, a large territory fell into anti-Communist hands almost by accident. During the war, the future leaders of Czechoslovakia had been allowed by the Russian government to organize a legion from Czech and Slovak prisoners of war in order to assist in the conquest of their future state. This Czech Army Corps, as it became, numbered some 50,000 men and fought on the Ukrainian battle front. In May 1918 they intended to make their way across Russia to Vladivostok, en route for Europe where they meant to add their weight on the much harassed Allied Western Front. Although the journey was authorized by *Sovnarkom*, relations between the Czechs and the Communists were not good, and there were armed clashes. The Communists attempted to disarm the Czechs, and when on 25 May Trotsky ordered that 'any armed Czech found on the [Penza-Omsk] railway is to be shot' they revolted. The Communists were at the time virtually unarmed and the Czechs rapidly occupied vital towns which gave them control of a large area of Russia and put them astride the Trans-Siberian Railway — Chelyabinsk on 26 May, Omsk on 7 June, Samara on the Volga on 8 June.

The success of the Czechs had important consequences. One was that it strengthened the Allies in their decision to intervene. Still more importantly, it won the immediate support of the Socialist Revolutionaries, who were strong in the area: they could cooperate with democratic fellow-slavs as they could not with reactionary Russian officers. Two governments emerged: in Samara and in Omsk. Socialists predominated in the Samara government, which accepted without question the Constituent Assembly elected in November 1917 as the foundation of authority. But its radical land policy alienated the landlords, and there was also friction between it and the army officers. The government at Omsk, socialist at first, was by the end of June superseded by the right-wing Provisional Government of Western Siberia, which declared the independence of Siberia. In spite of this political divergence between the two governments, a conference at Ufa on 8 September was successful to the extent of setting up an 'All-Russian Provisional Government', or Directory, of five members. This threat to Communist rule, on the face of it a formidable one, was in fact doomed to failure from the start, since neither the left nor the right, whom it purported to unite, was prepared to give it honest support.

In addition to military reverses, the Communists faced serious internal threats to their power, which reached a climax by the summer of 1918. If the promise of land had been fulfilled in a fashion, the peasants were now infuriated by forcible requisitioning of their produce. There was little prospect of either 'bread' or 'peace'. Those who had trusted Bolshevik promises of democracy were becoming disillusioned. Communist salvation lay in the fact that the opposition was sporadic, and neither organized nor united. But it was considerable. There were frequent reports in the press in the summer of 1918 of 'Kulak' resistance to requisitioning — 'Kulak' was fast becoming the usual term for peasants who did not accept Communist policy. There were strikes and demonstrations among workers against Communist rule, as well as the systematic Menshevik opposition which will be described in the next chapter. An armed worker revolt against the Communists took place in the adjoining towns of Izhevsk and Votkinsk, north-east of Kazan' in the Volga region. It began on 8 August with the overthrow of the Izhevsk Soviet by local workers. By September, an insurgent army of 50,000 peasants and workers had come into existence, which controlled a population of over 700,000. Even when the Red Army recaptured the two towns, the 'entire' population (according to the Soviet historian of the events) withdrew with the anti-Communist forces, and continued for years to fight the régime.

In the spring of 1918 a number of anti-Communist political groups emerged, willing to avail themselves of Allied aid — and in the case of one group, at any rate, German aid — to overthrow the government. On 30 August Lenin was wounded in an assassination attempt by a woman with Socialist Revolutionary affiliations, and on the same day another Socialist Revolutionary killed a prominent Communist in Petrograd. The immediate response was the so-called 'Red Terror' (dealt with in the next chapter). For longer-term defence, it was necessary to build up an army.

The rapid advance of the Czech Army Corps, if nothing else, brought home to the Communists the need to create an army to replace the one they had so effectively laboured to destroy. An attempt was made in January 1918 to create the new Red Army on a volunteer basis, but it met with little success and on 22 April compulsory military training was introduced. Trotsky, who had become People's Commissar for War, rightly perceived that without centralized control of the army the civil war could not be won. But he met with opposition from the anarchical partisan bands of Red Guards and peasant and worker fighting detachments which, until the end of 1918, made up the bulk of the Communist fighting force. Trotsky succeeded in creating some of the preconditions necessary for centralized command. On 8 July an ex-colonel of the imperial army became Commander in Chief, and a Revolutionary War Council was set up on 2 September.

With the introduction of conscription, the size of the army steadily increased, from under 400,000 (343,100 infantry, 40,060 cavalry) early in 1919, to over three million by the end of 1920, growing to five and a half million. The bourgeoisie, which term included former lawyers (after the abolition of the bar), priests, monks and bourgeois (i.e. non-Communist) journalists were, on 20 July, mobilized for 'clearing up dirt' in Trotsky's words. The libertarian principles which had destroyed the old army were now abolished. Election of officers, officially introduced in December 1917 and in practice in existence since March, was repealed, and strict discipline was restored, including the death penalty (which was ruthlessly applied) for desertion in battle. Officers of the imperial army — 'specialists' as they were called — were brought in on a large scale, usually by threats against them and their families if they refused: at the end of the civil war, according to Professor Erickson, out of 446,729 commanders,* including doctors, 314,180 were former imperial officers.

In addition to ruthless discipline, Trotsky brought a system of

*In the Red Army officers were known as commanders.

strict political control to the new army. This consisted of complete centralization, freedom from interference by the civilian party machine, and the stifling of the initiative of local party cells. Above all, the organized shifting of military party members from one part of the country to another, to meet emergencies as they arose on the widely scattered fronts, made possible the breaking up of troublesome cliques. Transfers took place on a large scale — over 24,000, for example, between April and November 1920 — and there is no doubt that they were a powerful weapon on the side of centralized control.

Political departments were now set up in Fronts and Armies, attached to the revolutionary war councils and headed by the Political Administration of the RSFSR — the PUR— established in May 1918. The main opposition to this apparatus came from the local party cells which hankered after the anarchical freedom of the early days, and whose activities were relentlessly put down by the new organs. In January 1919, an instruction on party cells made clear that their function was not interference in military affairs, but the creation within units of a nucleus of shock troops who, by their example, would strengthen the morale of the rest of the unit. (The presence of Communists in a unit does seem to have markedly increased its combat efficiency.) A further aspect of centralization, in February 1919, involved removing the 'special branches' responsible for security from the *Vecheka* and placing them under the control of the PUR. In order to make the employment of former officers less hazardous, a system of political commissars who had to countersign every command was introduced. Even so, officers managed to desert to the White forces.

The army was the scene of much political strife during the civil war, to which Trotsky's arrogant and high-handed manner contributed. Bitter antagonism developed between him and several other leaders, Stalin in particular. There were conflicts with Stalin and Voroshilov in 1918 when they were in charge of a food collecting expedition at Tsaritsyn (later Stalingrad) which grew into a military operation. By October 1918 Trotsky demanded and obtained Stalin's recall — a slight that was never forgotten. By March 1919, at the Eighth Party Congress, a military opposition movement to Trotsky had developed, rallying those Communists whose privileged positions had been assailed by his policy of centralizing party control. There were also heated discussions on military doctrine between Trotsky, who stood for orthodox, disciplined, conventional tactics, and communist theorists whose doctrines derived from their experience in partisan warfare — notably Frunze and Voroshilov. The partisan 'unitary military doctrine' demanded training of the army in a spirit of offensive action in order to prepare it for its task in supporting the coming world revolution. Trotsky, who was impatient of criticism and, moreover, sceptical about the possibility of bringing world revolution about by military intervention, had no difficulty in resisting his critics during the civil war. But a powerful opposition was building up against him which was to play an important part in his downfall in later years when Lenin was no longer there to protect him.

For a time, while the new Red Army was forming, fortune continued to favour the anti-Bolshevik forces, although the tides of victory swung backwards and forwards. The Directory set up in Siberia in September 1918 and claiming to be an 'All-Russian Provisional Government' was torn apart by its discordant left and right elements, and on 17 November was overthrown by a conspiracy of right-wing officers. Admiral Kolchak, who happened by chance to be in Omsk at the time, was declared 'Supreme Ruler of all Russia' and assumed the title of Commander in Chief of all Russian land and naval forces. Kolchak, who had no political ambitions, was probably unaware of the conspiracy which put him in power. His avowed aim was to favour neither reaction nor Communist extremism, but to restore order in the country so that it could choose its government. He was a man of complete integrity, but lacked both the military skill and the political flair for the difficult tasks which faced him. The British and French representatives approved of the coup, and prevailed on the Czech Corps, which did not, not to oppose it. The Czech troops were withdrawn from the front and assigned the task of guarding a portion of the Trans-Siberian Railway, along which Allied military supplies were carried from the port of Vladivostok where they were disembarked. The Socialist Revolutionaries, in hiding in Ufa, disowned the Corps but were unable to do much more. Some of them made precarious peace with the Communists; the Socialist Revolutionary members of the Directory, Zenzinov and Avksentiev, were forced to emigrate; and Chernov eventually escaped abroad.

Kolchak's army achieved some success in December 1918 with the capture of Perm', though this was offset by Red Army victories further south, which eventually resulted in the conquest of Ufa and Ekaterinburg. In March and April 1919, the numerically superior Kolchak forces made a successful advance which threatened the Volga towns of Kazan' and Samara. The Red Army, although menaced by peasant risings in the rear, was reinforced by a vigorous recruiting campaign and from April onwards drove the White front backwards, recapturing Ufa on 9 June. The vigour of the Soviet advance was enhanced by fears that the Allies were considering recognizing Kolchak as the legitimate ruler of Russia.

A major factor in Kolchak's defeat was the low morale of his forces; there were frequent desertions to the Communist side in the course of battle. Another was his failure to win over the population, which, although far from pro-Communist, preferred Soviet rule in the last resort. There were no landlords in Siberia on whom support of a sort could be built, and the peasants saw little to choose, so far as severity was concerned, between the Communists and Kolchak's military commanders. In its retreat, the White army moved into hostile guerrilla territory. The peasants' revolt was an expression of grievances against recruitment and against a war which interfered with their normal way of life.

The advances of the Red Army continued. In August, fifteen thousand of Kolchak's troops were captured by the Reds in a battle for Chelyabinsk, and on 14 November 1919 the capital of Kolchak's government, Omsk, was captured. Kolchak and the remnants of his dispirited army retreated in disorder, struggling to escape. Kolchak eventually placed himself formally under Allied protection, having abdicated as Commander in Chief in favour of Denikin. He was taken, under a Czech guard, to Irkutsk, where a Political Centre consisting of non-Communist opponents of the Kolchak régime had established itself in precarious power at the end of December. To this body the French military representative and the Czech guard handed over Kolchak. The motives of the Frenchman are incomprehensible; the Czechs presumably hoped to facilitate their main aim — transit eastward. They were also incensed by the fact that Kolchak had dismissed the Czech general Gajda from his post as commander of his Northern army, following severe defeats. Within weeks the Political Centre was taken over by a Communist revolutionary committee. Kolchak was interrogated by a commission and shot without trial on 7 February 1920.

In the south, General Denikin's Volunteer Army, now renamed the Armed Forces of South Russia, was winning considerable successes in the summer of 1919. This army had been founded on the Don in November 1917 by General Alekseev, who was soon joined by other military leaders, including Kornilov and Denikin. Driven from the Don by the Bolsheviks, after enduring great hardship and stubborn fighting, in which Kornilov was killed, the small army eventually reached the borders of the Kuban. The death of Alekseev from ill health in the autumn of 1918 left Denikin in command. With great difficulty he built up an army of some 150,000.

His first advances were in the Ukraine, where a series of victories culminated on 31 August with the capture of Kiev. Of all the waves of anarchy that beset Russia during the civil war, none was comparable to that which prevailed in the Ukraine. A succession of régimes served to destroy all respect for state authority. As we saw earlier, the nationalist Rada, which succeeded the Provisional Government, was for a short time replaced by the Bolsheviks, only to be followed by German occupation and a puppet government under Hetman Skoropadsky. This was overthrown by a vast peasant army, formed of the countless guerrilla bands that had operated in the country throughout its existence. A nationalist Ukrainian government was formed, but succumbed once again to the Communists, whom in turn Denikin drove out in the summer of 1919. In 1920, the Poles and Denikin's successor, General Wrangel, occupied parts of the Ukraine, before Communists successfully put through their policy of centralized Russification, outwitting nationalist trends both within and outside the Ukrainian Communist party, apparently against the efforts of Lenin. In the twenties, nationalist turmoils were to revive within the Ukrainian Communist party, to be put down by an even stronger party in Moscow.

The main causes of anarchy were the numerous partisan bands which operated in rural areas and harassed the towns, which, to them, represented the source of all their misery. The guerrillas were commanded by 'atamans' who at times controlled considerable parts of the countryside. Since pogroms were usually encouraged by the atamans and insufficiently discouraged by Denikin's army, the Jews were among the main sufferers. Jews were identified in the peasants' minds both with the Communists and with the bourgeoisie; they were also, as small traders, an attractive target for looters.

When, in the summer of 1919, Denikin turned his forces northwards, in an avowed drive on Moscow, his rear was severely harassed by partisans, especially those under a colourful anarchist guerrilla leader named Makhno, which captured town after town. Until the early autumn Denikin's forces were in the ascendant. They captured Odessa on 23 August, Kiev on 31 August, and Orel, an important city on the railway 250 miles south of Moscow, on 14 October. But the tide was turning. The Red Army now had superior forces and a few days later it recaptured Orel. It was the beginning of the rout of the Armed Forces of South Russia.

Denikin has been much criticized for launching his advance on Moscow without adequate preparation and without securing his rear, but the reasons for the White defeat were social and political as much as military. Denikin was not a monarchist and, as the son of a former serf, did not belong to the landlord class; but his patriotic appeal for a great and indivisible Russia evoked little response from peasants, least of all in the Ukraine. The military rule of his officers was no less unpopular in the villages than that of the Communists. Contemporary accounts tell of widespread speculation and corruption, which

Denikin, for all his personal integrity, was unable to suppress. His promise of land reform was vague and carried little credence in the light of actual administrative practice, and in face of the allocation of land, however modest, made by the Communists. The next six months witnessed the progressive defeat and demoralization of Denikin's army. On 4 April 1920 he resigned his command and nominated General Baron Wrangel as his successor.

In addition to the armies under Denikin and Kolchak there was a third force, the North-Western Army under General Yudenich. In October 1919, while the Red Army was mustering its forces for a determined attack on Denikin's successful advance, Yudenich launched a surprise assault on Petrograd which all but succeeded in capturing the city and reached its outskirts by the end of the month. However, the attack was held, in large measure through the energy of Trotsky, who rallied the whole city for defence from within and was able to muster reinforcements from outside. One of the causes of Yudenich's defeat was the failure of Estonia and Finland to provide the military assistance for which he had been hoping. They were unwilling to come to his support without adequate guarantees of their future independence. Both Kolchak and Denikin were opposed to this, and the Allied Powers were unable or unwilling to offer it. After the defeat of Yudenich, the Baltic states all signed separate peace treaties with Soviet Russia, in which their independence was recognized.

The Caucasus had a troubled history during the years of the civil war. The Bolshevik revolution stimulated national and separatist feelings, but an independent Transcaucasia proved shortlived in the face of the conflicting interests, both territorial and political, of its component parts, and in May 1918 three separate states, Georgia, Armenia and Azerbaijan, came into existence. A small German force occupied Georgia in 1918, and Turkish troops were in Azerbaijan, but these left at the end of the year after the defeat of the Central Powers. A British force now occupied Transcaucasia. The allegation that their occupation of the oil city Baku was aimed at capturing the Caucasian oil fields is belied by the fact that they left Baku long before the first Soviet troops appeared on the frontier of Georgia and Azerbaijan. The British announced that their aim in Georgia was to maintain order, but their rule was unpopular with the natives and inconsistent.

The three Caucasian republics were eventually reincorporated in the RSFSR by military force. The case of Georgia was particularly instructive. Independent Georgia was ruled by a Menshevik government, and the Mensheviks had a strong, traditional hold there. They won an overwhelming majority in the elections to the Constituent Assembly in November 1917, and in the election to the Georgian National Council in February 1919 they collected 72 per cent of the urban, and 82 per cent of the rural vote. The Georgian government probably veered more to the right when in power, and certainly showed nationalistic trends both at home and towards its neighbours, but it carried out an extensive policy of land reform and put into effect a socialist labour policy. Agrarian unrest nevertheless erupted from time to time, encouraged by the Communists and especially by Communist-propagandized soldiers returning home from the Western Front (Communist agitation was less successful on the Caucasian front.)

However, on 7 May 1920, after an abortive attempt to conquer Georgia, the RSFSR, to the dismay of the Georgian Communists, signed a treaty with her. Russia recognized her independence and promised to abstain from any interference in her internal affairs. Georgia undertook not to prosecute those who had engaged in activities on behalf of the RSFSR or the Communist party. In a secret supplement, the Menshevik government very unwisely recognized the right of free activity for the local communist party. Before long, the treatment of the Communists in Georgia, who continued to work for the overthrow of the government, became a subject of bitter dispute. On 11 February 1921, a rebellion, fomented by the Communists, broke out, and a 'revolutionary committee' asked for Soviet help. The Russian Eleventh Army, which had been preparing for a full-scale attack on Georgia for some time, marched in and conquered the country by force, overthrowing the Mensheviks. Lenin may have had some hesitation about this act of treachery, but his fears were mainly of Allied intervention and he was reassured when the British Prime Minister, Lloyd George, informed the Soviet diplomatic envoy, Krasin, that the Allied forces, in spite of the fact that they had recognized Georgia's independence *de facto*, would not make any move.

There was one other important field of action — Poland, which had become independent after the collapse of Germany in November 1918. The leading figure was Marshal Pilsudski, who became the first head of state and commander in chief of the armed forces. Pilsudski regarded Russia as the main threat to Polish independence and accordingly, in the spring of 1920, rejected Soviet offers of peace, believing that the weakness of Russia was Poland's opportunity to ensure her security by fostering the creation of independent Lithuanian, Belorussian and Ukrainian states. On 25 April, by agreement with the weak nationalist government which was then in power in Kiev, Polish forces launched a surprise attack into the

Ukraine. It met with little effective resistance, and Kiev was occupied on 6 May. But the foreign invasion stimulated a patriotic upsurge in the country and led to a strong counter-attack by Budenny's famous cavalry army, while further to the north the Red Army advanced, pushing the Polish forces back towards Poland. Great euphoria took hold of the Communist leaders, who saw this advance as the prelude to a Communist-ruled Poland and to the eventual spread of communism to Germany, where right-wing socialism predominated. At the end of July, a Revolutionary Committee headed by a veteran Polish Communist, Dzerzhinsky, was set up as the supreme authority in Poland in the first Polish town captured in the campaign. Subordinate committees were progressively established and an intense propaganda drive was inaugurated.

The spread of communism to Poland was a dismal failure, due as much to peasant hostility as to general anti-Russian sentiments. There was a rapid shift in military fortunes, and the Poles, with the aid of a French military adviser, halted the Soviet advance before Warsaw. A counter-attack was now launched and made rapid progress, ending in defeat for the Red Army, one reason being that the RSFSR did not put all of its mobilized forces into the field against superior Polish numbers. On 12 October 1920 an armistice, later followed by a peace treaty, was signed at Riga.

While the Red Army was preoccupied with the Polish campaign, the White Army under General Wrangel (General Denikin's successor) broke out of the Crimea and occupied territories on the mainland. Unlike previous White commanders, Wrangel had succeeded in restoring discipline and morale among his forces and he also proclaimed a more liberal land policy. But it was too late. On 13 October he was driven back across the Dnieper with heavy losses and by this time, with the armistice in Poland signed, the Red Army was ready for the assault on this last hope of the White armies. On 14 November 1920 General Wrangel evacuated his forces from the Crimea. Effectively, the civil war was over.

The end of the Soviet dream of world revolution probably dates from the defeat in Poland. The Bolsheviks had taken power in the confident expectation that the revolutionary proletariat in Germany and in the other industrialized countries of Western Europe would come to their aid, and these hopes remained high, in some quarters at least, until the Polish débâcle. Thereafter, Soviet policy envisaged a long period of coexistence with the capitalist powers before revolution could be expected. As Lenin pointed out, the ultimate hope lay in the coming revolt of the colonial peoples and in the economic aid to Russia which the capitalists could confidently be expected to provide for their own destruction.

What the Bolsheviks hoped for was what their opponents feared. The dread that communist revolutions in their own countries might be sparked off by a successful revolution in Russia was a powerful motive with the Allied powers in the decision to intervene militarily. Much has been made of this intervention and it is worth investigating here.

Limited Allied forces were in Russia before the capitulation of the Central Powers in November 1918. A small British force was landed in Murmansk on 5 March, and was for a short time not unwelcome to the Soviet authorities, who were still apprehensive of a German advance. Up to June 1918 the British force numbered only 500 Royal Marines and 600 other troops, but on 2 August about 13,000 troops, mainly British, Canadian and American, disembarked in Archangel, the main scene of Allied intervention. Two days later Japanese and British troops landed in Vladivostok, followed shortly by two US regiments and a small French force.

The United States was at all times a hesitant and reluctant participant in the Russian civil war. The Japanese, whose forces in Siberia eventually numbered 70,000 and who did not withdraw until 1922, had no interest in the conflict inside Russia beyond securing for themselves certain economic advantages in a weakened country, and there was considerable friction between Japan and her allies. The French were always the most vociferous in their demands for intervention, but their actual contribution was minimal. The brunt of the effort of aiding the anti-Soviet forces in the Russian civil war fell on the British, whose troops were eventually reinforced to a total strength of 18,400.

The Soviet reaction to the Allied moves was violent. There were many arrests of Britons and Frenchmen, including R.H. Bruce-Lockhart, Chief of the British Mission in Moscow, and raids on the embassies which resulted in a lurid charge of conspiracy to overthrow Bolshevik power. There were to be frequent protests, but they were always accompanied by professions of willingness to reach accommodation and there was no declaration of war. All this contrasted with the relatively mild reaction to the overrunning of large parts of Russia by the Central Powers: evidently, the Bolsheviks were reluctant to provoke them. It was also possibly of relevance that they had accepted large sums of money from the Germans in the past.

From the Allied point of view, intervention before the armistice of 11 November 1918 was justified by the intention of depriving the Central Powers of vital ports and of preventing Allied stores inside Russia from falling into enemy hands. The Allies were sore pressed on the Western Front, and their position in 1918 was not improved by the defection of Russia, which had resulted (as already recorded) in 50 divisions and 5,000 guns being moved from the east to the west.

With the defeat of the Central Powers, the position changed. A decision to maintain or reinforce the troops in Russia now became an act directed against the Communist régime. The Allied Powers, and the one most involved, Great Britain, had little love for the new rulers of Russia, for what they knew of their methods of government, and in particular for their avowed purpose of spreading their revolutionary doctrine to other countries. In the British Government, however, only the Minister of War, Winston Churchill, advocated maximum effort deliberately aimed at the overthrow of communism, arguing that otherwise the Allied Powers would be faced with a much greater menace in the future. However much events may seem sixty-five years later to have justified his prediction, the fact was that, all other objections apart, there was no possibility in 1918 or 1919 of raising the troops that would have been required for effective intervention. There was the greatest reluctance in the British Army to be sent to fight in Russia, and further conscription would have resulted in mutiny. The position in France was, if anything, worse.

The support given by the Allies to anti-Communist forces was therefore limited, and mainly restricted to supplies — over a hundred million pounds' worth, according to the lowest estimate, from Great Britain alone, with further quantities from France and America. Some of these supplies went to help Admiral Kolchak and the British government also sent two battalions to fight with him, before deciding, after his defeat at Chelyabinsk, that Kolchak's was a lost cause. The battalions were evacuated on 8 September and 1 November 1919.

On Denikin's front, British aid in supplies was substantial — 1,200 guns and nearly two million shells, for example, and 200,000 rifles and 500 million rounds of ammunition — but theft, waste and spoilage of supplies were common. A British tank battalion and two squadrons of the Royal Air Force were also present at the front for purposes of instruction and took part in actual fighting. Relations with Denikin, however, were not happy. The pogroms that took place in territories under his occupation were one reason for the disharmony: a more important one was the British commitment to a series of independent states in the Caucasus. This commitment, which was quite contrary to Denikin's ambitions, led to intervention in that area by a small British force, which was withdrawn by mid-October 1919. The French also occupied Odessa on 18 December 1918, after the departure of the Germans, but this was a disaster and lasted only five months.

This conflict with Denikin was typical of a basic inconsistency in British policy. On the one hand, believing that a dismembered Russia would be less of a menace to British interests, Britain supported the border states in the Caucasus and the Baltic which had declared independence,* though her support did not go so far as military aid against the Communist take-overs. On the other hand, she backed the White generals, who were determined that the future Russia should be restored to the frontiers of the former empire.

The truth was that the Allies' support for the Whites was never whole-hearted. They distrusted the White commanders, whom they regarded as undesirable future rulers of Russia and indeed little better than the communists, and though they felt a moral obligation to the Whites and were prepared to help them win, they were not prepared to do the winning for them. If the Whites lost despite Allied help, it would prove that the country wanted the communists.

On 4 March 1919, the British War Cabinet decided that its troops should be withdrawn the following summer. The reasons were mainly domestic, such as the unpopularity of the operations in North Russia both with the troops and with the working class at home. The evacuation from Archangel was completed on 27 September, and from Murmansk on 12 October, but before leaving the Northern areas, the British force made a successful attack on Soviet positions, inflicting over 6,000 casualties. This was virtually the only instance of British troops in combat in any strength against Soviet forces. Total British casualties throughout the civil war (including Australians and Canadians) were: in North Russia, where the troops were in action, 178 killed, 401 wounded; elsewhere, 2 killed and 2 wounded.

In the upshot, Allied intervention in the civil war was a complete failure. At most, the military supplies slightly prolonged the survival of the White forces, and it is arguable that this prevented Soviet forces from going in time to the aid of Communists who had taken over precariously in the Baltic states, or to help the short-lived Communist régime of Bela Kun in Hungary in March 1919.

On the other hand, it would be naïve to argue, as is sometimes suggested by those who fail to understand the nature of Soviet policy, that intervention prevented the burgeoning of friendship between the RSFSR and Great Britain: avowed Soviet hostility to the capitalist powers always precluded anything more than temporary accommodation between them — such as the Anglo-Soviet trade agreement of 16 March 1921. What intervention did do was to strengthen Soviet morale enormously: it gave the Soviet leaders a

*This policy was opposed by Churchill, who wished to see a united non-communist Russia as a counterweight to Germany.

powerful theme for propaganda appealing to Russian patriotism, and enabled them to claim that the Red Army had defeated the combined might of the White Armies and the Allied Powers.

There were many reasons for the victory of the Red Army in the civil war, but most of them add up to one simple fact: the people as a whole, in spite of the unpopularity of the Communists, preferred the Soviet régime to the available alternatives. The peasants disliked both sides and wished above all to be left alone; but when it came to the choice, they preferred the Communists who gave them land to the Whites who took, or threatened to take, it away. Trotsky regarded this as the main cause of victory.

There is, nevertheless, ample evidence that, throughout this period, the first choice of large sections of the population — probably a majority — would have been some form of moderate socialism. Unfortunately this was not a possible option. The socialist parties were unable or unwilling to organize resistance at the time when they could still have done so, and it was the tragedy of Russia in 1917 and after that both sides in the civil war were intent on destroying the moderate left, on which the only hope of a rational régime for the country rested.

One must also, of course, consider the state of the armies themselves. Banditry, corruption and desertion were rampant on both sides, but the better morale was on the side of the Red Army, and especially in those units where there was a fair contingent of Communists. These Communists were at any rate united on what they were fighting for: there was no common aim on the White side between, say, Socialist Revolutionaries and officers of the Imperial Army.

Towering above other reasons were the energy, skill and ruthless determination of Trotsky, the main architect of the new Red Army. His name is expunged from Soviet histories to this day, because he was out-manoeuvred by Stalin half a century ago.

Chapter Twelve

The Triumph of Leninism

Before the Bolsheviks took power in October 1917, there was nothing in their writings to suggest that the victors in the proletarian revolution would require a political security police force. Lenin's writings repeatedly emphasized that when the people seized power the maintenance of order would be a simple task, easily accomplished by a people's militia, and there is nothing to suggest that he did not believe this utopian fantasy. No doubt he was carried away by his own propaganda that the proletarian revolution would signify the victory of the enormous majority over a small minority of exploiters. What he does not seem to have envisaged was that, in order to survive, the new régime would require an instrument of arbitrary repression much more powerful than that of the old one.

The All-Russian Extraordinary Commission for Combating Counter-Revolution and Sabotage, universally known as the *Vecheka* or the *Cheka*, came into existence in response to the conditions that arise when a minority is determined to rule alone. Before it was set up, security functions were already exercised by the Military Revolutionary Committee (the MRC), which, at Dzerzhinsky's suggestion, organized a Commission for Combating Counter-Revolution and Sabotage on 21 November 1917. This was, however, attached to the Central Executive Committee of the Soviets. The *Cheka* was, from the start, subordinated directly to *Sovnarkom*, which created it on 7 December, acting on the report of a commission chaired by Dzerzhinsky, together with Lenin's comments on it. The *Cheka* was conceived as an administrative organ, and its powers were expressly limited to the investigation of cases which, if need be, were to be passed for trial to revolutionary tribunals set up at the same time.

Attachment to *Sovnarkom* meant that the *Cheka* escaped interference by the non-Communist elements which were still included in the Central Executive Committee. On 8 January 1918, however, the LSR — apparently opposed by Lenin — joined the *Cheka* and remained there until their final clash with the Bolsheviks the following July. Their unrealistic view that an unpopular minority could hold power in such circumstances without recourse to terror meant that while they remained members of the *Cheka* they exercised an unwelcome restraint on its activities. It was Steinberg, the LSR Commissar for Justice, for example, who on 18 December released a number of socialists detained by the *Cheka*.

The *Cheka* rapidly expanded both in size and in scope. By mid-1921, in the estimate of its historian, G.H. Leggett, its total strength was over a quarter of a million. Of this, civilian staff numbered some 30,000, while internal and frontier security troops were respectively over 137,000 and 94,000 strong. During the period of its existence, until 6 February 1922, when it was replaced by a body named the State Political Executive (GPU), its powers continued to expand, and in the main it successfully resisted attempts by the Commissariat of Justice and the Central Executive Committee to limit its scope. Nor did the GPU, in spite of its more formalized powers, cease to be an instrument of terror. As Lenin repeatedly asserted in the course of debates when the GPU was constituted, dictatorship of the proletariat was not possible without terror, including, as he put it, terror against 'agents of the bourgeoisie (especially the Mensheviks and the SRs)'.

A decree of 5 September 1918 conferred sweeping powers on the *Cheka*, which it never in practice lost. This extension of power, which was officially known as the 'Red Terror', was instituted in response to the assassination of Bolshevik leaders in June and August, and an attempt on Lenin's life in August. Lenin's claim that it was made necessary by Allied intervention was false. It was, in fact, an extension of what had gone on before. In July, before any Allied landing, 407 captive insurgents had been shot after a rising in Iaroslavl, and over 500 hostages were murdered in Petrograd before the decree on Red Terror. Attempts were made from time to time, by legislation, to transfer some of the *Cheka*'s powers to the Revolutionary Courts, but it was never more than nominally subject to the law. As Lenin openly acknowledged, it had been regularly shooting its victims and practising mass repressive action since February 1918 at least. On 16 July the ex-Tsar and his entire family, his physician and his servants, were massacred at their place of confinement in Ekaterinburg by the local *Cheka*, on orders from the district Soviet concerted with Moscow — ostensibly for fear that they would be rescued by the approaching White Army. This also took place well before intervention or the Red Terror.

The *Cheka* also assumed the power of administrative deportation to forced labour camps. These, run in conjunction with the People's Commissariat for Internal Affairs (NKVD) were first officially instituted by a decree of 15 April 1919, though confinement by the *Cheka* had long preceded the legislation. By October 1922 there were 132 camps with approximately 60,000 inmates. Judging by available statistics, a large proportion of the prisoners were workers or peasants. Estimates of deaths caused by the *Cheka* in the four years of its existence are necessarily difficult. The most recent figure (arrived at by Leggett) is 140,000 by execution, and a further 140,000 in the course of suppressing insurrections. (Executions in the last Tsarist period, from 1866 to 1917, on the basis of detailed Soviet statistics, numbered 14,000.)

Bolshevik leaders were addicted to drawing analogies with the French Revolution, and they certainly followed the Jacobins (to whom the common bond of fanaticism united them) in such practices as the mass murder of hostages. They also copied the French terror by waging war not against individuals but against a whole class — in this case the bourgeoisie — as numerous statements by their leaders showed. (They tended, however, to exempt those bourgeois whose skills they needed.)

On the other hand, among the many cases which only the imagination of the *Cheka* could regard as genuine counter-revolution, it did uncover a few real attempts to overthrow the Bolshevik régime in the course of the civil war. The *Cheka* also developed a counter-espionage section (KRO) in response to what was believed to be the threat presented by the influx of foreigners, following upon diplomatic recognition of the Soviet Union. The major successes of the KRO were the capture and show trial of Savinkov* and the destruction of his anti-soviet organization, as well as an elaborate deception operation, known as 'The Trust', which infiltrated the emigré monarchist movement and culminated in the seizure of a British spy named Reilly.

Opposition to the Communists was both economically and politically motivated. When they took power they were faced immediately with the simultaneous collapse of industry and a catastrophic drop in grain supplies to the towns — from 641,000 tons in November 1917 to 46,000 in January 1918. They therefore declared a crusade of enforced confiscation against the peasants and relentless war against the illegal private trade which sprang up between the towns and the villages. It was, as we saw, the excesses committed in the execution of this policy that caused the first break between the Bolsheviks and their recently so enthusiastic allies, the LSR. The forcible collection

---

*Savinkov was a prominent SR terrorist, appointed Deputy Minister of War by Kerensky but dismissed for his alleged part in the Kornilov affair. The most active of the anti-Bolshevik conspirators, he organized insurrections in Iaroslavl and two other places in 1918. He was tricked and captured by the *Cheka* in 1921.

of food was centralized at the end of 1918 under the Commissariat of Food and Supply, acting through commissars who organized the armed detachments of workers and poor peasants who exacted grain from the reluctant villages. This was a prime cause of the peasant violence that flared up during the civil war. The peasants, having obtained the land under the distribution effected by the Bolsheviks in one of their first acts, the land decree, no longer had anything to hope for from the new rulers.

In terms of the theory known as 'war communism', which prevailed until March 1921, the market had been abolished, and the industrial products of the towns were to go to the peasants in return for their food. In reality, industry had collapsed, and the peasants refused to part with food when no products were available in return. Right up to 1920, the survival of the country was dependent on the illegal market, not only in food but in raw materials as well. Nationalization of industry was completed on paper by the end of 1920, but in practice the central machinery proved incapable of managing the vast network of large and small enterprises. Surpluses accumulated in one area, for example, while production was halted for lack of raw materials in another. The losses which the Russian economy had suffered as a result of the peace treaty with Germany, and through the ravages of civil war, added to the self-induced chaos.

By the end of the civil war, which was virtually over by November 1920, even such support as the Communists could expect from peasants who, however reluctantly, preferred them to the Whites who threatened to take away their newly-acquired land, came to an end. The recalcitrant peasants were sowing less, and the break-up of the large estates meant that they were now producing for their own consumption. In some parts of the country, the town population was consuming only 41 per cent of the pre-war level, and even peasants in the food-consuming areas were worse off than state-assisted victims of famine had been before the war. In the food-producing areas their level of consumption remained unimpaired (up to the bad harvest of 1920) but this only exacerbated relations with the towns. Starvation told on industry. By 1920 manpower was halved by the drain of workers to the villages in search of food; Petrograd, for example, lost over half its population. Production fell drastically, especially in heavy industry. Light industry was better able to short-circuit the state bureaucracy, and produce for the black market. The general death rate more than doubled: over seven million are estimated to have died from malnutrition and epidemics between January 1918 and July 1920.

Politically, the opposition of the workers was exercised through the trade unions and, among the political parties, mainly through the

Mensheviks — the Russian Social-Democratic Labour Party, as they now called themselves. By May 1918 they were reunited with Martov's Internationalists and he had become the acknowledged leader of the party. Their policy remained steadfast to the end: to uphold the ideals of social-democracy, to oppose Communist one-party rule by all possible constitutional means, to demand freedom for workers, but to give no support to armed resistance or to foreign intervention. By October 1917 their influence in the country had sunk to insignificance, but as the reality of Communist rule became apparent to those who had backed it in the belief that it stood for genuine socialist soviet government, support for the Mensheviks grew. By the middle of 1918 they could claim with justification that, but for systematic dispersal and packing of soviets and arrests at workers' meetings, their following among the proletariat would eventually have brought them to power. The Communists responded with a policy of force and fraud, of false accusations and fake trials. In a period when a group of fanatics was destroying the foundations of social democracy in the belief that it was building a new and better world, the Mensheviks, for as long as they were able to survive, struggled for the traditional ideals of Russian socialism.

There was a certain ambivalence about Communist policy towards the Mensheviks — possibly due to the fact that not all the leaders shared the passionate fear and hatred of socialism that characterized Lenin and Zinoviev. Although the Mensheviks, along with the Socialist Revolutionaries, were expelled from the Central Executive Committee on 14 June 1918, on the ostensible charge that they had fomented risings, they were readmitted in September and action against them was thereafter confined to administrative rather than legal means. But they never recovered their press, which was closed down in June, and thereafter had to make their case by the skilful distribution of leaflets and pamphlets, largely made possible by the wide support they continued to enjoy among the printers. It was a tribute to their skill and courage that, as late as 1920 and in spite of persistent Communist obstruction, they won sizeable delegations in some of the provincial soviets — 205 in Kharkov, for example, and 120 in Ekaterinoslav.

The Communist charge, repeatedly made, especially by Lenin, that the Mensheviks engaged in violence against the régime (an accusation still to be found even in some Western histories) was palpably false. The few individuals who engaged in armed action were expelled from the party. Two 'trials' intended to establish Menshevik guilt failed in their avowed purpose. The best proof that the Communists knew the charge to be fraudulent was that throughout the civil war there were Mensheviks working in prominent official positions; and that, although constantly harassed, the party was allowed some degree of political tolerance and was only finally liquidated when the civil war came to an end. The real offence of the Mensheviks in Communist eyes was their constant advocacy of libertarian principles such as freedom for the workers or the abolition of the *Cheka* and the death penalty. (In accordance with Russian social-democratic tradition, they did not object to 'the complete or partial forfeiture of civil rights' by social groups other than 'those who take part in public productive labour'.)*

Menshevik influence grew steadily in the trade unions in 1919 and 1920. Zinoviev estimated Menshevik and anti-Communist sentiment in the union rank and file in 1921 at ninety per cent. He was prone to exaggerate, but even Trotsky had to justify Communist dictatorship on the gounds that it 'was more important than some formalistic principle', since it defended the true interests of the working class — a very familiar Communist argument, convincing to those who believe that intellectual theorists are better able to judge what workers want than the workers themselves.

It was, perhaps, convincing to the delegation of the British Labour Party that visited Moscow in June 1920 and had a full opportunity of meeting representatives of the socialist parties. It even witnessed the forcible dissolution, with forty arrests, of the Moscow Printers' Union, which had dared to organize a free meeting for the benefit of the visitors. Though it included an account of this incident in its reports, the delegation failed either to publish secret appeals with which socialists (at the risk of their freedom) had entrusted it, or to point out that repression of freedom applied in Russia to all the delegation's fellow socialists. This mealy-mouthed report contrasted sharply with an account given later by one member of the delegation who said that the proletariat in Russia had no freedom, and that the Russian people were as severely repressed as they had been under tsarism.

By 1921, when the final assault on the Mensheviks began, congress after congress of trade unions on which Mensheviks had secured majorities was closed down, and replaced by suitably rigged bodies dominated by Communists. In the first months of 1921, roughly two thousand Mensheviks were arrested, including the whole of their central committee. It was the virtual end of the party. In 1922 some ten prominent leaders were allowed to emigrate, and for a time they became the best informed and most accurate source outside Russia on the Soviet régime. Had Zinoviev not been over-ruled by the Central Committee, they would have been shot.

The fate of the Socialist Revolutionaries and the LSR was dealt

*Quoted from their manifesto of Summer 1919.

with in the previous chapter. The anarchists, a varied conglomeration of eccentric idealists, active terrorists, anarcho-syndicalists and plain criminals, must also be included among the political opponents of the Communists if only because of their steadfast resistance to all authority and their strong libertarian tradition. Many of them had proved valuable allies of the Bolsheviks during their rise to power — indeed, the political slogans of Bolsheviks and Anarchists were often identical — but, once in power, the Communists were above all anxious to establish the discipline which, in combination with the Provisional Government, they had helped to destroy. The Anarchists not only proved an obstacle to this; given the natural attraction which their beliefs held for the Russian people, they presented a danger to Communist power. They therefore suffered severely at Communist hands — though the fiction was always maintained that such operations by the *Cheka* as an armed raid in April 1918 on their Moscow premises, which resulted in some six hundred arrests, were directed solely against common criminals. They managed to survive the constant administrative harassment until the end of 1920, to keep their clubs going and even to publish a few periodicals, and to propagate anarcho-syndicalist ideas. They were destroyed by arrests at the end of 1920. After that they were able to enjoy one day of freedom, on 13 February 1921, when they were released from prison in order to attend Kropotkin's funeral. The Anarchists in exile could with justice complain that they were treated worse in Soviet Russia than in any capitalist country. The emigrés listed no fewer than 180 prominent Russian Anarchists, with circumstantial details of their fate up to 1921. Of these 38 had been shot, 70 were in prison or in exile, and the remainder driven by persecution to their death or to flight from Russia.

By the end of 1920, with victory in sight in the civil war, general signs of discontent were discernible within the Communist party. This party had changed considerably since, with some 240,000 members, it had seized power in October 1917. It now numbered over 600,000. Since the main increase took place in 1919, it followed that only a little over a third could be reckoned among the 'old guard', who had joined when the issue was still doubtful. The revolution had encouraged a system of unbridled licence for Communists in authority, and this inevitably attracted to the party men who were out for what they could get. There is ample evidence to show that only a small proportion of the forty per cent of party members classified as 'workers' were other than professional party administrators of worker origin. If these bureaucrats are added to the thirty per cent officially listed as 'employees etc.' it is a fair inference that by 1920 the majority of the party was fairly remote from the people whose interests it was supposed to serve.

In its report to the Tenth Party Congress in March 1921 the Central Committee lamented the growing discord in the party between workers and intellectuals and between townsmen and peasants, and attributed the disappearance of the former party solidarity to exhaustion from hardship, to over-rapid expansion and to the 'rift in the case of a significant number of the party leaders in the centre and in the provinces . . . between them and the hard-working masses'. The leaders, said the report, were gradually ceasing to attend party meetings and were losing the confidence of the rank and file. Inequality of living conditions and privileges for the higher party officials, which at first had been the exception, 'were beginning to become widespread' and increased discontent.

There was also trouble brewing in the trade unions by early 1920. Their seven million membership included half a million Communists, but since virtually the entire party was enrolled in the unions the number of Communist workers must have been relatively small. The non-Communist rank and file were becoming in-creasingly alienated from their Communist officials and committees, as indeed Lenin, among others, admitted; but this 'temporary wavering', as it was usually described, was regarded as a security, rather than a political, problem. The trade union Communists at first accepted without question the centralized control imposed on their unions by the Communist Party: persistent criticism of this practice by Mensheviks and other opposition groups was enough to persuade them that talk of union freedom was in reality counter-revolution. There was also the promise contained in the party programme, adopted in March 1919, that 'the unions must achieve the actual concentration in their hands of all management of the entire national economy as a single economic unit.' As time went on, this promise became a source of acrimonious debate. The rank and file Communist workers began to long for the 'workers' control' which Lenin and the Bolsheviks had encouraged during the rise to power in 1917 as a way of causing maximum disorganization, but which after they came to office was being increasingly sacrificed to efficiency. Both Communist workers and the trade union officials joined in opposing the system of one-man management, which in practice meant that the enterprise was run by a non-Communist specialist — the workers from basic hostility to 'bourgeois intellectuals', the officials because it dimin-ished their authority.

In March 1920, at the Ninth Party Congress, Lenin with the skill for compromise which he could show in dealing with party disputes, succeeded in appeasing all concerned, as well as smoothing over the rivalry that was rapidly developing among the top party leaders, and winning what looked like full support for his policy. The peace was deceptive. Two trends of opposition, generally critical of Central Committee policy, had formed in the party. One, which later acquired the name of 'Workers' Opposition', grew up among the trade union Communists in the course of 1919. The followers of this group of critics not only opposed the increasing rôle of the bourgeois specialists but deplored what they regarded as the tendency of the Communist leadership to become bureaucratic and out of touch with the working masses. They also claimed the right of the union Communists to have a bigger voice in the control over industry. As time went on, their criticism broadened to include complaints about the dictatorial behaviour of the central party organs.

The other opposition was intellectual, mainly among the Communists in the soviets. It acquired the name of 'Democratic Centralism' and stood for the democratic principles embodied in the constitution, but long abandoned in practice, such as a more representative Central Executive Committee, real power for the soviet Communists independently of the central party organs, and the right of minorities to express their views. It should be emphasized that neither of these groups had any sympathy with the Mensheviks or other socialists. Above all, they never disputed the monopoly of power which the Communist party had assumed for itself — only the disciplinary means that were necessary to maintain it.

By the end of the year Trotsky, flushed with victory in the civil war, had persuaded some of the big trade union bosses to accept his proposals, which involved virtual militarization of the unions. This brought the party to a state of turmoil, with the Central Committee split into two factions. It should be emphasized that no one in the Central Committee had any sympathy with the kind of rank and file resistance to discipline which was at the root of the Workers' Opposition and Democratic Centralism; but the issue of more or less compulsion, of more or less conciliation, was one that genuinely worried some party leaders. There followed, during 1920, a period of unrest in the party to which several elements contributed. There was little difference in aim between Lenin and Trotsky so far as the trade unions were concerned — both regarded them as essentially instruments for putting through a state policy emanating from above. But whereas Trotsky was impatient, impetuous and unaware of the meaning of tact, Lenin had made himself expert in getting his own way without his followers realizing it. He had by such means won over the trade union bosses in March 1920. Trotsky, on the contrary, made no secret of his conviction that the dictatorial methods with which he had built up the Red Army should now be applied to industry and to transport, both of which emerged from the civil war in a catastrophic state. Another element which contributed to the crisis was the intense hatred and rivalry which Zinoviev had developed for Trotsky, and the unscrupulous means by which he exploited the growing resentment of central discipline in the party in order to achieve his own ends. In this ploy he was, in general, supported by Lenin, who resented the trouble Trotsky was causing by his lack of diplomacy.

The third element in the crisis was the growth of the central apparatus of the party, and the unpopularity of much of its activity. The Eighth Party Congress in March 1919 created a Politburo, which eventually developed into the main policy-making summit of the party, replacing the Central Committee. The congress also set up a Secretariat, which until then had only existed informally but which now became the body mainly responsible for dealing with dissension and discontent inside the party. By 1920, the number of secretaries was increased to three, and its staff grew rapidly (to 602 by February 1921). Even so, party records remained fairly primitive until 1922, when the advent of Stalin as General Secretary made its impact. The other body, known as the Orgburo, which included Stalin and the three secretaries, was responsible for the extensive moving around of party members — over 25,000 transfers by September 1920. While the great majority of these postings were dictated by the need to infuse energy at different points of the country, some were beyond doubt punitive, and all were unpopular.

In 1920 the three secretaries appear to have been genuinely conciliatory in their attempts to pacify an ever more turbulent party, though throughout the year Zinoviev led a violent campaign, attacking the secretaries for what he alleged to be their dictatorial and oppressive methods, as well as vilifying the Orgburo. The dishonest nature of a call for freedom emanating from Zinoviev, a notoriously dictatorial character, could not deceive the more intelligent party members, but demagogy was always sure of success among the rank and file, and was therefore likely sooner or later to win adherents at the top. Hence, on 30 December, in a vote on the Orgburo in the Central Committee, an open split was revealed, with Trotsky, two trade union bosses and the three secretaries on one side, and Zinoviev, Stalin and other close supporters of Lenin on the other. Lenin was apparently not present.

Zinoviev's activities were not confined to this championship of democracy in the party. In the course of 1920, as head of the Petrograd Communist Party organization, he conducted an intemperate attack inside the Baltic fleet against the naval political directorate, for which Trotsky was responsible. One of the consequences of this was to fan the unrest in the Baltic navy which culminated in the Kronstadt revolt in March 1921. His other campaign was waged against another of Trotsky's institutions, a joint central transport committee, which cut across the authority of the railway union leaders, was dictatorial in its methods and intensely unpopular. On the other hand, the committee (called *Tsektran* for short) had been set up by a vote of the whole Central Committee, including Zinoviev, and it is difficult to avoid the conclusion that Zinoviev's intense campaign against *Tsektran* was an exploitation of its unpopularity in order to discredit Trotsky. By the end of the year this campaign had produced a crisis in the party, which the Tenth Party Congress, meeting on 8 March 1921, had to resolve.

A vote in the Central Committee taken on 9 November showed opinion fairly evenly divided between the views of Trotsky and Lenin on *Tsektran*. Analysis of the two positions suggests that where Trotsky bluntly demanded open compulsion, Lenin stressed that the primary method was persuasion, although 'proletarian compulsion' could not be excluded. The difference between the two lay in the method adopted in trying to get the union leaders to submit to compulsion from the centre. A commission was now set up to reconcile the two formulations: Zinoviev was appointed its chairman, and Trotsky, not surprisingly, refused to serve on it. If Zinoviev's attempts at conciliation were genuine, they failed. In the Central Committee on 7 December, with Lenin's backing, he demanded the abolition of *Tsektran*. The Central Committee split on this issue. On one side were Lenin, Zinoviev and Stalin, and their supporters, ten in all; on the other side, Trotsky, Bukharin and others, including the three secretaries. This open division necessitated an all-party discussion, which lasted for two months.

For large sections of the party the trade union issue soon proved to be of secondary importance, and the debate was exploited for the ventilation of the deeper grievance over the decline of party democracy. This was particularly evident in the case of the Workers' Opposition which, with the adherence to its ranks of the colourful figure of Alexandra Kollontay, Shliapnikov's mistress, was transformed from a dull trade unionist lobby into a dramatic movement of rank and file discontent with central party dictatorship. Madame Kollontay voiced the familiar and popular complaints that only the peasants had benefited from the revolution, that the party was dominated by middle-class elements, estranged from the workers, and that the leaders had lost faith in the working class. Among the very first to rally to Lenin in 1901, she must have been surprised when he and others accused her of Menshevism, petty bourgeois ideas, and even, on one occasion, of 'Catholic beastliness'. On the trade union issue, eight 'platforms' in all appeared, but only three survived to be debated at the congress: the Platform of the Ten, backed by Lenin; and the 'platforms' supported respectively by Trotsky and by the Workers' Opposition. By an astute move of Zinoviev, the Central Committee was persuaded to order that the delegates had to declare which platform they supported before election to the congress. This effectively ensured the victory of the Platform of the Ten. Trotsky's unpopular policy would make his defeat certain, while in spite of the popularity of Kollontay and the occasional turbulence of the party, its generally deferential character would make it difficult for the 'platform' of the Workers' Opposition to score many votes without the backing of any Central Committee member, let alone of Lenin. By the time the congress met, however, it was faced with a crisis which far exceeded in gravity the dissensions inside the party.

In the last week of February 1921 industrial unrest began in Petrograd which soon started to assume the character of a general strike. The main motive seems to have been the extreme food and fuel shortage from which the city was suffering, though some of the resolutions passed reflected Menshevik and Socialist Revolutionary influence. The local Communist party responded by the dual methods of rushing food to the capital and arresting all the socialists still at liberty, and the strike collapsed.

A far more serious revolt broke out in the naval base of Kronstadt. Here food shortage was probably not a cause: rations in the fleet were higher than in industry and the sailors, who mostly came from the villages, did not share the townspeople's resentment of the peasants. (There is, however, no evidence to support the contention, mainly emanating from Trotsky's instant sociology, that the Communist party in the Baltic fleet contained a much higher proportion of peasants than elsewhere.) One reason for the revolt was that the authority of the naval commissars had been undermined by Zinoviev's campaign against Trotsky who controlled them through his nominee Raskol'nikov. Besides, anarchist influence had been strong in Kronstadt for a long time: in 1917, the local Communists had been quite beyond the control of the Central Committee. Finally, the Kronstadt revolt was sparked off by the sailors' confident expectation, in view of what was happening in Petrograd, that their rebellion would spread to the mainland.

On 28 February the crew of the *Petropavlovsk* voted the resolution which became the charter of the rebels. It demanded re-election of the soviets by secret ballot; freedom of speech and press for 'workers, peasants, and for the anarchists and the left socialist parties'; freedom of meeting and free trade unions and peasant unions; liberation of all socialist, worker and peasant political prisoners, and a review of all those detained in prisons and concentration camps; abolition of all special political departments (e.g. in the army and navy) 'since no one party can enjoy privileges for the propagation of its ideas and receive money from the state for the purpose'; equal rations for all; full rights for the peasants to do as they pleased with their land and the right to individual small-scale manufacture, but 'without employment of hired labour.'

The obviously popular and primitive nature of this programme did not prevent the Communists at the time, and since, from branding it as bourgeois, or as a disguised demand for the restoration of capitalism; nor from alleging, without any evidence, that the rebellion was inspired and led by White Guard officers. The resolution was voted at a mass meeting, at which the sole dissenting votes were those of Kalinin, the Chairman of the Central Executive Committee of the Soviets, and the Chairman of the Local Kronstadt Executive Committee. At the lowest estimate, 30 per cent of the local Communist party supported the rebellion and 40 per cent were neutral. On 2 March a Provisional Revolutionary Committee was set up, headed by a naval clerk, which rejected the Soviet government's demand for surrender. On 7 March, a military operation commanded by Tukhachevsky began.

Kronstadt is situated on an island in the Finnish Gulf about twenty miles west of Petrograd, but in winter the sea freezes over and Tukhachevsky's men were able to advance across the still frozen ice. The fortress was finally stormed on 18 March by reluctant Red Army men, driven on by their commissars and encouraged by some two hundred delegates from the Party Congress. The victims of reprisals numbered hundreds, if not thousands. A list was published of thirteen carefully selected ringleaders, consisting of a priest, five ex-officers, and seven peasants, but no public trial was ever held.

Although this revolt of the proletariat against the dictatorship of the proletariat was a severe humiliation for the Communist leaders, it does not seem to have presented a danger which military action could not solve. The party rallied as one man in face of this challenge to its privileges — many, no doubt, believed that the very foundations of socialism were at stake. Not a single member of the Workers' Opposition supported the rebels — indeed, its adherents were among the delegates sent to egg on the Red Army. The same army cadets who not many weeks before had voted for Kollontay's fiery resolutions were among the most reliable fighters on the ice in the Finnish Gulf.

From Lenin's point of view the Kronstadt revolt could not be allowed to fester, particularly since he was engaged in the full dismantling of the disastrous 'war communism' and the introduction of the New Economic Policy (NEP). This reversal had been decided on by Lenin before the outbreak in Kronstadt, and was motivated by the peasant guerrilla war. It involved replacing the confiscation of food quotas by a tax in kind and permitting free exchange of the products remaining in the peasants' hands. With much of the party in a state of left-wing ferment, this decision to abandon socialism called for an entirely new degree of central discipline if the party's hold over the country was to be maintained. This new party stranglehold was forged at the Tenth Congress, which voted NEP right at the end of its sessions after a debate consisting of four ten-minute speeches. The introduction of NEP also signalled the final destruction of the Mensheviks: they had for so long been advocating a policy similar to NEP, and therefore had to be deprived of the rudiments of political toleration that they still retained.

The panic into which the Kronstadt revolt had flung the delegates when they met in congress on 8 March 1921 made it possible for Lenin to achieve his policy with striking ease. Voting by 'platforms' produced some 45 or 50 Workers' Opposition delegates, but only 18 in the end supported their policy. The overwhelming victory of the Platform of the Ten was a foregone conclusion. On the second day, Lenin had given a warning about opposition: 'It's not the time for it,' he said, and went on: 'No more opposition now, comrades. And in my view, the congress will have to draw the conclusion that the time has come to put an end to opposition, to put the lid on it, we have had enough opposition.'

On the very last day, 16 March, when the congress had apparently finished its business, Lenin produced two resolutions directed against the Workers' Opposition. The first, on 'Party Unity', declared that there were signs in the party of the formation of 'groups with separate platforms and with the determination, to a certain extent, to become self-contained and to create their own group discipline'. (This was totally untrue of the Workers' Opposition, which had only emerged with its own 'platform' when ordered to do so by the Central Committee, and which fully accepted party discipline.) The resolution proceeded to hint that the opposition had given encouragement to the enemies of the revolution, and enjoined restraint on criticism, bearing in mind the enemies by which the party was surrounded. It went on to demand, on pain of expulsion, the immediate dissolution of all groups with separate platforms. By a secret clause, members of the Central Committee could be expelled for factionalism by a two-thirds vote.

The second resolution condemned the views of the 'so-called Workers' Opposition', and proclaimed that 'marxism teaches us' that only the Communist party is capable of uniting, educating and organizing the working masses to enable them to resist petty bourgeois waverings — in other words, the doctrine of *What is to be Done?* of 1902. The effect of panic was evident in the voting: the Workers' Opposition delegates did not vote up to their strength and the rest of the congress was solidly behind Lenin. The general mood was probably summed up by Karl Radek, in later years one of Stalin's many victims: 'In voting for this resolution, I feel that it can well be turned against us, and nevertheless I support it . . . . Let the Central Committee even be mistaken! That is less dangerous than the wavering which is now observable.'

Eloquent resolutions were proposed to the congress that were certainly calculated to calm the apprehensions of those who were still naïve enough to believe them. The Platform of the Ten, in two passages, proclaimed the need 'to do away with the method of appointment from the top'. Another long resolution that was adopted asserted that the military form of centralization dictated by civil war conditions was no longer necessary, and stressed the need in future for complete freedom of criticism inside the party and of election in place of appointment from the top.

The new régime in the party made itself felt immediately. The three secretaries were removed, and replaced by Molotov, who worked under Stalin's direction. The Central Control Commission, which had been appointed in September 1920 and which endeavoured in the first months of its existence to act impartially, was now charged with 'the consolidation of unity and authority in the party'. Even so, it continued for some time to maintain relative impartiality, and the extensive repressions against oppositionists which began soon after the congress were, in the main, carried out by other central party organs.

The iron hand of the Central Committee was also evident over the trade unions. One resolution on democracy passed at the Tenth Congress had included a clause to the effect that 'the reconstruction of trade union organization from the top is completely inadmissible,' and in May 1921, true to the spirit of this resolution, the Metal Workers' Union, the oldest Bolshevik union, showed its sympathy with the Workers' Opposition by rejecting the Central Committee's list of candidates for the controlling committee of the union by 120 votes to 40. The Central Committee thereupon appointed a union committee consisting entirely of its own nominees. Such instances could be multiplied. *Tsektran*, for example, was restored with full powers immediately after the party congress at a carefully packed congress of transport workers. Suggestions have been made, mainly by Trotsky in exile, that the new régime imposed on the party by

Lenin was intended to be temporary. If so, he did not retain his strength long enough to change what he had brought about in 1921.

From the start of Bolshevik rule, it became evident that real power was to be exercised by *Sovnarkom* (which for the short period between December 1917 and March 1918 included a few LSR commissars but after that was wholly Bolshevik). For the conduct of matters relating to the civil war, a Council of Workers' and Peasants' Defence was set up in November 1918, consisting of five Bolsheviks, including Trotsky and Stalin. Lenin was chairman of both councils. Theoretically, *Sovnarkom* was supposed to be the executive body: legislative power was vested in the Congress of Soviets and, between the infrequent meetings of that gathering, in its Central Executive Committee (CEC). As elected at the Second Congress of Soviets (after the socialists had walked out) this consisted of 67 Bolsheviks and 29 LSR, with 20 seats allocated to various small left-wing groups of no significance or influence. In practice, the CEC was dominated by the Bolsheviks and its Bolshevik chairman. This situation was not altered when the CEC was expanded by merger in November 1917 with the Peasant Soviets' CEC, since in practice the deputies who entered the merged body were mostly Bolshevik and pro-Bolshevik soldiers. Its legislative activity was virtually confined to endorsement of measures submitted to it by *Sovnarkom*. For some time, however, debates in this body did provide the opportunity for fairly frank expression of critical views of Bolshevik policy.

The evidence suggests that it was Lenin's intention that the government of the country should be concentrated in *Sovnarkom*, in its standing committee, the Lesser *Sovnarkom*, and in the Council of Labour and Defence (STO) for economic and supply matters. Lenin was chairman of all these organs and their members were leading party members. But after the improvement of central party machinery in 1919, the Politburo and Orgburo increasingly became the main centres of policy decision. The process was accelerated after Lenin's incapacity in May 1922: no one could replace Lenin in the art of holding a businesslike coalition together, and the centre of power shifted to the uneasy alliance of Zinoviev, Kamenev and Stalin.

Chapter Thirteen

Lenin's Last Years

Soon after the Tenth Congress, it had become apparent that its promises of democracy in the party and the trade unions were a sham. The hated *Tsektran*, whose abolition had been urged by Lenin, Zinoviev and Stalin, was restored. The packing of the Metal Workers' Union has been noted. Victimization of supporters of the Workers' Opposition became particularly intense. The attacks on them, such as discrimination in appointments, transfers from one district to another, and even expulsion from the party, were not based on ideological grounds but followed on any kind of criticism of the party's shortcomings, even at private meetings. The Workers' Opposition, headed by Shliapnikov, appealed to the Central Committee, but its complaints were flatly rejected as untrue. Its leaders thereupon decided to enlist the support of the Communist International.

The Third Communist International (*Comintern*) came into being on Lenin's initiative in 1919, and was from the first overshadowed and dominated by the Soviet Communist Party. This was not surprising, in view of the prestige and authority acquired by the first extreme left-wing movement that had actually come to power. The nascent European Communist parties were hypnotized by the 'First Socialist State', and the Executive Committee of the *Comintern* could scarcely be expected to sympathize with complaints about the flouting of democracy in the Soviet party or its growing non-proletarian composition. A commission appointed to examine the charges duly exonerated the party and claimed that accusations against it merely provided encouragement to Mensheviks and 'counter-revolutionaries' generally.

Lenin himself was particularly infuriated by the fact that the Russian oppositionists had also established contact with left-wing splinter groups in the European Communist movements, who argued that the *Comintern* was dominated by Russian interests, and not those of the working masses. But Lenin's health was failing. He was to suffer his first stroke in May 1922, and he had been able to attend only the opening and closing sessions of the Eleventh Communist Party Congress, which met on 27 March of that year. At that congress the Central Committee virtually got its own way on the issue of the Workers' Opposition, which it condemned, although the delegates refused to expel the oppositionist leaders, as the Central Committee demanded. This virtually marked the end of what still remained of democracy in the party. The most important decision of the congress was to elect Stalin as General Secretary, apparently with Lenin's approval, and to add a number of his known supporters to the Central Committee. Under Stalin's overall control, the hold of the central party was considerably extended.

The spread of Communist influence over the life of the country, which began in 1919, was accelerated. Two processes were of primary significance in this development. One was the setting up of departments of the Central Committee which, under the direction of the General Secretary, were eventually to dominate the whole life of the country. The other was the extension and improvement of the records on party members. The assignment of the right men to all appointments, the disciplining of individuals by exile or dismissal, and the selection of officials and delegates necessarily depended on such records. By 1923 considerable progress had been made towards the establishment of the system of party domination which has remained essentially the same ever since: the control over postings, which enabled the central apparatus to place well-screened and trusted nominees in key positions; strict discipline over party members and over local organizations; and the establishment of supremacy over state institutions.

While this was going on, the New Economic Policy was transforming the life of the country. The resolution of the Tenth Congress, as extended by subsequent legislation, virtually restored a system of small-scale commerce in the country. The fact that the peasants could now keep and sell on the free market what remained after the payment of a tax encouraged them to increase their production. (It was also a powerful factor in calming them down, although even so the Red Army had to spend about a year putting down guerrilla activity.) Restricted leasing of land and hiring of labour were also introduced and brought prosperity to the more ambitious peasants — the so-called 'kulaks', who were to become the first of the countless victims of collectivization in 1929 and 1930. Eventually the monetary system was rationalized, with the assistance of a former Kadet Minister of Finance, and legal codes were enacted which were intended to provide stability for commercial transactions. The aim of this policy was to attract the investment of foreign capital in Soviet enterprises, although the new rulers' determined repudiation of all the debts incurred by the tsarist government continued to deter outside entrepreneurs from sinking money in Russia.

Small-scale trade and industry flourished, and in this the return of enterprises to private management was an important factor. Around three-quarters of retail trade would eventually be in private hands, but the state kept an extensive hold on large and medium-scale industry, on finance, and on foreign trade. NEP was, in fact, a great material success. After a disastrous crop failure in 1921 and 1922 — of which the consequences would have been much worse but for the generous help provided by the American Relief Administration of Herbert Hoover — the Soviet economy made rapid progress, although the revival of industry was slower than that of agriculture, and the real incomes of workers in heavy industry in 1922-23 were still less than half their earnings in 1913. All this was to lead to economic and political complications.

As the release of what Bukharin called 'the demon' of capitalism became increasingly apparent, so opposition to NEP spread inside the Communist Party. There were many who had accepted it only reluctantly as a temporary necessity in 1921: when it became clear that NEP had come to stay for some time, the left opposition inside the party, of which Trotsky eventually became the leader, gathered force. It was, in any case, always a powerful argument among the rank and file that the revolution had brought benefits only to the peasants, and none to the workers. But by the time of Lenin's death arguments in the party were no longer won or lost by reason of their content. The improvements in the central apparatus of the party, largely effected by Stalin during his first years of office, had ensured that political issues would be decided not by debate but by manipulating the election of delegates to party congresses and conferences, and by the exercise of party discipline. The question of NEP, and of policy towards the peasants, became interwoven with Stalin's bid for sole power and his personal conflict both with the left of the party under Trotsky, and later the right of the party, headed by Bukharin and Tomsky. But this development was to take place after Lenin's death. NEP was also a period of flourishing intellectual life. Large numbers of Russian writers and scholars had repudiated communism, and had either emigrated or joined the White side of the civil war. On the other side there were some Communist writers and academics, but for the most part literature and learning in the early twenties were maintained by those who, while rejecting communism, were prepared to cooperate with the government — either from patriotism, or because they hoped that the régime would eventually change for the better. This suited both those party leaders who, like Bukharin, expected to win over the intelligentsia by the merits of communism, and those who, like Stalin, viewed cooperation with non-Communists as an unavoidable necessity until such time as they could be replaced by Communists or pro-Communists.

The NEP years were something of a golden age in Russian intellectual life. For the time being, the universities and the Academy of Sciences (formerly the Imperial Academy) retained a good deal of their freedom. But parallel Communist institutions were set up, with the intention of training a future academic élite — the Red Professors' Institute, set up in 1921, and the Socialist Academy. These two bodies produced works of distinguished marxist scholarship, especially in the legal and historical fields.

In the case of literature, there was the difficulty of reconciling the party's desire to control creative activity with the writers' equally strong determination to retain their freedom. Marx and Engels had held conventional views on literature, and Lenin did not conceal his dislike of modern experimental schools. In due course, his pronouncement on the subject of 'literature' made in 1905, which seems to refer to party political rather than creative writing, was much canvassed in support of complete control over writers. But, in general, literature remained relatively free, apart from rough censorship by the security forces. Alexander Blok, possibly the greatest poet of his generation, supported the Bolshevik revolution to the dismay of his friends, but was soon disillusioned, and died in 1921, consumed with disappointment and remorse. The most talented writers formed a group called the Fellow Travellers: they were the constant object of attack by the extreme left-wing 'Proletarian' writers, but during the early years of NEP the party remained mainly neutral in this struggle.

Religion fared less well. Lenin had always been a militant atheist, though he wisely remained silent on the subject during the struggle for power in 1917. After the Bolshevik victory, anti-religious activity was stepped up by the *Cheka* and by amateur bodies of anti-religious fanatics. The Constitution of 1918 proclaimed the separation of the church from the state, but recognized the freedom of both religious and anti-religious propaganda. However, there was much harassment of priests, frequent expropriation of church property, and refusal of legal recognition to church marriages. In 1922 a staged trial took place of fifty-four high dignitaries of the Orthodox and Roman Catholic churches. Nevertheless, the assault on religion made little real progress during the NEP period. In the case of the Jews, the official policy was to encourage assimilation. Manifestations of anti-semitism (which, since so many leading Communists were Jewish, often meant anti-communism) were repressed in the early years.

The effect of NEP on the foreign policy of the RSFSR was soon to become apparent. Hitherto its relations with the outside world had been largely those of an outcast fomenting world revolution, and itself the object of intervention by the capitalist powers. But by 1921 the prospects of revolution had receded: attempts to stir them up in Poland, in the independent Baltic states and in Germany had failed. The immediate need of the Soviet state was for normal trade relations with the capitalist world: it was hardly a coincidence that an Anglo-Soviet Trade Agreement was signed in London on the day after Lenin's announcement of NEP to the Tenth Party Congress. At the Third Congress of the *Comintern*, in June and July 1921, the Russian delegation, firmly led by Lenin, sounded the retreat from world revolution. Considerable opposition to this policy was voiced by non-Russian left-wing critics, and there is no doubt that their views found sympathy among members of the Soviet delegation, even if they did not voice it. The RSFSR sensed the danger of this. The disciplinary powers of the Executive were strengthened, and before long the dissident left-wingers were expelled. A resolution adopted on the structure of Communist parties went even further in assimilation to the Russian party than the so-called Twenty One Points voted by the Second Congress in 1920.

At the next, much more obedient, Fourth Congress in 1922, the keynote was the need to direct all action towards helping the Soviet state. Lenin, already very ill, astonished his colleagues by criticizing the resolution on party structure adopted in 1921 for being 'too Russian' and unintelligible to non-Russian comrades. However, the congress ignored him and adopted an even more 'Russian' resolution on party structure.

The RSFSR also made progress in conventional diplomatic relations. It is true that a conference in Genoa in April 1922, from which the RSFSR hoped to obtain both recognition and loans for the development of her industry from the capitalist powers, ended in failure, foundering on Allied claims in respect of debts repudiated by the Communists, and the nationalization of foreign-owned enterprises. But a political and commercial alliance was clandestinely concluded at Rapallo with the other outcast, Germany. This alliance was further bolstered by certain secret agreements — tentative negotiations had gone on in 1921 for the manufacture by Germany in Russia of military equipment prohibited to Germany by the Treaty of Versailles.

By the end of 1921, illness had compelled Lenin to abandon full-time work. His public appearances in 1922 were very few, and by March 1923 he was totally incapacitated. At intervals until then he had continued to dictate memoranda and articles, but his party colleagues were by now pursuing their policy in many ways in disregard of his views, and his relations with them were strained. Many matters were kept from him, ostensibly out of consideration for his health. His two secretaries were reporting on him to Stalin — or so he believed. Even his wife (as will be seen below) failed to carry out his wishes on one vital occasion. His confidants were Bukharin and Trotsky — though the latter could not always be relied on to keep his promises to the sick man.

One of the causes of conflict between Lenin and his fellow-communists was the policy pursued towards the non-Russian minorities of the former Russian empire. It will be recalled that, in spite of opposition from his colleagues, Lenin had insisted on making self-determination for all the component elements of the empire part of Bolshevik policy, and this principle was embodied in an early decree of the new government in 1917. But, as the control of the Red Army was progressively extended during the civil war over border areas which had secured their temporary independence, it became evident that traditional Communist insistence on centralized control would prevail over theory as propounded by Lenin. Communist organizations, with the aid of troops, were used to overthrow national governments. The constitution of 1918 described the RSFSR as a 'federation of national soviet republics'. In March of the following year, as we saw in Chapter 10, the party programme, while reaffirming the right of minorities to self-determination and secession, had qualified this by explaining that the soviet pattern of federation should become 'one of the transitional paths to complete unity', and that in every case who precisely had the right to choose separation must be decided 'according to the historical stage of the development of that nation'. In practice, this usually came to be interpreted as meaning that the 'bearer of the will' was the small, Moscow-dominated, mainly Russian local Communist Party. Even where Communist Parties in national territories enjoyed a measure of local support, the principle embodied in the party rules in December 1919, that the local national committee was a regional committee sub-ordinated, like any other, to the Central Committee, inevitably led to friction.

Lenin, although fully behind the policy of centralization, became increasingly disturbed by national tension which he attributed not to the unpopular policy of Moscow's control, but solely to the lack of tact in handling non-Russian minorities on the part of Stalin as Commissar for Nationality Affairs, and his Great Russian, or assimilated non-Russian, emissaries.

By the end of 1922, it was decided to give formal recognition to the reincorporation which had in fact taken place. On 29 December, articles of union were signed by representatives of the Communist parties of the four republics concerned — the RSFSR, the Ukraine, Belorussia and Transcaucasus (the latter comprising Georgia, Azerbaidjan and Armenia). The Constitution of the USSR (Union of Soviet Socialist Republics), as it was now to be called, was approved by the CEC on 6 July 1923 and ratified by an All-Union Congress of Soviets on 31 January 1924. In internal matters it followed that of the RSFSR of 1918. As regards federation, it included the now derisory right of secession, left the union republics sole competence in certain areas, such as health and education, and provided for a federal Council of Nationalities. Party control of administration and election ensured that centralization would be preserved.

Party discipline had made certain that the opposition to central-ization of local communists had been kept from expressing itself. This was especially strong in Georgia, and on 21 October 1922 the entire Georgian Central Committee had resigned in protest against the failure of the Central Committee's emissary to discuss with them the plan for creating the Soviet Union. In December, Lenin, who had been increasingly critical of the treatment of the Georgian Com-munists by Stalin and his emissaries, dictated three notes on the national question. In these, he roundly blamed Stalin and his associates for their 'Great Russian chauvinism', and urged that the possibility should be considered of leaving independence to all commissariats in the republics, except those for foreign and military matters. He particularly cautioned against chauvinism in questions relating to the right to use the native language — a matter on which nationalist sentiment is always particularly sensitive. He ended with a warning of the havoc that would result 'on the eve of the emergence of the East' from adopting 'something like imperialist relations' to Soviet Russia's own minorities. He said nothing, however, about the centralized control of the party, which made a mockery of any independence left to the government machinery in the republics.

Stalin became aware of Lenin's notes, and attempted to see him. An effort by Krupskaia to shield her husband led to a 'rude outburst' from Stalin, and on 5 March, to a letter to him from Lenin, demanding an apology. Three days later a stroke put Lenin out of action for good; but before then he had forwarded his notes to Trotsky, apparently as the result of Trotsky's agreement to take up the case of Georgia at the Twelfth Party Congress, due to meet in April. He had also sent a letter of strong support to the Georgian Communist leaders. Stalin was able to ward off the threat to his own position, largely owing to Trotsky's failure to take any action on the notes at the Congress, and also helped by Lenin's secretary, who fowarded the notes to the Politburo with a warning that Lenin had not had time to revise them. Stalin was thus able to avoid publishing the notes — much to his regret, as he said. The decisive factor, however, was probably Trotsky's silence, for which there is no satisfactory explanation. In spite of bitter opposition speeches, the victory of Stalin's policy by an overwhelming majority was ensured by the fact that the congress was packed with his supporters. In a concluding speech, which was a masterpiece of hypocrisy, Stalin praised the unity of the party, adding how much he regretted Lenin's absence.

Lenin's conflicts with his colleagues in 1922 and 1923 were not confined to the national question. The most serious attack on Stalin, with whom he had expressed disagreement on a number of other important issues, was contained in several memoranda which he specifically stated were intended for the 'forthcoming' Twelfth Congress of the Party, due to be held in the spring of 1923. In the first note, dated 25 December 1922, Lenin warned that the main threat to the stability of the leadership lay in the bad relations between Trotsky, 'the most able man in the present Central Committee', and Stalin, who had concentrated 'enormous power' in his hands and was not always sufficiently cautious in using it. On 4 January 1923, after Stalin's attempt to speak to him on the nationalities question (and the clash with Krupskaia) he dictated a postcript to the effect that 'Stalin is too rude' and that 'I propose to the comrades to think out some way of removing Stalin' from the post of General Secretary.

The other matters in these and subsequent memoranda (which became known as 'Lenin's Testament') related mainly to his views on the need to restock party organs with workers and peasants, so as to put an end to corruption and inefficiency. He seems to have shown no realization of the threat to the party posed by the growing power of the secretariat, but remained convinced that the trouble lay with the moral character of the incumbents of offices. So far as our evidence goes, he never considered that if once you place uncontrolled power in the hands of an élite, abuse of it is certain to occur — a principle underlying all the checks and balances invented to control governments throughout the centuries.

We can get a fairer picture of Lenin's thoughts on the future as he saw it from a number of articles which he wrote during his lucid period in 1922 and early 1923. One cannot, of course, know how he would have conducted affairs had he returned to power in 1924; but in his state of disability, with no real prospect of recovery, he got nearer than ever before to constructive thought on the future of the régime which he had played so big a part in creating. In the first place, he recognized that the attempt to construct socialism in a country as backward as Russia had been out of line with orthodox marxist thought, which frequently warned against such action. In the conditions of 1917, he maintained, there had been no alternative; but this had meant that the political revolution (by which he meant the seizure of power by the Bolsheviks) had taken place before the necessary social conditions had matured. Now that political power was in the hands of the proletariat (meaning the Communist Party) a long period would be required in which the peasants could be raised to the level of social consciousness that a socialist revolution demanded. This meant many decades, and this time should become one of peace between town and countryside, since conflict between these two parts of society was the greatest danger which could befall the Soviet state. During this long era of peace in the villages, the peasants must learn the benefits of cooperation: with power in the hands of the 'proletariat', cooperation could ensure real progress towards socialism, and play a big part in raising the educational level of the peasants.

A constant refrain in these late writings is complaint at the inefficiency of state institutions, which he blamed on the fact that these were the pre-1917 ones, 'only slightly anointed with Soviet holy oil,' as he put it. What he failed to point out was that the 'holy oil', in the form of the Communists who penetrated the institutions, made life and work impossible for the old civil service by their interference. There was also some reflection on the future of the RSFSR on the world scene. The dream of swift revolutions in the industrial countries had collapsed — evidently capitalism was stronger than had been believed. What was imminent now was the inevitable ultimate conflict between the imperialists and the awakening colonial peoples. In this clash of forces, the exploited were certain to win, and it was essential that the Soviet state should survive until the defeat of the capitalists by the subject colonials came to its rescue. The upshot of all this was to justify NEP and the limited market economy which it entailed, and to see it not as a short-lived effort to get out of trouble, as many in the party regarded it in 1921, but as a serious long-term policy for the foreseeable future. How many were persuaded by these arguments it is difficult to say. What is certain is that Bukharin was convinced by Lenin's vision, and did his best to put it into practice in the years before NEP was killed, and he and his allies politically defeated, by Stalin in 1929 and 1930.

On 21 January 1924 Lenin died, three months before his fifty-fourth birthday. From the age of seventeen his life had been devoted to the aim of revolution. He played no part in February 1917 when the monarchy collapsed: his sights were set on the only kind of revolution that he acknowledged, one in which the Bolshevik party, created by him in 1903, would hold the monopoly of power in the name of the working class. Other socialist parties, claiming to be workers' parties, were to be excluded as fraudulent pretenders. All methods were justified to achieve this end, because Lenin and his close supporters believed with fanatical intensity that their success in Petrograd on 25 October 1917 would inaugurate a new era in the history of mankind, and would bring forth a new and happier world. This faith may have diminished as the practical problems of office accumulated: notes of doubt or disillusionment seem to sound in the last writings of Lenin that we know, and in 1921 NEP had indicated an abandonment of the intransigent 'war communism' and a recognition that theory had to be tempered by common sense. But to ignore the faith that dominated Lenin and his close followers like Trotsky, Dzerzhinsky, Sverdlov or Stalin is to misunderstand the history of the Russian revolution.

In the actual organization of the final stages of the Bolshevik revolution, Lenin's rôle fell far short of Trotsky's, for example, who saw the importance of linking the Bolshevik seizure of power to the meeting of the Second Congress of Soviets. Yet there is no doubt that without Lenin the Bolshevik coup would have been postponed, and might conceivably have failed. Even more significantly, the whole notion of the Bolshevik monopoly of power was Lenin's, as well as the vital device of using the party as the instrument for maintaining it. Moreover, in inventing a system in which a disciplined, centrally controlled party is used to manipulate a façade of ostensibly freely functioning and popularly elected institutions like soviets or trade unions, Lenin added to the store of political devices an entirely new type of mechanism, and one which has since been imitated in many parts of the world. No doubt the debate will continue for years whether Lenin's doctrine and practice were a perversion of the doctrines of Marx, or the inspired implementation of the theory in practice. Perhaps the answer does not matter all that much. What is important is that the refusal to compromise with the socialist parties, and the headstrong implementation up to 1921 of dogmatic policies from which great hardship and misery flowed, were the direct result of the fanatical confidence of Lenin and his followers that they alone held the key to making Marx's theories work.

The first party congress after Lenin's death, the Thirteenth, was due to meet on 23 May 1924. A few days before that date Krupskaia forwarded to the Politburo the notes which Lenin had dictated between 22 December 1922 and 23 January 1923 — the so-called 'Testament'. She explained the delay by the statement in an accompanying letter that Lenin had expressed the 'definite wish' that these notes should be submitted to the next congress 'after his death'.

No explanation has ever been offered of this assertion, which flatly contradicts what Lenin dictated in the notes themselves. The year's delay in dealing with the explosive 'Testament', of which Stalin must certainly have been aware, was presumably not wasted by him. At any rate, the threat posed by the notes, which could have meant his downfall in 1923, now seemed to present no danger to him. In the end, the notes were not laid before the congress, but only read, with suitable comments, to leaders of delegations. The congress was a model of unanimity. Immediately after it, at a meeting of the Central Committee, Stalin offered to resign. The entire committee pressed him to remain at his post. Most probably, under the effect of the shock of Lenin's death, the leaders of the party feared that if Stalin were removed from the helm it would endanger their own survival in power.

Since Lenin's departure in 1922, power had been in the hands of a triumvirate consisting of Stalin, Zinoviev and Kamenev. Trotsky, together with forty-six of his supporters, mainly old left-wingers, had come out openly against what they described as the 'inadequacy of the party leadership' in economic policy and the 'completely intolerable' régime within the party. In mid-October 1923, they had served on the Politburo a document containing these charges, which became known as the Declaration of the Forty Six. Trotsky was now the main object of attack by Stalin and his supporters. Shortly after Lenin's death, a journal called *The Bolshevik* came into existence with the avowed object of combating 'Trotskyism'.

Minor attacks by Stalin against Zinoviev and Kamenev began in June 1924. By the autumn of that year relations between Stalin and his ostensible allies were near breaking point. Before long, Trotsky was to join forces with them, in a struggle to defeat the formidable machine which Stalin had built up — a struggle that was to culminate on 19 January 1928 with the announcement that some thirty oppositionists, headed by Trotsky, had gone into exile. From the outset the attempt had been hopeless. By that time Stalin's predominance was beyond challenge.

Epilogue

Those who have got as far as this will have realized that the author's main purpose has been to examine the methods by which the Bolsheviks achieved power in 1917, and the ways in which they succeeded in subsequent years in holding on to it. In other words, this book is concerned with the working out in practice of what Lenin believed to be the principle underlying politics — 'Who whom?' — who overcomes whom? On this assumption, compromise with political opponents is impossible: if one is to survive oneself, they have to be destroyed, at all events politically. This was also the only logical position that could be adopted by a group of men who believed intensely that they, and they alone, knew how to create Utopia in Russia, and soon after in the whole world. Lenin certainly held this faith, at any rate in 1917. The discerning reader will also have realized that the theme of this book centres on human beings — not social trends, economic theories or sociological analyses, but on what men and women did or tried to do in the circumstances they faced.

No one who lived through the February revolution and the fall of the monarchy in Petrograd in 1917 will ever forget the hope with which those events were greeted. Before long, popular enthusiasm became centred on the soviets, rather than on the Provisional Government, which in any case was regarded as only a place-holder for the Constituent Assembly. The soviets, however rough and ready, were elected bodies; their reason for existence was plain for all to see. The Provisional Government, on the other hand, had no legitimate basis for its existence from the very start. Its links with the Duma, from which it claimed its right to exist, were of the slenderest. Its members were, in effect, self-appointed — Miliukov's empty rhetoric, 'The revolution appointed us', was an admission of this. The logic of the popular view at the time — that the Provisional Government was the executive, while the Petrograd Soviet was the legislature — is easy enough to understand.

There were many, both in the Provisional Government and in moderate circles in the country — intellectual, commercial, legal —

who viewed with dismay the mounting chaos resulting from the policies pursued by the Soviet, often in cooperation with the Provisional Government, which in many respects shared its aims. But, except for those of avowed right-wing sympathies, they were restrained in their actions by constant fear of counter-revolution, with which they associated any attempt to limit the extremism of the Soviet. These fears were unrealistic, in the sense that there never was during 1917 any serious threat of the restoration of the monarchy, nor of the old order generally; but they operated to create extreme suspicion of the army leaders, for example, who were concerned not with restoring the Tsar or preserving the rule of the landlords, but with stopping the anarchy and disorder that were sweeping the country in general and the armed forces in particular. This was constantly exploited by the Bolsheviks, with great success.

There was ample material elsewhere for the Bolsheviks to exploit in a country where the mass of the population had for centuries been kept outside participation in politics, and was the more readily susceptible to demagogy. The desire for peace had been building up in the army and navy for years, and had been kept in check by discipline and patriotism. When discipline was removed by the combined measures of the Soviet and the Provisional Government and patriotism was undermined by uninhibited debate, pressure to end the war at any cost became intense. On the land, the peasants, often encouraged by deserters trained by Bolshevik propagandists, were eager, amidst the general breakdown of public order, to seize from the landlords the land and produce of which they were persuaded they had been unjustly deprived. In the factories, workmen were easily won over, not only by Bolshevik but by much socialist rhetoric, to believe that all the economic ills of the country could be cured by depriving the owners of their ill-gotten profits. An atmosphere of righting all the wrongs of the past at a stroke was in the air. The political agitators believed that justice was on the side of those who had been the underdogs in the past, and that the day had now dawned when all that would be remedied. Their words fell on ready ears. There were also, of course, many to whom the prospect of banditry and violence held great attraction, bolstered by the fact that they could easily be persuaded that such conduct was a fitting reward for injustices suffered in the past. Bolshevism, during its rise to power, when violence was openly advocated, appealed to such people. The Bolsheviks claimed to have made a proletarian revolution. In reality, their revolution was in large measure that of the *'Lumpenproletariat'*.

The picture of Russia in 1917 is not complete without recognition of the fact that there was at the same time a widespread desire in the country for effective resistance to the Central Powers in the war. It was partly through patriotic feeling that there was a widely prevalent suspicion of the Bolsheviks, to be found among people of every class, because they were suspected of being German agents, or if not actually agents, then serving German interests by their defeatism. Amidst extremism and violence, there was also a longing for reconciliation and compromise, and for an end to interminable conflict. But the many opponents of Bolshevism lacked unity of purpose or determination. They did not believe with any conviction that a Bolshevik take-over was a serious possibility, still less that it would be more than a brief transient episode if it took place. And so, in the end, the Bolsheviks, who knew what they wanted, came to power on a wave of popular desire for the soviets to assume the reins of office as the only alternative to a government which was palpably incapable of governing — and then usurped soviet authority in favour of the rule of their own party. They exploited the widely prevalent hope for the Constituent Assembly to put an end to uncertainty — and then swept away the Constituent Assembly in favour of the pseudo-soviets which their party dominated. Those, and there were many, who wished for, or were ready to tolerate, socialism which respected the principles of freedom and justice, accepted Bolshevik rule partly because they thought it could not last in its extreme form; and in part because they feared that opposing it they would open the way to reaction and to the return of the old order.

The Bolsheviks enjoyed certain overwhelming advantages in their pursuit of power. They were prepared to use any deceit or stratagem, any demagogic device. They were not restrained by any scruples or doubts of principle — Lenin repeatedly explained that the only criterion of a moral action in politics was whether or not it helped to further the revolution. Above all, Lenin devised the means by which a chaotic democratic system could be harnessed to carry out the will and to further the interests of a group of fanatical enthusiasts — the Bolshevik party. This party, which at the time was a new and unique device in politics, could be used to make institutions conform to the intentions of the ruling élite, by short-circuiting the unpredictable inconvenience of majority decisions. Certainly, in the early stages, Bolshevism enjoyed a large measure of popular support; but when Lenin's promised Utopia failed to materialize, when the score of broken promises of bread, peace and freedom mounted, the machinery of the party proved indispensable in holding on to power in the face of growing opposition. At no stage in the period covered were the Bolsheviks or Communists unanimous on questions of policy. But all, almost without exception, were agreed that preservation of power was the first priority, in order to implement their Utopia. Dissension invariably melted away, whatever the principle involved, in the face of any danger to the survival of the monopoly of rule instituted after the departure of the LSR from the government.

Subversion of the armed forces was a vital part of Bolshevik strategy. It was essential from the Bolshevik point of view to counteract the military committees which were, for the most part, dominated by socialists, who were liable to oppose the Bolsheviks. It was for this reason that so big a propaganda effort (as far as our evidence goes, probably paid for by German money) was devoted to the army at the front. It was essential from Lenin's standpoint to neutralize the army as a fighting force for two reasons. First, because a victorious offensive could restore shattered morale, and so remove the most powerful factor operating in favour of the Bolsheviks — the desire for peace. And secondly, because an army of unimpaired morale could provide the Provisional Government with a force to resist the Bolshevik take-over when it came. The Bolsheviks did not start the decline of morale in the army at the front: they certainly did their best to accelerate it.

The Petrograd garrison was an equally vital factor in Bolshevik plans. Here, Lenin's party enjoyed certain advantages. For one thing, it was the most persistent opponent of any attempt to move garrison troops to the front. Besides, troops who had committed acts of mutiny and violence against their authorities had a strong vested interest in the survival of the revolutionary order and were therefore particularly susceptible to Bolshevik talk of counter-revolutionary threats. It was, perhaps, surprising that the Bolsheviks never succeeded in winning the active support of more than a small part of the garrison; but the neutrality of the troops proved sufficient for their purpose, and the soldiers' overwhelming support for the soviets was, in the end, all they needed for the capture of power.

It can be argued that it was not so much the case that the Bolsheviks won, as that their opponents lost. Or, as it is sometimes put, that power 'lay in the streets' for anyone to pick up. Certainly, in retrospect, the Provisional Government would seem to have done everything to bring about its own downfall. It failed to discover, or to act upon, the evident danger of a Bolshevik *coup d'état*. To a degree that seems incomprehensible in a time of war, it tolerated Bolshevik agitation at the front. It introduced, in the midst of hostilities, extreme libertarian measures in a country that had virtually never known anything but police rule, that was still far off from complete literacy, and that as yet lacked institutions of self-government. It took no effective step to bring to an end a war which it could not fight. It failed to act speedily in convoking the Constituent Assembly which alone could have given it the legitimacy it so patently lacked. It failed to stem the tide of peasant unrest by taking any decision on land distribution before the long-delayed Constituent Assembly met, and so let agrarian disturbances play into the Bolsheviks' hands. The list could be multiplied.

Yet, when all allowance is made both for a large measure of incompetence and indecision on the part of the Provisional Government, and for the built-in incompatibility in many respects between the government and the more radical Petrograd Soviet, the policy of Kerensky, however misguided, was dictated by principle. The persistence in the war and the ill-fated June offensive did have the effect of keeping the forces of the Central Powers away from the hard-pressed Western Front of the Allies. It ill becomes the French and the British to reproach the Provisional Government on that score. The failure to curb the Bolsheviks sprang from reluctance, now that the old police régime was overthrown, to use its repressive measures against political opponents, however violent and unreasonable. The failure to convoke the Constituent Assembly and to deal with the land problem, as well as the future of the non-Russian nationalities, may in part have been due to reluctance to tackle unwelcome questions and to the desire to postpone the evil day; but there is no doubt that the main reason for the delay was the sense of grave responsibility which called for meticulous preparations for what were seen as momentous events in the history of Russia.

Was Stalin Lenin's heir? Was his horrendous period of rule a direct consequence of the régime instituted by Lenin? These questions have much preoccupied historians, and there is no agreement on the answers. The matter is complicated by the fact that those who seek to preserve the idea of communism from contamination by Stalin's misdeeds, which few now defend, try to place the greatest possible distance between Lenin and his successor.

The differences between the two eras of Soviet history are indeed very great. For one thing, the scale of victims exacted is scarcely comparable — a few hundred thousand by Lenin, tens of millions by Stalin. Stalin, who lacked the moral authority which gave Lenin so much control over the minds of men, could assert himself only by killing great numbers of people. Again, for all his authoritarian methods of getting his own way, Lenin never put an end to the functioning of institutions like the Communist Party or the machinery of soviets: congresses of each met regularly during his lifetime, as well as the subordinate committees. Debates at the meetings still retained some reality, in spite of considerable control from the centre at party occasions and effective Communist manipulation of soviets. Under Stalin, towards the latter part of his era, meetings of soviet and especially of party organs became rare and irregular, and were formalized and stage-managed to such a degree that it is impossible to discern real debate in the reports. In fact, Stalin's method of rule offers the closest example we can find in modern times in a developed state of a personal dictatorship. He did not govern through the party, the security service or the government apparatus, but through his personal secretariat and a small group of trusted henchmen. Each of the institutions was used as seemed most appropriate to implement a policy. Again, unlike Lenin, Stalin was inordinately vain, and much of his tyrannical behaviour is traceable to his desire for self-aggrandisement, or to vengeance for a past slight. None of this kind of conduct can be remotely associated with Lenin.

The last chapter noted what appeared to be a theoretical change of direction by Lenin during the lucid months which remained to him in 1922 and 1923. These last writings, those that have come down to us, suggest that he realized that what Russia now needed was not further internal conflict, but a long period of reconciliation, that it was a time for persuasion rather than compulsion. It is, of course, impossible to say if he would have implemented this intention had he returned to power. Bukharin, who believed he was carrying out Lenin's intentions after his death, appeared to be following his precepts to some extent. On the other hand, Lenin was a dying man in 1922 and 1923, with no hope of resuming work, and there can be no certainty that he would have held the same views had he been in normal health. They were, moreover, opinions which were very uncharacteristic of his beliefs as we know them up to then. Also, there is no reason to suppose that the compromise which he had in mind extended beyond reconciliation between the peasants and the towns to tolerance of the surviving socialists. On the contrary, venomous attacks on Mensheviks figure in the very last of Lenin's notes that have come down to us.

It was by means of the party machine Lenin had forged that Stalin rose to power in the twenties, and defeated his rivals. It was by exploitation of Lenin's system of Communist control that Stalin established his mastery over the country. Even if he abused it in a way that was not originally intended, it was from Lenin that Stalin inherited the instrument of rule; and once provided with the means, Stalin was as unlikely as Lenin to be restrained by moral considerations: neither of the two men ever accepted moral factors as a limit on his course of conduct. The party mechanism which Lenin invented and developed contained no real safeguard against the emergence of a man like Stalin who would use it for his own ends. In his so-called 'Testament' Lenin did propose certain improvements in party institutions: these improvements were made in the end, and they were completely ineffective in restraining Stalin's abuse of power. Indeed, the fact that Lenin suggested the removal of Stalin as General Secretary implies that he did not believe in the efficacy of any devices to circumvent misuse of the party apparatus by one who was determined to do so.

Stalinism was not a necessary consequence of Leninism, but it was nevertheless a possible result. There was nothing inevitable about the emergence of a man of Stalin's character: yet if once it happened, the tools were ready to his hand.

My readers will, I hope, forgive me for closing this book on a personal note. I am one of the diminishing number of surviving contemporaries, outside Russia, of the events described in the preceding pages. In 1917, aged nine, I lived with my parents in Petrograd. We stayed there until late 1920. My family did not fall into the category of enemies of the régime, nor did they enjoy any priorities of privilege. Life was exceedingly hard. Diet was near starvation level, in the winter we suffered from freezing conditions for lack of fuel, breakdowns in public services were a normal occurrence. Stories of terror and brutality abounded. Yet my recollection, no doubt influenced by the adults around me, is one of enthusiasm and excitement. Life was new, hopeful, it was moving forward to some great future. In spite of hardships and the brutality of the régime, the spirit of euphoria evoked by the fall of the monarchy in March 1917 was not yet dead.

Decades later, it fell to me as a historian to look at those years in the light of the evidence. It was only then that I realized the extent to which the régime was shaped by the determination of a small, still largely unpopular party to secure and hold power for itself and its supporters alone, in defiance of other parties and of large sections of the population. A return to the study of these early years in the course of preparing this book has reinforced my view of this inherent vice in Lenin's doctrine, from which derive the vicissitudes through which his unhappy country has passed.

The Main Political Parties

SOCIALIST PARTIES

The Socialist Revolutionary Party (SR) came into existence at the turn of the century and held its first Congress in 1905. It was an openly revolutionary party, which engaged intensively in terrorist activity. It had a wide following among the peasants but sought to extend its support among the industrial proletariat. Its members were mainly defencist during World War I, but a left internationalist wing developed, which in October 1917 became the separate Left Socialist Revolutionary party (see below).

The Left Socialist Revolutionary Party (LSR) supported the Bolsheviks for a time, but eventually clashed with them on the issue of policy towards the peasants and over the separate peace with Germany.

The Maximalists were a splinter party of the Socialist Revolutionaries after 1904, who found the main party too mild for their liking. They collaborated with Bolsheviks in 1917, but fell out with them and suffered persecution thereafter.

The Social Democratic Party (known in full as the Russian Social Democratic Labour Party) was founded in 1898 as a marxist revolutionary party. In 1903 it was effectively divided into *Bolsheviks* and *Mensheviks*. After that the Bolsheviks maintained a separate organization, though the party remained in many respects united, with the Bolsheviks claiming to be the sole legitimate holders of the title. After March 1918 the Bolsheviks adopted the title of *Communists*, while the Mensheviks continued to use the old name of the RSDLP.

The Anarchists. There was a great variety of anarchist groups and parties. Originally close allies of the Bolsheviks in their rise to power, they were severely persecuted after the Bolshevik take-over.

LIBERALS

The Constitutional Democrats, or *Kadets*, were established in October 1905. Their fundamental aim was to work for real civil liberties and for a full constitution. In this sense, they were more radical than liberal in Russian conditions.

The Octobrists came into existence after the issue of the October manifesto in 1905 with the express aim of working with the imperial régime to implement the promises of the manifesto. Their programme supported civil rights, including the extension of full civil rights to the peasants. The Octobrists attracted merchants, industrialists and landowners, and became a conservative, centre party, committed to slow-paced reform.

RIGHT WING

The Union of the Russian People was an extreme right-wing party, which enjoyed the support of the Emperor. It came into existence in the autumn of 1905. Its aim was to remove what it regarded as the radical trend of the Fundamental Law of 1906.

Bibliographical Note

A full bibliography, dealing with all the sources which I have used, is beyond the scope of this book. The reader is referred to existing bibliographies of the literature covering the period — for example, that in the third volume of the work by Browder and Kerensky, cited below, or the one in my *Origin of the Communist Autocracy*. These and other bibliographies list works in Russian, including much source material. In the present note the main works in Russian which have been used are referred to, but many more are omitted, both for lack of space and as of little value to the non-specialist reader for whom this book is primarily intended.

General Works

The best comprehensive history of the two revolutions of 1917 and of the civil war is still W.H. Chamberlin, *The Russian Revolution*, 2 volumes, New York, 1935. E.H. Carr's, *The Bolshevik Revolution*, Volumes 1 to 3, London, 1950-1953, does not deal with the collapse of the monarchy, which occupies much of this book, and has also been criticized for somewhat too ready acceptance of official statements on policy; but it summarizes a great deal of material with great skill and elegance. There is a useful symposium, entitled *Revolutionary Russia*, edited by Richard Pipes, published in 1968 by Harvard University Press. Individual contributions will be referred to later as appropriate.

A number of collections of documents exist, which are of the greatest value to the student, including the following: O.H. Gankin and H.H. Fisher, *The Bolsheviks and the World War, The Origin of the Third International*, Stanford, 1940; James Bunyan and H.H. Fisher, *The Bolshevik Revolution 1917-1918, Documents and materials*, Stanford and Oxford, 1934; James Bunyan, *Intervention, Civil War and Communism in Russia, April-December 1918, Documents and materials*, Baltimore and Oxford, 1936; Martin MacCauley, *The Russian Revolution and the Soviet State 1917-1921, Documents*, London, 1975; R.P. Browder and A.F. Kerensky, *The Russian Provisional Government 1917*, 3 volumes, Stanford, 1961.

There are many collections of documents published in Russian in the Soviet Union. I have found the earlier publications more valuable and reliable than the later ones, in which, with some notable exceptions, scholarship is sacrificed to party requirements, with the result that names of 'unpersons' are omitted, and documents tampered with, truncated or omitted. The two collections which I have found most useful are the six volumes published in 1923-30, edited by N. Avdeev and others, entitled *Revoliutsiia 1917 Goda (Khronika sobytii)*; and the ten volumes edited by M.N. Pokrovskii and Ya. A. Yakovlev published mainly between 1925 and 1931 under the general title *1917 God v Dokumentakh i materialakh* (Volume IX on the State Conference appeared in 1939), which deal with all the main aspects of the year, such as peasants, workers or the army; and institutions such as the Petrograd Soviet or the Second All-Russian Congress of Soviets.

Among the earliest histories of 1917 which are all valuable sources are: P. Miliukov, *Istoriia vtoroi Russkoi Revoliutsii*, Sofia 1921-23, in three parts, not available in English; N.N. Sukhanov, *Zapiski o revoliutsii*, 7 volumes, Berlin 1922-23, translated and abridged by Joel Carmichael, under the title *The Russian Revolution, 1917*, London, 1955; Trotsky's *The History of the Russian Revolution*, written in 1930 and published in translation in London in 1932-33, though frankly pleading the Bolshevik case, is another valuable source.

Memoirs form an important source of our knowledge of events. The British and French Ambassadors, Sir George Buchanan and Maurice Paléologue, have both left their records (the latter is available in translation). P.N. Miliukov's memoirs of 1905-17, those of W.S. Woytinsky and the earliest volume of Shliapnikov dealing with the eve of 1917 are now available in English. The memoirs of Tsereteli, Chernov, Zenzinov, Zinaida Gippius and Stankevich, among many others, must be read in Russian. This also applies to the important four volumes of Shliapnikov's memoirs, which cover 1917 and after. Alexander Kerensky published extensively, and not always consistently, in exile. His last book was *Russia and History's Turning Point*, New York, 1965; *The Catastrophe* appeared in 1927 in London and New York, and *The Crucifixion of Liberty* in London in 1934. The 22 volumes of *Arkhiv Russkoi revoliutsii*, in Russian, published in Berlin in 1921-1937, are an important source for memoirs and documents, as are also the Soviet journals *Krasnyi arkhiv* and *Proletarskaia revoliutsiia*.

The works of Lenin and Trotsky are a most important source. The English edition of Lenin's *Collected Works* is full, but not complete. The most complete, Russian, edition, the fifth, in 55 volumes, finished publication in 1966; but the most scholarly edition is still the

2nd/3rd, published in 30 volumes in 1935-57. There is no complete edition of Trotsky's Works. The most important single work for the historian of the revolution is probably his autobiography, *My Life*, which is available in English translation.

The early parts of the biographies of leaders are often an important source of information. The lives of Lenin are referred to later. Bertram Wolfe, *Three Who Made a Revolution*, New York, 1948, deals with the early lives of Lenin, Trotsky and Stalin with rare brilliance and insight. The best life of Stalin is still that by Boris Souvarine, published in French in 1935, though available in an imperfect English translation. The first volume of Robert C. Tucker's *Stalin as Revolutionary*, published in New York in 1973, is of great value.

Two works, covering the activities of major political parties in 1917 are of importance: Oliver H. Radkey, *The Agrarian Foes of Bolshevism*, New York, 1958, on the Socialist Revolutionaries; and William G. Rosenberg, *Liberals in the Russian Revolution*, Princeton, 1974, on the Kadets.

Chapter 1

A most essential documentary compilation on events which preceded the revolution of 1917 is Volume 3 of *A Source Book for Russian History from Early Times to 1917*, edited by Georgy Vernadsky and others, New Haven and London, 1972.

The best history of the decades before the revolution is Hugh Seton-Watson, *The Russian Empire 1801-1917*, Oxford, 1967. On various aspects of pre-revolutionary Russia, the reader may with profit refer to *Russia Enters the Twentieth Century, 1894-1917*, edited by George Katkov and others, London, 1971. Other books which may with advantage be consulted include: G.T. Robinson, *Rural Russia under the Old Régime*, second edition, New York, 1949; T.G. Stavrou (editor) *Russia Under the Last Tsar*, Minneapolis, 1969; George Tokmakoff, *P.A. Stolypin and the Third Duma: An Appraisal of the Three Major Issues*, Washington, D.C. 1981; Richard Charques, *The Twilight of Imperial Russia*, London, 1958; Parts I and II of George Katkov, *Russia 1917: The February Revolution*, London, 1967, deal with the events which preceded the revolution. Much source material on the years preceding the fall of the monarchy and government is contained in the seven volumes (in Russian) of the interrogation of former ministers and others by the Provisional Government. Bernard Pares, *The Fall of the Russian Monarchy*, London, 1939, is based on this material.

On the 1905 revolution there is Sidney Harcave, *First Blood*,

London, 1965; and Solomon M. Schwarz, *The Russian Revolution of 1905*, Chicago and London, 1967.

On the constitutional period consult Jacob Walkin, *The Rise of Democracy in Pre-Revolutionary Russia: Political and Social Institutions Under the Last Three Czars*, New York, 1962; and Geoffrey A. Hosking, *The Russian Constitutional Experiment: Government and Duma 1907-1914*, Cambridge, 1973.

On Russia in the First World War, see Winston S. Churchill, *The World Crisis: The Eastern Front*, London, 1931; and N.N. Golovine, *The Russian Army in the World War*, New Haven, 1931. The reader should also consult Marc Ferro, *The Russian Revolution of February 1917*, translated by J.L. Richards, London, 1972.

Chapter 2

The main information is contained in Lenin's own writings.

The best history of the early years of Russian social democracy is J.L.H. Keep, *The Rise of Social Democracy in Russia*, Oxford, 1963.

On the early Lenin see the essay by Richard Pipes in his symposium *Revolutionary Russia*. The best biographies of Lenin are *Lenin* by David Shub, New York, 1948, and by Adam Ulam, *Lenin and the Bolsheviks*, London, 1966. Much information of interest will be found in the essays which make up the symposium edited by Peter Reddaway and myself entitled *Lenin: The Man, the Theorist, the Leader; A re-appraisal*, London, 1967, and in Israel Getzler, *Martov: A political biography of a Russian Social Democrat*, Cambridge, 1967. For an original assessment of Lenin, which differs from much Western scholarship, see Neil Harding, *Lenin's Political Thought*, two volumes, London, 1977 and 1981. Readers may also find the early chapters of my *The Communist Party of the Soviet Union*, 2nd edition, London, 1970, of some use.

Chapter 3

The February Revolution is now superbly studied in George Katkov's *Russia 1917* and in T. Hasegawa's *The February Revolution, Petrograd 1917*, Seattle and London, 1981. Very different in treatment, these two books provide as complete a picture of the revolutionary days of February and March 1917 as we are likely to get. Katkov's is the more dramatic and imaginative, with much hitherto unknown material; Hasegawa's is a more factual and detailed analysis of events. His access to Soviet archives, however, does not seem to have contributed much new information.

The pre-Social-Democratic revolutionary movement can be

studied in F. Venturi's classic *Roots of Revolution*, London, 1952. On the evolution of Russian radical thought see Andrzej Walicki, *A History of Russian Thought*, Stanford, 1979.

Sukhanov's memoirs, as well as those of Buchanan, Paléologue, Gippius and Stankevich, contain much material. The reader is also referred to Volume I of Browder and Kerensky, *The Russian Provisional Government 1917*. Miliukov's History and the four volumes of A.G. Shliapnikov on the year 1917 (only in Russian) are of great importance. S.P. Mel'gunov's history of March 1917, only available in Russian, is a study of vital significance.

Chapter 4

A great deal of the documentation on which much of this chapter is based will be found in Browder and Kerensky, Volumes 1 and 2.

The following works are useful on special topics: on freemasonry: G. Aronson (in Russian), *Russia on the Eve of the Revolution*, New York, 1972. On the Romanov family: S.P. Mel'gunov (in Russian) *The Fate of the Emperor Nicholas after Abdication*, Paris, 1951; I have also used the minutes of the Cabinet and War Cabinet for 1917 in the Public Record Office. On the peasants: John L.H. Keep, *The Russian Revolution: A study in Mass Mobilization*, London, 1976; Graeme J. Gill, *Peasants and Government in the Russian Revolution*, London, 1979. On national problems: Richard Pipes, *The Formation of the Soviet Union: Communism and Nationalism*, Harvard, 1954.

Chapter 5

The successive crises of the Provisional Government are documented in Volume 3 of Browder and Kerensky, and fully described in the general works cited above. The July crisis has been admirably studied in depth in A. Rabinowitch, *Prelude to Revolution*, Bloomington, 1978. The First All-Russian Congress of Soviets is documented (in Russian) in Volume 2 of the series edited by Pokrovskii and Yakovlev.

While the issue of German financial subventions to the Bolsheviks is discussed in Chaper 6, it was one of the dominating questions of the July crisis. For the German official documents, which now form the basis for the allegation, see Z.A.B. Zeman (editor), *Germany and the Revolution in Russia*, London, 1958. The question is examined in the contribution of G. Katkov to *Revolutionary Russia*, edited by Richard Pipes; and in B.V. Nikitine's memoirs, translated from the Russian under the title *The Fatal Years: Fresh Revelations on a Chapter of Underground History*, London, 1938.

Chapter 6

Material on the decline of morale in the armed forces will be found in Volume 2 of Browder and Kerensky. The early stages of the process are discussed by Allan K. Wildman, in *The End of the Russian Imperial Army: The Old Army and the Soldiers' Revolt*, Princeton, 1980 (another volume is in preparation). The most thorough study of the question is in Russian, by M. Frenkin, entitled *The Russian Army and the Revolution 1917-1918*, published in Munich in 1978. Although written in emigration, the work is based on a great mass of material collected from the archives while the author was still in the Soviet Union, and brought with him when he left. There is a valuable collection of documents (in Russian) in Volume 6 of the series edited by Pokrovskii and Yakovlev.

Chapter 7

On the Kornilov affair the definitive work is G. Katkov, *The Kornilov Affair*, London, 1980. Readers can also consult Browder and Kerensky, Volume 3; and Chapters 6 to 8 of Alexander Rabinowitch, *The Bolsheviks Come to Power: The Revolution of 1917 in Petrograd*, New York, 1976.

The report of the Democratic Conference (in Russian) is in Volume 9 of the Series, edited by Pokrovskii and Yakovlev.

Chapter 8

There are two outstanding works on the Bolshevik take-over in English: A. Rabinowitch *The Bolsheviks Come to Power*, New York, 1976; and the translation of S.P. Mel'gunov, *The Bolshevik Seizure of Power*, 1972. The first volume of the Soviet edition of the minutes of the Military Revolutionary Committee of the Petrograd Soviet is a vital source, as well as Sukhanov and Miliukov (all in Russian, though an abridged translation by Joel Carmichael of the seven volumes of memoirs by Sukhanov was published in London in 1955). Memoirs of participants (listed on eight pages by Rabinowitch) form an important source, as well as Lenin's works, and Trotsky's autobiography. Readers may also wish to consult Marc Ferro, *October 1917*, London, 1980; and my *Origin of the Communist Autocracy*, London, 1955.

Chapter 9

I found Volumes 2 and 3 of the Minutes of the MRC invaluable. G. Leggett, *The Cheka: Lenin's Political Police*, Oxford, 1981, is an excell:nt work of meticulous scholarship. I have dealt with many aspects of the consolidation of power by the Bolsheviks in my *Origin of the Communist Autocracy*. Two works by Oliver H. Radkey are indispensable: *The Election of the Russian Constituent Assembly*, Harvard, 1950; and *The Sickle Under the Hammer*, New York and London, 1963. Lenin's writings and the minutes of Central Committee meetings are an essential sourcè. (A translation by Ann Bone of the minutes for the period August 1917 to February 1918 was published by the Pluto Press, London, in 1974.)

Chapter 10

Numerous compilations on this topic have been published in recent years in various cities of the Soviet Union: though occasionally useful, they lack for the most part any serious claim to scholarship. More valuable are three long articles by V. Leikina in *Proletarskaia revoliutsiia* for 1926 (Nos 49, 58 and 59). John Keep has made meticulous use of Soviet materials both in his *The Russian Revolution: A Study in Mass Mobilization*, London, 1976, and in the paper which he contributed to *Revolutionary Russia*, edited by Richard Pipes. Relevant aspects are discussed in Roger Pethybridge, *The Spread of the Russian Revolution*, London, 1972. An excellent pioneering monograph by Donald J. Raleigh on the take-over in Samara and District (which I have read in manuscript) is forthcoming. There is also much relevant information on the activity of MRCs in the provinces in Frenkin, *The Russian Army and the Revolution 1917-1918*.

Chapter 11

The treaty of Brest-Litovsk was studied by John W. Wheeler-Bennett in *Brest-Litovsk: The Forgotten Peace, March 1918*, London, 1938.

There is an excellent introductory volume on the civil war by David Footman, *Civil War in Russia*, London, 1961, and there exists an English translation of the official Soviet history, *The History of the Civil War in Russia*, edited by M. Gorky and others, Moscow, 1942-1960. General Denikin's *The Russian Turmoil*, London, 1922, is available in English, but his complete memoirs, published in Paris 1921-1926, are in Russian. On Kolchak there is a valuable compilation of documents entitled *The Testimony of Kolchak and other Siberian Materials*, edited by Elena Varneck and H.H. Fisher, Stanford, 1935; and, in Russian, two volumes by G.K. Guins on *Siberia, the Allies and Kolchak*, Berlin, 1921. On the new Soviet Red Army in the civil war there are Erich Wollenberg, *The Red Army*,

London, 1938; and D. Fedotoff-White, *The Growth of the Red Army*, Princeton, 1944; and in Russian the three volumes of Trotsky's *How the Revolution Armed Itself*, Moscow, 1923-5.

Chapter 12

On the *Cheka* see Leggett, *The Cheka.* On political opposition I have assembled the evidence in my *Origin of the Communist Autocracy*, on which much of this chapter is based, and the reader is referred to that book for sources. On the Kronstadt revolt the best history is Paul Avrich, *Kronstadt 1921*, Princeton, 1970. On *Sovnarkom* see T.H. Rigby, *Lenin's Government: Sovnarkom, 1917-1922*, Cambridge, 1979.

Chapter 13

This chapter is based on Russian sources too numerous to list here. They are studied in my previous books *The Origin of the Communist Autocracy* and *The Communist Party of the Soviet Union*, to which the reader is referred.

Index

MORE ABOUT PENGUINS, PELICANS
AND PUFFINS

For further information about books available from Penguins please write to Dept EP, Penguin Books Ltd, Harmondsworth, Middlesex UB7 0DA.

In the U.S.A.: For a complete list of books available from Penguins in the United States write to Dept DG, Penguin Books, 299 Murray Hill Parkway, East Rutherford, New Jersey 07073.

In Canada: For a complete list of books available from Penguins in Canada write to Penguin Books Canada Ltd, 2801 John Street, Markham, Ontario L3R 1B4.

In Australia: For a complete list of books available from Penguins in Australia write to the Marketing Department, Penguin Books Australia Ltd, P.O. Box 257, Ringwood, Victoria 3134.

In New Zealand: For a complete list of books available from Penguins in New Zealand write to the Marketing Department, Penguin Books (N.Z.) Ltd, Private Bag, Takapuna, Auckland 9.

In India: For a complete list of books available from Penguins in India write to Penguin Overseas Ltd, 706 Eros Apartments, 56 Nehru Place, New Delhi 110019.

A CHOICE OF
PELICANS AND PEREGRINES

☐ **The Knight, the Lady and the Priest**
Georges Duby   £5.95

The acclaimed study of the making of modern marriage in medieval France. 'He has traced this story – sometimes amusing, often horrifying, always startling – in a series of brilliant vignettes' – *Observer*

☐ **The Limits of Soviet Power** **Jonathan Steele**   £3.50

The Kremlin's foreign policy – Brezhnev to Chernenko, is discussed in this informed, informative 'wholly invaluable and extraordinarily timely study' – *Guardian*

☐ **Understanding Organizations** **Charles B. Handy**   £4.95

Third Edition. Designed as a practical source-book for managers, this Pelican looks at the concepts, key issues and current fashions in tackling organizational problems.

☐ **The Pelican Freud Library: Volume 12**   £4.95

Containing the major essays: *Civilization, Society and Religion, Group Psychology* and *Civilization and Its Discontents*, plus other works.

☐ **Windows on the Mind** **Erich Harth**   £4.95

Is there a physical explanation for the various phenomena that we call 'mind'? Professor Harth takes in age-old philosophers as well as the latest neuroscientific theories in his masterly study of memory, perception, free will, selfhood, sensation and other richly controversial fields.

☐ **The Pelican History of the World**
J. M. Roberts   £5.95

'A stupendous achievement . . . This is the unrivalled World History for our day' – A. J. P. Taylor

A CHOICE OF
PELICANS AND PEREGRINES

☐ *A Question of Economics* **Peter Donaldson**   £4.95

Twenty key issues – from the City and big business to trades unions –
clarified and discussed by Peter Donaldson, author of *10 × Economics* and one of our greatest popularizers of economics.

☐ *Inside the Inner City* **Paul Harrison**   £4.50

A report on urban poverty and conflict by the author of *Inside the Third World*. 'A major piece of evidence' – *Sunday Times*. 'A classic: it tells us what it is really like to be poor, and why' – *Time Out*

☐ *What Philosophy Is* **Anthony O'Hear**   £3.95

What are human beings? How should people act? How do our thoughts and words relate to reality? Contemporary attitudes to these age-old questions are discussed in this new study, an eloquent and brilliant introduction to philosophy today.

☐ *The Arabs* **Peter Mansfield**   £4.95

New Edition. 'Should be studied by anyone who wants to know about the Arab world and how the Arabs have become what they are today' – *Sunday Times*

☐ *Religion and the Rise of Capitalism*
    R. H. Tawney   £3.95

The classic study of religious thought of social and economic issues from the later middle ages to the early eighteenth century.

☐ *The Mathematical Experience*
    Philip J. Davis and Reuben Hersh   £6.95

Not since *Gödel, Escher, Bach* has such an entertaining book been written on the relationship of mathematics to the arts and sciences. 'It deserves to be read by everyone . . . an instant classic' – *New Scientist*

A CHOICE OF
PELICANS AND PEREGRINES

☐ *Crowds and Power* **Elias Canetti** £4.95

'Marvellous . . . an immensely interesting, often profound reflection about the nature of society, in particular the nature of violence' – Susan Sontag in *The New York Review of Books*

☐ *The Death and Life of Great American Cities*
Jane Jacobs £4.95

One of the most exciting and wittily written attacks on contemporary city planning to have appeared in recent years – thought-provoking reading and, as one critic noted, 'extremely apposite to conditions in the UK'.

☐ *Computer Power and Human Reason*
Joseph Weizenbaum £3.95

Internationally acclaimed by scientists and humanists alike: 'This is the best book I have read on the impact of computers on society, and on technology and on man's image of himself' – *Psychology Today*

These books should be available at all good bookshops or news-agents, but if you live in the UK or the Republic of Ireland and have difficulty in getting to a bookshop, they can be ordered by post. Please indicate the titles required and fill in the form below.

NAME _____ BLOCK CAPITALS

ADDRESS _____

_____

_____

Enclose a cheque or postal order payable to The Penguin Bookshop to cover the total price of books ordered, plus 50p for postage. Readers in the Republic of Ireland should send £1R equivalent to the sterling prices, plus 67p for postage. Send to: The Penguin Bookshop, 54/56 Bridlesmith Gate, Nottingham, NG1 2GP.

You can also order by phoning (0602) 599295, and quoting your Barclaycard or Access number.

Every effort is made to ensure the accuracy of the price and availability of books at the time of going to press, but it is sometimes necessary to increase prices and in these circumstances retail prices may be shown on the covers of books which may differ from the prices shown in this list or elsewhere. This list is not an offer to supply any book.

This order service is only available to residents in the UK and the Republic of Ireland.

● ● ●